W9-BWU-248

A PRIMER FOR UNIVERSITY PRESIDENTS

A PRIMER FOR UNIVERSITY PRESIDENTS

Managing the Modern University

BY PETER T. FLAWN

UNIVERSITY OF TEXAS PRESS
AUSTIN

Copyright © 1990 by the University of Texas Press
All rights reserved
Printed in the United States of America
First Edition, 1990

Requests for permission to reproduce material from this work should be sent to
Permissions, University of Texas Press, Box 7819, Austin, Texas 78713-7819.

The paper used in this publication meets the minimum requirements of American National
Standard for Information Sciences—Permanence of Paper for Printed Library Materials,
ANSI Z39.48-1984.
∞

Library of Congress Cataloging-in-Publication Data

Flawn, Peter Tyrrell.
    A primer for university presidents : managing the modern
university / by Peter T. Flawn. — 1st ed.
        p.   cm.
    ISBN 0-292-76522-3 (alk. paper)
    1. Universities and colleges—United States—Administration.
2. College presidents—United States.   I. Title.
LB2341.F52 1990
378.73—dc20   90-33350
                                                                        CIP

To my wife, Priscilla,
a "first lady" in every sense of the word,
who did it all with class

Contents

Preface

THIS "PRIMER" for university presidents is devoid of education theory or management theory. It is a practical guide to the management of the modern university. Although it is addressed to university presidents, or those who aspire to that position, it will, I think, be of interest to all those involved in the leadership and governance of the academic enterprise. To some, it may seem irreverent. It will not be considered for adoption as a text in any management course except in the unlikely event the instructor has actually managed something. If you are bemused by theory, this Primer will not help you; it may irritate you; and in all probability you will fail as a university president anyway. Moreover, it is written for the chief executive officer of an *operating* academic institution whether he or she is called "president" or "chancellor." It is not intended for the chief executive officer of a university system. The difference will be made clear.

It is a Primer for the president who wants the university to function successfully as an educational institution. It should be useful in defending against those who see the university as a social action agency and would conspire to use the institution in support of various causes to the detriment of its educational mission. If you as president have an agenda other than the advancement of higher education, I hope you will seek another calling.

I considered calling this work a Handbook on University Administration. But handbooks do not attract readers. They are usually full of data. The subject of this Primer is, in the broad sense, management. There is some support in the dictionary for interchangeability of the terms "administration" and "management." But, to me, "administration" is more remote, even cleaner, than "management." Administrators just do not get into it like managers do. So . . . if you think that you are too experienced to read a primer, think of this book as a handbook on management for university presidents.

I also considered more provocative titles, such as "A Farewell to Academic Innocence" and "Goodbye to the Scholar-President," but I decided that such titles might attract the philosophers of higher education who would surely be disappointed. I thought about calling it "Behind the Academic Rhetoric" but concluded that that title would mislead the critic searching for revelations of academic misconduct. So . . . even though some may complain that this book is not really a "Primer," I offer it as such.

For those who come into a university presidency from an academic position, such as vice-president or dean, this book should be very helpful. In the unusual case of a university president coming into the position from the chair of an academic department or a faculty senate or other committee, the probability is that he or she will not last a year. So there is little sense in your taking the time to read this Primer. After all, you have to know *something*. For those who come to a university presidency from the corporate world because the board of regents or trustees want the institution run in a more "businesslike" way, this Primer will be your bible. But, you will have to think about what it tells you more than just a little. For those who come into the position from the political arena because a politically appointed board of regents or trustees responded to a great opportunity to bring a distinguished public servant to lead the institution, the best advice is to hire a competent executive vice-president or provost and stay away from the campus. It is the executive vice-president who will find this book useful.

The college president may also find the work of interest. A college is smaller and less complex than a university, indeed universities are made up of colleges and schools. In universities, colleges and schools are headed by deans; in stand-alone colleges, the chief executive is called a president. However, the distinctions between colleges and universities are not everywhere clearly drawn. Some colleges, in fact some schools, with inferiority complexes or great ambitions, or both, have renamed themselves "universities." This fools no one except perhaps some students and their parents who are so unsophisticated as to believe that universities are superior to colleges. In the case of publicly supported institutions, the change of name to elevate an institution that historically has been a teachers college or a normal school to a university is commonly undertaken to convince legislators that the institution merits state funding at the same level as universities that have earned the name. The result has been to make traditional distinctions meaningless. While universities are not necessarily superior to colleges academically, it is true that universities are generally superior to colleges in intercollegiate athletics. For this reason, a *student* with athletic talents who wants to participate in intercollegiate athletics may be well advised to select an academically distinguished college rather than a university. In big universities with nationally competitive athletic programs, the athletes are rarely students. Of course, real universities as distinct from in-name-only universities are easily distinguished from colleges by the number and quality of graduate programs they offer. And to finish with nomenclature and its connotations, within universities, colleges contain academic departments headed by chairs (formerly called chairmen), whereas schools are not departmentalized.

The reader might well inquire as to the credentials of the author. These are usually presented in exaggerated terms on the jacket of the book. However, not knowing what copywriters might make of my credentials, I present them here. I attended and took degrees from two private institutions, a small liberal arts college and a private university. Of course, you do not learn much about academic institutions by attending them. I built and served as president of a regional public university and subsequently served as president of one of the big ones. I have also served as a member of the faculty and in various administrative capacities from director of a research unit to executive vice-president. All in all, I was at it for thirty-six years. Moreover, assignments on various boards, commissions, and committees at the state and national levels have given me a broad perspective on universities through dealing with matters relating to their funding and their legislative and constitutional authority. In short, I do not believe that the critic who, without a sense of humor, finds this Primer lacking in proper respect for the nobility of the university enterprise will be successful in impugning the credentials of the author.

I was assisted greatly in the preparation of this book by Ronald M. Brown, Shirley Bird Perry, Beryl Buckley Milburn, and Carolyn Bacon, who read early versions of the manuscript and gave me very helpful advice and counsel. My assistant, Helen Holacka Oelrich, assisted me in editing and prepared the index. These friends and associates have my gratitude.

The information in this Primer is presented as a series of topics. The order of presentation has nothing to do with importance. Mr./Madam president, you may be attacked from any quarter at any time by any one of your many constituencies. Good luck.

A PRIMER FOR UNIVERSITY PRESIDENTS

CHAPTER 1

To Set the Stage

A QUOTATION attributed to the great English statesman, Edmund Burke, has graced the wall of my office for many years. It says: "Those who would carry on great public schemes must be proof against the worst fatiguing delays, the most mortifying disappointments, the most shocking insults, and what is worst of all, the presumptuous judgement of the ignorant upon their design." That describes the lot of the public university president in the last quarter of the twentieth century. To a somewhat lesser degree, it describes also the lot of the president of a private university because private universities are no longer very private. Private universities receive public funds in the form of research grants and student financial aid. If they are not-for-profit institutions they are tax exempt. Thus, they are subject directly or indirectly through the coercive threat of litigation to the civil rights and labor laws that burden public universities. Their "private" status shields them from open records and open meeting laws until such time as a litigant uses a court to open up their records and force disclosure of what went on in their meetings.

There are, of course, significant differences between public and private universities and among the public universities and private universities. Some of the very old private Ivy League universities in the Northeast retain traditions and procedures rooted in the centuries when accountability was to God rather than the federal government, a professor was an absolute master in his classroom, the senior faculty made the decisions on salaries, hiring, promotion, and tenure without involving the president except in a ministerial role, and students were grateful for the opportunity to learn. These institutions are unique in the United States in that they employ management practices and procedures that differ from the ways in which nearly all public and private institutions conduct their business. That some of these traditions and procedures are still with us is remarkable. Among the public universities there are also variations in the degree to which the president is directly involved in decisions on faculty hiring, promotion, and compensation. This Primer deals with university management as it exists in the vast majority of American universities; its observations and conclusions are not, in my judgment, prejudiced by the management practices of the few institutions that stray from the norm. All in all, in the area of management, universities have much more in common than not.

The public expects its institutions to be managed effectively and efficiently but at the same time supports laws that make effective and efficient management impossible. The president of a public university cannot confer privately with the board except on a few "protected" subjects. As anyone who has had the responsibility to manage any kind of an organization knows very well, the business of the organization cannot be conducted efficiently in a public arena where, in Burke's words, it is subject to "the presumptuous judgement of the ignorant." So, as the free press defends the public's right to know, business is conducted inefficiently and you, as president, must accept the burden of laborious execution of the simplest personnel action. If we as a democratic nation are so foolish as to believe that all institutions within our democracy must be run democratically, we shall see in a relatively short time a society that avoids all risk and in which the process of making decisions and taking action upon them is paralyzed. If you do not have the patience to endure lengthy grievance procedures and endless appeals, do not make a career in university administration.

The culmination of the move to democratize the management of the university is found in the initiative to make students members of governing boards. Young men and women are not qualified by training or experience to make management decisions, notwithstanding the success of Alexander the Great in conquering the world at a tender age. Alexander the Great understood how to use infantry and cavalry together in a disciplined order of battle; he did not have to deal with student regents leaking the substance of sensitive policy deliberations to a media that, contrary to the self-proclaimed nobility of its cause, is destructive in its actions. No rational society has ever admitted children to its councils of government. In fact, admission of children to councils of government is prima facie evidence of irrationality. Societies that include children on their councils of government make childish decisions and are not likely to be around very long. We in the United States not too many years ago were graced by a president who consulted his young daughter on nuclear policy, or at least built a media event around such consultation. That was a chilling experience. The inclusion of students on the governing board will make the president's job more difficult. Whereas the other members of the board have as their responsibility the effective and efficient governance of the institution, student members will believe that they are there to represent student interests. The governing board should not be a little legislature. The information the president needs from students can be gathered in other ways. Although it will not be a popular position, you should resist the addition of students to the board. You may very well lose on this issue. The fallback position is to support appointed student regents rather than elected student regents.

Language is very important in a university. The president must at all times be very careful of what he or she says and how it is said. Language, after all, is the working tool of the intellectual, and the university is the home, refuge, and citadel of the intellectual. Language reveals attitudes and ideologies . . . it may reveal elitism, egalitarianism, chauvinism, sexism, racism, or perhaps nothing more than cynicism. You will have already noticed the use of "he or she." Be advised that it is far better to use excess or cumbersome verbiage than to run the risk of being labeled "sexist" or "insensitive." Be very careful of extemporaneous remarks. Eschew humor. Ideologues are completely lacking in it and will regard anything but the most intellectual witticism as evidence of your insensitivity. The majority of the university community is of the liberal political persuasion. Many are cause oriented. Some are radical. If you, as president, elect to take a position on an issue as a conscious decision, all well and good. But if, for example, you carelessly refer to an "undocumented worker" as an "illegal alien" you may be taking a political position without being aware of it.

If a group of protestors undertakes a hunger strike to extort some concession that cannot be gained through regular governmental or judicial process, do not say, "Well, if they want to starve to death, that's their choice." In the academic community, that indicates a callous disregard for the sanctity of human life. It is the academic view that, for those on a hunger strike, society should be willing to do whatever is necessary to coax the strikers to eat. As president you should express grave concern for their health. You can be sure that hunger strikers on university campuses will, overtly or covertly, be well nourished. When asked in interviews what you do for recreation, never confess to enjoying hunting, fishing, horse racing, or bull fighting. You will have enough trouble with animal rights groups over the care of laboratory animals.

It is a very good idea for the president to commit to memory basic facts about the university and to form a position on major issues that can be articulated on demand. It is better to have a well-reasoned response than to give a random response or to appear evasive, or to be or to appear ignorant. University presidents are supposed to be knowledgeable. Basic data on enrollment, tuition costs, room-and-board costs, makeup of the student population, composition of the faculty, number of books in the library, number of parking spaces on campus, make, model, and capacity of the university's main computer, and a profile of the alumni will need to be immediately recoverable without consulting notes. You should know the name of the football coach. Any other information you can put in the ready file about the university's athletic program is all to the good. If you know the names of the first-, second-, and third-string quarterbacks along with some performance data, you will be way ahead with an important constituency. But perhaps most important is a cogent, well-reasoned argument as to why society should support universities in general and your university in particular.

While tolerance is considered a prime virtue in the academic community, that same community is intolerant of any deviation from the academic shibboleths, dogmas, or norms of the moment. Universities are consistently inconsistent in the practice of the virtues they espouse. The president must at all times display a benign tolerance of fools and nonsense. Both abound on university campuses. In the social sciences, five thousand years of accumulated wisdom about human behavior appear to count for very little, and research projects commonly are proposed to demonstrate what anyone who has been alive and reasonably sentient for forty years already knows. If, for compelling reasons, such as a strong expression from the governing board, the president must take a position against fools and nonsense, it must be carefully crafted after consultation with university lawyers and thorough staff analysis and review. I remember once, at a brown-bag, off-the-record lunch with a group of law students, I was drawn into a conversation with a young man who was distinguished by having a very large number of outstanding parking tickets. After listening to some creative legal theories on why he should be allowed to park whenever and wherever he pleased, within the informal context of the luncheon, I advised him to "pay the goddamn parking tickets!" This unseemly use of profanity by the president of the university provoked a great deal of editorial comment in the student newspaper and many letters to the editor. The lesson is . . . be benign at all times, you cannot be a good fellow with students, and remember that nothing is ever off the record.

As part of the educational process, universities discriminate among those students who succeed at the academic enterprise and those who do not. Those who do, pass their courses and take a degree that is supposed to certify to a level of academic accomplishment. Those who do not, receive failing grades in their courses and, if they cannot improve their performance, leave the institution without taking a degree. Schools and educators have been engaged in this kind of discrimination since the process of education began. However, although discrimination based on academic performance is still considered to be within a university's mission, discrimination based on race, sex, national origin, age, or other constitutionally protected attributes or behavior is certainly not acceptable. Unfortunately, there are occasions when a student who has not performed academically alleges that he or she is the victim of other kinds of discrimination. The student may allege that he or she failed an examination not because of academic weakness but because the instructor violated his or her constitutional rights. This calls into question even the traditional right of an instructor to make judgments about the performance of his or her students and to discriminate among them in assigning grades. Unless the student is related to or knows a plaintiff's attorney, these cases are usually handled within the academic community through academic appeals processes and a hierarchy of committees, departmental chairs, deans, vice-presidents, and, ultimately, you, the president. If dealt with in house, these disputes consume a great deal of time but do not impose other costs on the institution. If they find their way into court, the institution's grading procedures and the academic judgments of its faculty will be subject to judicial review and in rare cases monetary damages may be assessed against the university. The word *discrimination* has acquired such a pejorative connotation that it is best not to use it except to refer to unacceptable behavior.

Discrimination resulting from racism or sexism is a very big issue on campus and in our society. It is an issue that occupies a great deal of the president's time. There are bureaucracies at the federal and state levels whose business is the detection of discrimination. With the authority granted to them under law, they will be examining all of the university's operations to find any evidence of discriminatory actions—in hiring, promotion, grading, housing, or admission to university organizations or activities. Their investigators will not know what a university is, what it does, how it operates, or why it operates as it does. Moreover, they will not care. They will not appreciate the difference between quantities and qualities. They will charge that informed qualitative judgments made by faculty and academic administrators on the promotion of young faculty are arbitrary and capricious because they themselves are not qualified to evaluate the criteria upon which university decisions on promotion are made. They will urge the adoption of a point system whereby an assistant professor who earns 80 points will be promoted while one with only 75 will not. They will weave elaborate theories of racist or sexist conspiracies based on statistics. When faced with patently absurd charges of racism or sexism as a result of the fair application of established university procedures, you as president should not be afraid to go to court. The record shows you will win such cases.

These bureaucracies are not dissimilar to those that grew up around the Holy Inquisition about five hundred years ago. Their business was heresy. And, of course, everywhere they looked they found heresy. After all, that was their business and if they did not find it they were out of business. You can be sure that our latter-day federal and state agencies charged with ferreting out discrimination will find it. That is their mission. Your responsibility as president is to defend the merit-based systems of the university against the thinly disguised quota systems that they will attempt to force upon you.

I will take as given that, whether male or female and whatever your ethnicity, you as a university president are an enlightened, educated individual who stands firmly against racism or sexism and for equal opportunity for all members of our society. If in searching your soul you detect any deep-seated prejudices, you should resign. You will not be happy or successful as a university president. But it will not be enough for you to know in your own mind that you are innocent of racial prejudice or other biases. If you are an Anglo-Saxon president, male or female, you must be patient in the face of the most shocking and bizarre charges of racism that will be leveled against you and your institution by those members of ethnic minorities who have failed to perform well enough to earn promotion or passing grades, or win positions in organizations and on teams where excellence of performance is the sole criterion for membership, or by those seeking political or economic advantage by exploiting the civil rights legislation. One of the inconsistencies in our society is that it is deemed right and proper for all ethnic groups save one to exhibit pride in race and make decisions based on race. The exception, of course, is the Anglo-Saxon race. It is racist in the pejorative sense for Anglo-Saxons to show pride in the accomplishments of their ethnic group. Anglo-Saxons are too close to the sins of empire for their accomplishments to be universally admired. The only acceptable behavior for an Anglo-Saxon university president is to graciously accept personal and institutional guilt for historical injustices.

If you are an African American or Hispanic American president, you face an even more difficult problem. The racial minorities will perceive you as their advocate and have great expectations of what you will do for them. But since you as president will have to work within the policies, procedures, and traditions of the institution to achieve the institution's goals and objectives and carry out the institutional mission, you will stand accused of not doing enough for "your people" . . . of betraying your heritage. The university president who belongs to a minority group must walk a difficult and narrow path between university constituents and the board of regents or trustees. The president can and should be an advocate for principles; he or she cannot be an advocate for a single constituency.

The aspirations of ethnic minorities are expressed as a desire to improve their social, economic, and political position. Those aspirations are understandable and commendable and deserve your support. But you have a problem when the realization of those aspirations threatens the intellectual integrity of the university that provides the opportunity to realize them. Your most difficult job as president is to recognize and support the legitimate aspirations of the ethnic minorities without yielding on the imperative for merit-based standards by which reward, recognition, and advancement come through excellence of performance.

The most recent campus-based attacks on university traditions of free ideas, free speech, and academic standards based on merit take the form of "sensitivity" seminars or workshops designed to "correct" the thinking and attitudes of students, faculty, and staff. Based on the radical premise that the traditions of the university, indeed of Western civilization, are inherently racist, sexist, capitalist, and designed to deprive people of freedom, these "sensitivity" sessions have promulgated a "newspeak" that so distorts the common meanings of the terms "racism," "sexism," "harassment," and "abuse" as to make them useless for communication. When a proselyte from one of these workshops mystifies you by accusing you of harassment and abuse, or worse, it is probably a waste of time to attempt a rational dialogue. He or she is speaking a different language in which "to abuse" is synonymous with "to disagree"; there is no common ground for civil discourse.

In dealing with the troublesome issues of discrimination on campus, you should be heartened by the knowledge that universities have done far more to provide opportunities for minorities and women than all of the mission-oriented agencies created by the government to enforce social policy. The long-term solution to the racial tensions that prevail in our multicultural society is education. The university is in a position to make a great contribution. Take comfort in that.

In a democratic society, the motivation to pander to students varies directly as the number of young people in society and indirectly as the age of the franchise. Legislators that represent university districts have a great sympathy for student issues no matter how sophomoric they may be. In every session of the legislature, senators and representatives who know better introduce legislation to put students on governing boards. There have been even more absurd bills introduced into state legislatures that would prohibit state universities from recording failing grades and in other ways would degrade academic standards of performance. A few years ago legislators from some university districts were persuaded to introduce legislation to permit activist students to collect fees from all students to finance so-called public interest research groups. Fortunately this rip-off to finance cause-oriented political activists was not generally successful. Legislators from districts that did not include universities were not eager to give taxing authority to groups likely to cause consternation among their own constituencies. In private universities the level of presidential discomfort caused by student political activists is not as high as in public institutions because presidents of private universities do not get as much help from legislators in managing their institutions. But even in private universities the president is well advised to pay attention to the nature and direction of student political activity. It can affect adversely the relationships between the university and the larger society, particularly the alumni.

In both public and private institutions perhaps the best way to keep a lid on political activity is by reminding students that the purpose of a university is to provide them with an opportunity for intellectual development. The best way to remind them is through maintenance of high academic standards of performance and a requirement that they take at least three courses a semester to continue as a student in good standing. This puts the students under stress. They should be under stress. Despite a great deal of nonsense from professional educators about shielding students from stress, history demonstrates clearly that no resource, human or natural, was ever developed without stress. Students should be anxious about the quality of their academic performance. It does not benefit the campus environment for large numbers of people with an agenda other than education to hang around year after year taking one course and calling themselves students. A student taking a full and demanding academic load is not likely to be planning a take-over of the president's office.

The same legislators from university districts that want to micromanage the institution through creative bills and riders will also be the ones who most vigorously oppose increases in tuition and fees necessary in a time of inflation to finance adequately the operations and capital needs of the institution. The state must depend on legislators from districts that do not have universities to protect the public against student lobbies that work so vigorously in their self-interest. In general, the agenda of student lobbies is straightforward. Put simply, and with only mild overstatement, they want a first-class education free and they want students to run the institution. Since World War II nearly every district has either a public junior college, a college, or a university in it and enrollments are increasing. Student lobbies are not to be taken lightly.

Do not make the mistake of referring to the university as a place. This will brand you as a Philistine. The university is a community. It is a community of teachers and scholars. The campus is the place. For those outside the academic world this may not seem to be a "big deal," but it is symbolic to the institution's intellectual elite. These are the people who decry investments in "bricks and mortar" as antithetical to those values for which a university stands. The money should go into faculty salaries or to support academic programs in the humanities and social sciences (but not in the professional schools). Investments in bricks and mortar are all right, even applauded, when made to build a new library or provide a new building for the complaining faculty member's own department.

From time to time, the president will be waited upon by groups of faculty who will gravely inform him or her that "faculty morale is at an all-time low." Indeed, the president may have already read that distressing news in the campus newspaper. Orations in the faculty senate may have deplored the low state of faculty morale. Be not overly concerned, Mr./Madam president. Faculty morale is always "at an all-time low." The reason for this collective faculty depression, depending on the group making the case, is commonly represented as a failure on the part of the administration to provide leadership, take a high moral position with regard to a current national issue, such as capital punishment or a hawkish initiative taken by the president of the United States, or provide additional faculty parking. Or perhaps the malaise is caused by the decision of the president to deny tenure to a popular young professor. Whatever the reason, if the university's annual budget contains a respectable increase for faculty salaries, the perennial concern about faculty morale will be muted. If not, it will be exacerbated. Salaries are very important. Very few faculty members will confess to feeling guilty about being paid a good salary with job security inferior only to federal judges for pursuing the most satisfying career in the world. However, the university community exists as part of the larger society (much as it might prefer to be an ivory tower in fact) and therefore there will be times when faculty morale . . . and administration morale and staff morale . . . will be low for good reason. It occurs in the difficult times when the president must effectively lead the institution so as to minimize the impact of untoward external events on the institution. The president must convince the university community that even when resources are few it is a privilege to be part of such a great enterprise.

From the outset, it will be clear to you as president of the university that intercollegiate athletics as they are "produced" today for national audiences bear no relation to the mission of a university, notwithstanding specious arguments to the contrary. I shall have a good deal more to say about this in a separate section. As a general observation, however, you are advised to learn the specious arguments.

If you come into a university presidency from the inside, with the blessing of a search committee that included faculty and students, you will have a honeymoon—but it will be short. You will have the advantage of knowing the players both inside and outside who influence the course of events. If you come from outside the institution, with the same search committee endorsement, you will have a slightly longer honeymoon during which time you should make an all-out effort by studying local histories and genealogies to learn about the antecedents and traditions of the new world in which you find yourself. If you do not have the support of the search committee, do not accept the job. Without that endorsement, you will begin your presidency under a big, dark cloud.

Assuming that all of the relevant constituencies support your appointment, your success will depend to a large extent on the skills and insights you employ in selecting your administrative team. You must have a clear, preferably written, understanding with the board that hires you about your authority to hire or replace vice-presidents. Go slow and be careful. During the interview process with members of the board of regents or trustees try to get a reading on how they regard the sitting vice-presidents. As a general rule, any vice-president that you might want to keep will submit his or her resignation to you the first day you are in office. Those that do not probably feel secure in their own constituencies and personal relations with board members. At this point you are at a critical juncture. A vice-president with an agenda that differs from yours can destroy your presidency. You must engineer a departure in a decisive but graceful way.

Management of a university is, like management of other organizations, largely a matter of common sense. However, common sense is so rarely encountered on university campuses that it may not be recognized among the various constituencies that are affected by the president's decisions. Thus, in a university, a decision based on common sense and for which the rationale is obvious should be presented in an elaborate form that details the most elementary of assumptions and derives the decision in minute detail. This is absolutely necessary in faculty senates and university councils where common sense is usually vigorously attacked. Those social scientists who are wedded to socially just causes are less rigorous in methodology than their more objective colleagues. They make decisions through a kind of backward process that begins with theory, always popular, liberal theory, and employs only those data that fit the theory. Data that might prejudice the theory are considered questionable or irrelevant and are explained away or discarded. The ultimate conclusion is based on selected, biased, or weighted data. The behavior of social activists in faculty senates and the method of their reasoning are upsetting to physical scientists and engineers. The physical scientists remain quiet for fear of being labeled conservatives or reactionaries. The engineers become disenchanted with the entire process and stop attending the meetings because they regard them as a waste of time. Consequently, the only regulars at meetings of faculty senates or university councils are the activist social scientists and humanists along with the student representatives. Although activist by nature and dedicated to causes, the student representatives for the most part exhibit more common sense than is to be found in those faculty representatives who make a career out of the faculty senate. Thus, when the president comes to a decision arrived at through the exercise of common sense, he or she should rehearse an explanation of exactly how it was made. One useful exercise is to practice how to explain it to a reporter from the campus newspaper. With rare exceptions, the reporter will be so ignorant of what universities are all about that the president may well have to begin the explanation with the premise that "knowledge is better than ignorance" and follow the chain of reasoning from that point. This is why a university president who has been in the classroom has an advantage over one who has come from outside the institution from a world in which an interrogator is expected to have some standing to question a decision. Not so in the university.

One of the great dangers faced by the president of a university, or any other chief executive for that matter, is the danger inherent in the *ad hoc* decision. No matter how harassed by the pressures of the moment, no matter how tempted by expediency, no matter how exasperated by what appears to be endless debate, you should not make *ad hoc* decisions . . . unless, of course, you are planning to leave the presidency in the very near future. Even then, if you have a concern for how history will judge you, it is better to leave the decision to your successor than to "*ad hoc* it" in the interests of a clean desk.

The *ad hoc* decision is one that may satisfactorily resolve a problem of the moment but sets a precedent that may hang you down the road. Decisions should rest on principle—on a guiding principle or philosophy that will establish a sound basis for future decisions and provide for predictability and continuity in the making of decisions. Decisions that rest on principle will stand against charges that they were made arbitrarily, whimsically, or capriciously. When you are called upon to explain and defend why you expelled Smith but put Jones on probation, you should be able to articulate the principle under which Smith was expelled while Jones was not. Once that is clearly set forth and understood, it will establish a precedent for future decisions and perhaps even diminish Smith-like behavior.

A principle should be defensible and the defense should be understandable, if not acceptable, to a rational person. A decision-controlling principle should not be legalistic nor should it be drawn on too fine a line. In fact, in making a "tough call" it is helpful to review in your mind how you will explain it to an adversary. If you cannot come up with a convincing defense it may very well be the wrong decision. Areas where *ad hoc* decisions can get you into a great deal of trouble include admissions, student discipline, acceptance of gifts to the university, the awarding of honorary degrees, financial aid for students, registering of student organizations, use of campus facilities, and, of course, personnel matters in general. Legislative bodies are particularly vulnerable to the *ad hoc* decision and you should review the products of the faculty senate for actions that will solve a problem today but get you into trouble tomorrow.

If the university furnishes you with a president's home, always referred to in the press as a "mansion," make it clear that you are really "living over the store" . . . that is to say that you occupy a modest bedroom suite and use the rest of the house for official occasions. Be sure that you use the structure for official purposes and keep a detailed log of the events taking place there, including who was present at the various functions. If you do not use the president's home for official occasions, move out. Otherwise, you will not be able to justify the maintenance.

Before the years of student activism, the president's home was usually on or immediately adjacent to the campus. Following the decade of the 1960s, however, universities, either through purchase or gift, acquired homes for their presidents beyond easy marching distance from the campus. Notwithstanding this separation, the president's home, properly used, is a very important resource for building a sense of community within the institution and building a bridge between town and gown in the larger society. Faculty and student organizations should be entertained frequently in the president's home, there should be informal meetings of faculty and staff in the residence, the alumni should be invited to the president's home on appropriate occasions, and, of course, the president's home is where links with the business and political communities can be forged. Holding such meetings on campus in conference rooms never has quite the same ambiance. You should have a working office in the home. If your university is a large one and you have a director of special events (someone other than a spouse who plans official functions), you might build an office for her or him in the official residence. That helps to sustain the image that it is a working university building rather than a luxurious "perk" for the president.

Student newspaper interviewers commonly pose the question, What do you do all day? This is a form of the basic question, How can you sit here in this big office and justify your obscene salary? It is perhaps the most difficult of all questions because the interrogator does not know enough to understand what you tell him or her. The best approach is a "for example" response in which you take the reporter through your calendar for a week. He or she may not believe you should be paid for some of the things that you do, but there will be no doubt that you are fully occupied. If you are a male president whose spouse is the university's "first lady," make the point that she works full-time without compensation and therefore your handsome salary is for two. It will be true enough.

Experts on management talk about how important it is for a chief executive officer to have outside interests. This is all very well in theory, but there is not much time for outside interests in the life of a university president. The demands on a president's time are all-consuming and never-ending. If you have outside business affairs of some magnitude, someone else will have to look after them. If you are still making out your own income tax returns, you had better hire an accountant to take over that responsibility. Since you will have obligations to support the university's athletic programs, your passion for sports can be satisfied on the job.

Other recreational activities, such as golf or tennis, will be combined with your responsibilities in university development . . . in other words, play with people at clubs where you can mix with university benefactors and potential benefactors. Those lovely fall afternoons that you used to spend in the country or at the lake will now be spent in the football stadium. The time you used to devote to such hobbies as photography or woodworking will inevitably be diminished. You had better plan to take leave from the professional obligations you had in your own discipline. Your colleagues will understand that. It will benefit the university if you continue with your charitable activities . . . up to a point. Serving on a hospital board will help the image of the university. Serving on a corporate board will likewise put you in association with people who can help the university. In other words, during your tenure as a university president, time will be at a premium, and there will always be something else that you could be doing to advance the affairs of the university. A university president who lounges behind a clean desk without a paper in sight and appears to have all the time in the world to spend with you is either playing a game or is president in name only.

The president of a university has occasion to travel frequently. There are state and national meetings, visits to alumni clubs, and calls on federal funding agencies, foundations, and potential donors. If the university is public, there will be numerous trips to the state capital, particularly when the legislature is in session; if your institution is part of a system, you will find yourself at meetings at system headquarters more often than you want to be. Operations at off-campus facilities, such as observatories or marine stations, will from time to time benefit from a visit. To be effective in recruiting students, the president should visit high schools and junior colleges. The prospects for success in recruiting a very distinguished faculty member or academic administrator are materially increased if the president makes a call on the candidate.

But travel is a great consumer of time and there are competing demands for literally every minute of a university president's time. The problem of making time-efficient travel arrangements is exacerbated if, as is so commonly the case, the university is located in a small town or city without a major commercial airport. Overland travel is too slow for distances of more than one hundred miles, particularly in congested, urban areas.

The solution, of course, is a university airplane, either owned and operated by the institution or on charter. State universities may have access to state aircraft operated out of a pool under a central authority. University systems may operate aircraft upon which component institutions may call under system policies. What you want is a twin-engined, fully instrumented, pressurized airplane with two pilots, and you should not settle for less.

Operating such an airplane is not cheap. There will be those who do not appreciate the demands on your time or who will not be convinced that your time is worth very much. Your use of an airplane will be criticized as a luxury and a wasteful extravagance. It is neither. You will have to be prepared to justify its use and hope that your board and, if you are in the public arena, the legislature and the political leadership of the state, most of whom use state-owned and private aircraft extensively because they know how precious their time is, will understand the pressures on you to be in many different places over a very short period of time. Make sure that the aircraft's log and passenger manifest support the argument.

A good deal of the criticism can be avoided if an independent alumni organization, a wealthy alumnus or group of alumni, or a corporation can be persuaded to make an airplane available to you at no cost to the university or at a cost below what you would have to pay for a charter. Perhaps you can work out an arrangement for the university to pay only the cost of fuel and pilots. Look to your development board or your alumni association to help with this kind of arrangement. It may very well be among the most important things they can do for you.

Access to an airplane, whether university-owned, state-owned, system-owned, chartered, or through special arrangement with friends of the university, will save you an enormous amount of time and enable you to accomplish a great deal more than you can without it. It will also lessen the stress that comes from racing to catch a commercial flight, worrying about airport delays, and missing a connection when you are scheduled to make a speech to a waiting audience. There is enough stress in the job without adding the hassles of commercial air travel.

There may be occasions when an event on campus or in the world outside incites the passions of an element of the university community to the extent they are moved to protest. Depending on the nature of the situation, there may be disorder of a magnitude to threaten the civil discourse so essential to the conduct of the university's business. There may be marches, rallies and manipulation of a willing press to attack the university administration and its policies and procedures.

The protest may come as a reaction to a perceived social or economic injustice that involves a great many faculty and students. More commonly, the protest is sparked by an event that in and of itself excites only a few students but is expanded and magnified by other disaffected groups with their own agendas. Political activists will seize upon the issues and distort them for their own benefit. Some of those involved in a big protest will not be students or faculty. The press and media will exacerbate the problem with stories that will be founded largely on the protestors' viewpoints.

If the protests are not disruptive and do not appear to be moving in that direction, a benign tolerance may be the best response. But under no circumstances should the president sit by and permit violation of law or the disruption of the university's normal business.

Each crisis is different, so it is difficult to generalize on how the president should deal with crisis management. But here are some general rules.

The president must have good intelligence on just what is going on. Although much is to be gained by swift action to calm a potentially explosive situation, you should not react until you have the facts. If you take action based on a first assessment by an excited staff member or a rumor, you will make a mistake.

Identify the leaders of the protest and find out what it is they want. Develop a reasoned position on the issues based on an accurate assessment. Do not be immediately involved or visible. Put a dean or vice-president out front. That will draw less press attention and permit you to come in to hear the appeals in a calmer forum.

Depending on the facts, the president can be responsive, conciliatory, or even apologetic . . . but . . . in any confrontation on campus the president must control the agenda and set the terms of the engagement.

Whatever you do on campus, remember that the larger community, including your board, and in the case of a public institution, the legislature, will be watching. It is very important that the president is perceived to be in charge.

These opening observations I have made to set the stage may raise the question of why anyone would want to be a university president. It is a fair question and one that will be posed more than once as this Primer addresses the management challenges that face a university president. I have not yet introduced interactions with the board of regents or trustees. The board will see you as their chief executive officer. However, the faculty, staff, and students will see you as the mayor of university city and responsible to them. Even though they have not elected you, they will behave as though you were an elected official, but of course without the protection of a specific term of office. Indeed, students will have the idea that the university exists for their benefit and pleasure and that the tens of millions or hundreds of millions of dollars that society spends annually to operate the institution is some kind of "right" that has been conferred upon them. Even pointing out that the tuition they pay is only a part (in public institutions a very small part) of what it takes to operate the university does not dispel this idea that the president is employed by the students. The president does work for the students, for their benefit, but he or she is not employed by the students in the sense that their tuition pays the salary. It is only in the small, private institutions with very high tuition that tuition paid by students defrays a large part of the operating budget. In both public and private institutions students have contributed little to the capital investment that built the classrooms, laboratories, libraries, dormitories, and other improvements and equipment that grace the campus. Walking the path between the board and the constituencies that regard you as their mayor will not always be "fun," but it will never be boring.

So why take the job? The compensation will be fair to good, but you do not become a university president to make a lot of money. It may be a stepping stone to higher public office. Some university presidents become ambassadors or cabinet officers; some run for public office. But those opportunities are uncommon, if not rare, and should not be a deciding factor in your decision to seek or accept a university presidency. If you tend toward the technocrat, there is considerable satisfaction in taking hold of a complex system and making it work. But that satisfaction, although important, is probably not enough in itself to persuade you to take the position. As president of a university, you will probably be invited to serve on one or more corporate boards that pay directors' fees. This is a nice supplement to your university salary and gives you an opportunity to know individuals who can be of great assistance in building your university's endowments. You do not meet these kinds of people in the coach section of airplanes. However, before you accept the position as president, you should have a clear understanding with the board of regents on how you will respond to invitations to join corporate boards. You should be selective in which board invitations you accept. Do a little research on the other members of the board. If you are president of a public university you must be scrupulous in taking vacation time for any day for which you receive a fee from a corporation, foundation, or any other source. You cannot in good conscience be paid twice for the same period of time. If you do not keep detailed records of the time you spend on corporate business, you may find yourself in serious trouble. As president, you will also have available to you a certain amount of discretionary money to be used to support your office. Be absolutely certain that the money is indeed used for appropriate university purposes and not for anything that might be perceived to be a personal expenditure.

The job is a "bully pulpit." When university presidents say things, even though they may not be very profound, people tend to listen. This can be very rewarding. We live in a society where a great many people are saying things twenty-four hours a day to a great many people who are paying no attention whatsoever. The university presidency still carries an aura of credibility. If you have a strong desire to have people pay attention to what you say, by all means become a university president. Just be sure that you have something of substance to say, because if you do not the audience fades fast.

The central mission of the university is human development and that is a very good thing in which to be involved. As president, you are leading an institution that makes it possible for students to develop their intellectual abilities, their knowledge, their skills, and their ability to think and reason. If, in the process, students are prepared for particular jobs, that is also a good thing. But job preparation is not the principal purpose of the institution. The university is not a training corporation. It is probably best not to make this pronouncement publicly. Nearly all the people who support the institution, from elected officials to private benefactors, believe that the purpose of the university is to train students to hold jobs. The student who is successful in developing his or her intellectual abilities, knowledge, and skills will be prepared to play a useful role in society in a variety of ways. The successful graduate will be able to adapt to a changing social and economic environment and to function effectively. In other words, the student will have improved prospects for employment. Being involved in this very worthwhile social endeavor brings a sense of satisfaction.

The university is a very interesting place to be. The atmosphere of inquiry is fascinating. University support of the arts is traditional and very likely your institution will be involved with the performance of symphony orchestras and operas. There will be art shows in your museums and galleries. The business community of the region will be involved with your school or college of business and this will hold true of the other professional schools that make up the institution. There will be seminars, lectures, symposia, and conferences. University faculty and staff will be players in community good works projects. University faculty and students, in exercise of their constitutional rights, will be active in political and social causes and will attempt to involve the university as a social or political action agency. Containing these well-meaning people and keeping the university on course as an educational institution may not be all that enjoyable, but neither will it be boring. Contentious people are irritating but they make universities exciting places.

It is when you preside over your first commencement that you will understand why the position of university president is perhaps the finest position to which a man or woman can aspire. When the students who have successfully completed the requirements for a degree come across the stage to receive their diplomas, or in the very big institutions stand to be recognized, you will experience the enormous satisfaction of being part of, indeed, of leading, a great enterprise. On that occasion, all the administrative harassment, all the "fatiguing delays, mortifying disappointments, shocking insults, and presumptuous judgements" will fade into insignificance—that is until the next semester begins.

CHAPTER 2

Governance and Management

Nearly all universities are governed by a board. This is true of public, private, and church-related institutions. There is some kind of governing board. The members of the board are commonly called regents, trustees, or directors. This board is supposed to *govern* the institution, not *manage* it. Management is the responsibility of the president. If the board, for whatever reason, intrudes into the management function, the president is in serious difficulty.

In carrying out its proper governing function, the board, in the ideal case, selects and employs the president, establishes the broad policies under which the institution operates and within which the president manages, seeks to secure the resources necessary to the operation of the institution, approves the annual budget and the long-range plan, and supports the president as he or she attempts to build and advance the institution. In public institutions, perhaps the most important function of the board is to stand as a bulwark between the institution and the political fads and pressures of the moment. No public university that depends on public funds for all or part of its budget can remain apart from politics. But the board, depending on the authority granted to it under the state constitution or by law, can protect the president from holders of elected office who misuse their position to seek special favors for constituents. The first responsibility of the board is to defend the integrity of the institution. The board also has the responsibility to monitor the president's management of the institution and to step in if he or she fails to do a good job.

This, of course, is the ideal, but boards are not perfect instruments. Their members vary widely in competence and character. They come and go. Some seek to use their office to their own advantage. Beware the "born-again" regent who is given to know the truth and the right. Such a regent will not be happy with the compromises you will have to make.

From time to time a board will be graced by a very talented, knowledge-able, able individual with nothing to do but help the president run the institution. This regent, trustee, or director will be on campus frequently, commonly visiting your office unannounced and consuming a great deal of your time, dealing directly with vice-presidents, deans, and faculty pol-iticians, and even meeting with the officers of student organizations. This is a "rogue regent" and must be dealt with very carefully. With time, he or she may very well arouse sufficient hostility among colleagues on the board to lose their support, so be patient and time may take care of the problem. When the rogue regent holds a press conference to make a pro-nouncement about the football coach, even the most tolerant members of the board will have had enough and will rally to your support. There is always a chance, albeit slim considering the character and motivations of rogue regents, that their energy and knowledge can be channeled into useful and constructive activities. But do not ever make the mistake of believing that you can put a rogue regent in your pocket. He or she will stay with you only as long as it suits a purpose. In the event the rogue regent comes to chair the board, you should plan to make a graceful exit. It will just be a matter of time until you are found wanting in the quality of your leadership.

In private universities the authority exercised by the board derives from the institution's charter. In public institutions the authority may be constitutional or statutory or both. No public institution in the United States has ever achieved academic distinction without some kind of con-stitutional protection from the dictates of the state legislature. There are many mediocre state universities and a few good ones that do not have this constitutional shield, but history has demonstrated that it is those public institutions given some degree of independence by the state consti-tution, be it a constitutionally protected endowment or a degree of au-tonomy in allocating funds and in management, that have the potential to become great universities.

In private universities boards are usually self-perpetuating. The mem-bers serve defined terms and are replaced at appropriate intervals through a nominating committee appointed by the board through its chair. There are, of course, variations on the theme. There may be a provision that reserves a number of board seats for members elected by the alumni. In church-related institutions one or more seats may be held *ex officio* by des-ignated members of the church hierarchy. Major donors are commonly invited to serve on the board. Boards are usually large with the action vested in an executive committee. Thus, the president will have social and ceremonial duties with the bigger group, but will actually work with a relatively small number of influential regents. There will be other standing and *ad hoc* board committees charged with making recommendations to the executive committee or the full board. They will deal with nominations, audit, finance and investments, fund raising, curriculum, and other issues of current interest. Commonly, the president is a member of the board.

Boards of public universities vary widely in method of appointment, size, and organization. In some states, prospective members stand for election to their seats. In others, members are appointed to the board by the governor with the consent of the senate. There may be a legal requirement to assure a political balance by requiring that half the seats be occupied by Democrats and half by Republicans. There are states in which by law a certain number of board members must be appointed from a number of interested constituencies, such as faculty, students, alumni, industrial or agricultural societies. I have spoken in the previous chapter to the problems caused by student members or any members that believe that their first responsibility is to a constituency rather than to the institution. A good board of regents is not a legislature in microcosm. In some states the governor is an *ex officio* member of the board; other state officials or department heads may also hold *ex officio* membership. The president may be a member of the board or may be a paid executive without a board seat. Big boards consist of as many as thirty or forty members. Small boards are composed of seven to nine members. In the bigger boards there is usually an executive committee of five to seven with which the president works. The boards are organized into working committees concerned with academic programs, investments, buildings and grounds, audit, planning, and other issues of importance.

In general, it enhances the position of the president if he or she is also a member of the board rather than just a hired hand. However, in the case where the board is divided, either on political or philosophical grounds, and the president as a member of the board must break the tie in a number of significant votes, board membership can create the extra pressure that leads to early departure from the presidency. If you do find yourself a voting member of the board, begin the very first day to develop and sustain a friendly, collegial relationship based on the "we're all in this together" approach to your responsibilities. In a very short time you will be the regent who knows the most about your institution. Do not be patronizing; do not be impatient with the obvious failure of some of your fellow regents to do their homework. Do as much work as you can on an individual basis with the other regents before the formal meeting of the board so they will be up to speed on the material supporting the agenda. A few phone calls and an occasional lunch may be time consuming but they will pay big dividends. Remember that a university is a very complex, and in many ways unique, kind of organization. What may be apparent to you who have spent a large part of your professional life working in a university will not be at all clear to regents whose experience has been quite different. Take time to explain, but do not lecture!

Unless you as president are in the fortunate position of being able to influence the appointment of regents, you have to work with what you get. Some regents will be people who have been successful in a profession, such as law or medicine. They will include intelligent, well-meaning individuals who know nothing whatsoever about managing large organizations and they will be impatient at your inability to make things happen quickly. Some of your regents may have held high, responsible positions in corporations. They will know a great deal about the management of large organizations. Corporate officer regents can be of great help to you once they understand that a university is not a corporation. However, they too will be impatient at your inability to make things happen quickly. Some regents, unfortunately, will have no qualification beyond the ability to make large contributions to political campaigns. Do not write them off too soon. You may encounter political problems where they can lobby effectively in your behalf. Then there is the "gotcha" regent, or nitpicker. This is the bright regent with nothing much to do who pores over the material in support of the meeting agenda until he or she finds an inconsistency, an error, or just something dumb that has no business being brought before the board in that form. The "gotcha" regent takes a lot of tender care. It is worth the time, however, to prevent the "gotcha" regent from becoming a rogue regent. An individual who has had experience as a regent at another college or university will require explanations of why you have elected to do things differently. Be receptive. You may get some good ideas. From time to time, the appointment process may produce a fool or a jackass. A jackass regent is a fool who is also objectionable. You must suffer the fool and the jackass. They will quickly be perceived for what they are by their colleagues on the board who will commiserate with you. Fortunately, it is rare for the appointment process to produce this kind of burden.

Without exception, regents like the events in which they are involved to be well organized and well staffed. You are well advised to think through all of the details of a board function personally and for major ceremonial events to have a dry run or rehearsal to make sure that as the official party leaves the stage they do not encounter a locked door. The individual whom you select to handle these arrangements should be a high-anxiety, think-of-all-contingencies staff member who knows how to please important people. From smooth transportation arrangements to sensitive table seating to the ability to prepare remarks for regents who are called upon to speak at functions, your director of special events can earn you points that you will need. Attention to detail is essential if your administration is to build a reputation for doing things right.

Regents have spouses. Spouses, like board members, require a lot of attention. Some will be charming; others will need to be charmed. Some female spouses are likely to be sensitive to the style in which you entertain and the details of the functions in which they are included. Both male and female spouses may, as a result of their own business, professional, and cultural activities, take an interest in certain of the university's academic programs. In such a case, entrepreneurial faculty members will find them and make them into an advocate at the board level for a particular program. This may cost you some money. Go ahead and spend it. You may find it politic to cater to their interest.

It has been my experience that almost without exception regents grow into the job and with the job. They become strong supporters of the institution and its mission. Remember that they do not get paid for the long hours they put in on university business. Those that start out impatient with your inability to get things done quickly will learn what a university is and how it operates and, what is more, they will learn to appreciate why a university does not operate efficiently. In time, they may even understand the tenure system and why it is necessary to retain it if universities are to remain universities rather than become training corporations. There are exceptions, of course. If chance gives you too many regents who regard themselves as watchdogs or reformers, better move on and make your contribution to higher education at another institution.

Your first contact with what may become your board will occur when you are contacted about your interest in the presidency and agree to an interview. It may be with a search committee or with the full board. Do your homework. But come to the interview convinced that you do not want the job and would not accept it under any circumstances. You will know that they are seeking a man or woman to manage an institution that is unmanageable in any corporate or business sense. It is unmanageable in the same way that a city of the United States is unmanageable in our time. You must determine if they know that. If your initial contact is with experienced, sophisticated regents who have fought the battles with intrusive state and federal agencies and have been in court with faculty and student plaintiffs, you may have a basis for serious negotiations and, reluctantly, you may express some interest in the position. It is vitally important that both you and the board have the same understanding of what the job is and what the expectations are. At this point, you are in the "driver's seat" but this is the only time you will be able to define the job and set the terms.

The reality is that, although you must appear to the board to be a tough, firm manager in order to command their respect and support for any length of time, in most universities the authority of the president has been diminished to the extent that he or she can only cajole, persuade, wheedle, and occasionally intimidate. The management of a large public university in the United States may well be the most difficult job in the world. It is, for example, easier to administer a department of the federal government with its great layer of insulating bureaucrats than a modern university where the president, without significant authority and serving at the pleasure of the board, must deal directly with all of the university's many constituencies on demand. The president's problem is that, by law, court decision, and board action, authority in universities has been cut into a number of pieces; the pieces have been parceled out to various constituencies; no single piece is big enough to permit action without consensus; there is never ready consensus about anything in universities; and, therefore, decision and action are nigh impossible. The president who can devise tactics and strategies to bring academic matters to a decision is an effective and successful president. Do not expect to do it by issuing edicts from the president's office.

But while the authority of university presidents is diminished, the responsibility that goes with the position is not. As a result, fewer and fewer presidents stay in the job very long. The search for presidents thus becomes more frequent and more difficult. Boards of regents in this environment have not infrequently been burned by "a charmer." "Charmers" are accomplished candidates for presidencies who are charming, engaging individuals, eloquent about "the academy," politically astute, and who, once in the job, turn the management over to vice-presidents, enjoy the emoluments, entertaining, and social interactions for a few years, and then move on, leaving the institution as good as the vice-presidents can make it. Only in extraordinary situations does charisma endure for more than three years. In your initial interviews with the board, and in subsequent interactions with regents, do not be too charming. They will know, or they will soon find out, that you cannot manage an organization on charm for very long.

If you want to have a successful presidency, deal openly and honestly with the board. If there is a secret to a successful relationship with the board, it is that you should not be secretive. Do not try to keep the board out of your business. Board members do not like surprises any more than you do. As mentioned previously, you should cultivate the "we're all in this together" approach to management issues and problems. This is not inconsistent with the ideal separation of the board's responsibility to govern and your responsibility to manage. It is precisely through keeping the board informed about management issues and problems that you can make this ideal separation a working reality. The well-informed regent is the first to say, "Well, that's a management problem . . . good luck!"

There are occasions when a president will find himself or herself in a position to influence or control the board. You may be close to the governor or to powerful state senators who can influence appointments or even appropriations. You may be a great favorite with powerful alumni or university donors. You may have a close personal relationship with some regents. You should, of course, use this kind of political influence sparingly and wisely. It will be known that you have these relationships. You may strengthen your position by not using them. In the final analysis, however, your ultimate weapon is your resignation. You should use this only when faced with a board decision you cannot in good conscience accept. If you threaten to resign and do not follow through, you no longer have this weapon in your arsenal, in fact, you no longer have an arsenal.

The board of regents of a public university will probably make their decision on your selection as president in executive session and then announce it or vote again for the record in open session. It is to be hoped that their decision was unanimous. But if it was not and you were selected in a split vote with a substantial minority in opposition, you will have to think long and hard before you accept the appointment. You need the support and confidence of a large majority of the board. Without this kind of support you take a great risk in accepting the position. You can be sure that as time passes and you make hard, unpopular decisions your support on the board is likely to diminish. Very few board members will appreciate what you are up against in dealing with faculty, students, alumni, the legislature, state agencies that coordinate higher education, federal officials, litigants, and organized community groups. Some of the president's decisions will appear weak. Why, for example, did you recommend the sale of beer and wine on campus? Why did you agree to meet with protestors? Why can't you control obscenities in the campus newspaper? Some decisions will appear arbitrary. Why, for example, was the president so opposed to having the chairman of the faculty senate present at board meetings to speak for the faculty on agenda items? Then there is the really tough question: Why doesn't the president attend all of the out-of-town football games? Doesn't the president support intercollegiate athletics? When the president feels that he or she is losing a working majority of the board, it is time to move on. In view of all the problems of managing the institution out in front, you have to be confident that you have a good, strong support behind you . . . and that means support from the board. You cannot fight and win against attacks coming from all sides. In the final analysis, your decision in the case of a split vote on your selection will depend on who voted against you and why. If the "nay" votes came from the first appointments of a new governor with other appointments to come, you will have to make a realistic assessment of your ability to win their confidence and support. You do not want to be in the middle in a power struggle over control of the board. To their credit, the caliber of most boards of regents is such that, whatever the differences of opinion among the members, after a vote is taken the board comes together in support of the president and the institution. The minority does not carp in public.

In selecting a president, the experienced and knowledgeable board will look very carefully at the spouse. Except in those situations where the candidate is female, the board will be evaluating the wife for her ability to contribute to the presidency. The woman who is president of a university is handicapped by not having a wife who can serve as first lady and will freely admit it. The president's wife who works at the job plans and acts as hostess for innumerable official occasions; she makes and keeps up to date endless mailing lists and invitational lists; not uncommonly she will supervise a small staff; she will be expected to join and take a leadership role in women's clubs, garden clubs, fine arts groups, charitable organizations, and, of course, the university ladies club. She will have the responsibility to make sure that the president's home is suitably appointed. The president's wife has a key role in university development (fund raising). If the university's major donors do not like the first lady, the development effort may languish. For all of this the president's wife receives no compensation. So when the president takes the position that his salary is for two, it is an accurate statement. There are university president's wives who have their own careers and do not make an effort as a first lady. These male presidents have the same problem as the female president. They have to hire the job done. You can be sure that if these very important tasks are not well done it will damage your presidency. The office of the president must be efficient in dealing with the people who are important to the institution and, what is more, the office must exude a personal warmth toward and interest in the individuals who can make a difference.

In nearly all universities, and certainly in all prestigious universities, the board of regents has delegated to the general faculty, which in turn has delegated to a faculty senate or other deliberative body, authority to "legislate" in the area of academic programs and student life. The rationale is that the faculty are the most knowledgeable about academic and student affairs. The underlying assumption that is not questioned is that the faculty have the best interests of the institution at heart and want the university to succeed in its educational mission. Thus, unlike his or her executive counterpart in a corporation, the university president must interact with a faculty deliberative body in determining policy and making decisions that have to do with academic and student matters. The rationale for this delegation of authority to the faculty is sound in principle. But in reality many faculty members have little interest in the university's programs outside their own academic department and research projects as long as their salaries are satisfactory, monies are available to pay travel expenses to meetings of learned and professional societies, and the teaching load is not overly heavy. It is left to the president and staff, together with a small number of loyal and dedicated faculty, to worry about the overall direction and quality of the institution.

Observers of the higher education scene have commented that faculty loyalty is to a discipline rather than to an institution. Thus the term "general faculty" has little significance in the modern university and only rarely is a quorum achieved for a meeting of the general faculty. It takes a collective faculty anger about a university issue to turn them out. Similarly, the great majority of faculty members have little interest in faculty senates and their pronouncements. However, faculty senates are of great interest to activists who are so persuaded to an ideology or cause that they seek any opportunity to indoctrinate or proselytize. Their dedication is to their cause rather than to the educational mission of the university. They seek to use the institution to achieve their own purpose, but since their cause is always just, they are using the institution for noble purpose. Fortunately, there are few such faculty—but a few go a long way and they tend to concentrate in the faculty senate. If you are not inclined to let them use the institution to accomplish their own noble purpose, they will work against you very actively, proposing votes of "no confidence" and decrying your lack of leadership.

The president's job is also complicated because the faculty senate, in exercising the authority delegated to it by the board of regents, is not likely to limit its concerns to academic and student matters in the narrow sense. The faculty senate will extend, or attempt to extend, its purview to everything that goes on in the institution. The senate will offer gratuitous advice on management, seek to take a hand in preparing the annual budget, set up their own planning committees, and pass resolutions on any and all university issues. From time to time the senate will take positions on state and national issues. The positions taken will always attract the attention of the governing board and, if the institution is public, the state legislature. In extreme cases, the faculty senate may call for student strikes or work stoppages to protest this or that decision. The senate cannot in most cases persuade the faculty to go on strike because the faculty as a whole does not sympathize with the views of their colleagues who serve as members of the faculty senate. You can have confidence that only in the case of an extraordinary issue of great moment will the general faculty support activist colleagues in the senate on calls for actions to disrupt the normal business of the institution. It is up to you to see that campus issues do not become issues of great moment. You cannot, of course, control national or international issues that have the potential to arouse the faculty.

The existence of a faculty senate with authority over academic and student matters is one reason why the position of a university president differs from that of a business executive and has similarities with that of a city mayor, and it explains why the president cannot make things happen quickly in the area of academic programs. But if you deal openly and directly with the members of the faculty senate, if you do not overburden them with presidential rhetoric, if you take the time to explain to them the realities and limitations of the budget, if you bring important university issues to the faculty senate and ask for advice and counsel, and if you draw the lines of authority in a straightforward manner, it is not likely that you will have to deal with a hostile majority. This is not a task that you can delegate to a vice-president or provost. In order to build and maintain a good relationship with the faculty senate, you will have to give it your personal attention.

In addition to the faculty government within the university, there is the student government, known under that name or as the student association, the student assembly, or a variation on the theme. Boards of regents recognize that it is traditional and desirable to have a student government and expect the president to deal with it constructively and effectively. For many years, student government was a happy, sophomoric enterprise through which students did indeed learn something about the democratic political process by way of election of class officers and participation in a student congress or assembly. In those happy days student government for the most part concerned itself with academic issues important to students, organized social events, and did good works on campus and in the larger community. It rarely took positions on local and national political issues. But then the law-making bodies of the land declared that eighteen-year-olds were adults and enfranchised them. The courts followed along and eased residence requirements for voters. This changed the political complexion of university towns. Professional political organizers moved into the big universities. Young would-be politicians saw election to a student body office as the first step to a higher, real-world political office. And, sadly, some universities began the outrageous custom of paying salaries to the student body president and other officers.

In this new political environment, student government organized with different kinds of players and began to try to wrest management authority away from the administration, first in the area of student life and later in the area of academic programs and budget. The cry was, "The University is for the Students!" That ranks with some of the other great slogans, such as, "If an eighteen-year-old is old enough to fight, he's old enough to vote!" To equate the ability to serve in the armed forces with the capacity to exercise the franchise in a responsible way is like equating the ability to conceive a child with the capacity to support a family. Uni-

versities are not for students in the literal sense. They are established and
operated by society for a public purpose—to develop society's human
resources.

In those cities that were home to big universities, politically organized student bodies became a very real community force and local politicians were quick to pander to them. What was once a body of young
people getting an education became a constituency under more or less
professional political leadership.

Students are as a group bright but possessed of the innocence that
comes from ignorance. They thrive on an adversary relationship with the
president of the institution. Local politicians who once supported the university as a great asset to the community now make political capital out of
attacking the university administration to secure the student vote. Given
all of the rights conferred upon students by legislation and the courts,
there is no way that the president can control them as the board and the
larger community would like. The president cannot control their dress or
their habits; he or she cannot censor their publications, no matter how
lacking in taste or how obscene they might be. If students engage in bizarre, disruptive behavior, the president can move to suspend or expel
them but only under a due process procedure wherein the student's attorney prepares the case for a county or state court. The process may well
drag on for years during which the university is enjoined from removing
the undesirable student from classroom or campus. With competent counsel, an offending student may very well graduate before due process comes
to its ultimate conclusion. By that time, of course, all is moot. Such is the
consequence of the conferring by statute and case law of frivolous rights
upon students.

You as president are obliged to deal with student government. It is a
good practice to insulate yourself as much as possible from day-to-day
dealings with student officers by using a dean of students or vice-president
of student affairs in that capacity. It is now much more pleasant to deal
with student body presidents than it was some years ago. Activists with
state or national political agendas have given way to student presidents
whose primary concerns revolve around legitimate university issues. There
are still activists on campus but they are frustrated by what they call student apathy. The students are not at all apathetic. They may not be interested in an activist political agenda but they are very much interested in
the quality of their education and how well the student service departments of the institution operate.

You must firmly resist student attempts to intrude into the management of the institution. You do not have enough authority to give any
away, particularly to students who do not know enough to make management decisions. However, you can learn a great deal from students about

how your university is operating. Student evaluations of instructors provide important information on what is going on in the classrooms of your institution that cannot be obtained in any other way. That evaluation process should be institutionalized. Do not let the faculty leadership talk you out of it. When school and college faculties, under pressure from accreditation agencies, make recommendations to you on required courses for degree programs, by all means talk to the students. They will have insights as to the value of specific courses that will be invaluable to you in making those academic decisions.

Meet frequently with student groups in informal sessions and put questions to them about their experiences in the classroom, with registration, with student financial aid officers, and with parking problems—generally encourage a dialogue about university life. You will enjoy it. Take notes. Act on what you learn. But do not make the mistake of meeting only with students who hold elective offices in student government. They have their own agenda and what you learn from them will not be nearly as useful as what you will learn from meeting with other student organizations, or even groups picked at random by the computer. But even if you make a great effort to find time to meet with students, you will probably be criticized as too remote or isolated and not sufficiently student oriented. This is certain to be true in a big public university. The students will not know what you do and will not understand why you cannot accept all the invitations from student organizations that come your way.

The quality, loyalty, and dedication of your vice-presidents will have a big impact on the success of your administration. The initial decisions you make on these appointments will be among the most important you will ever make. They must be *your* people. They must work at your pace and have the experience and judgment that produce the right decision at least 90 percent of the time . . . at least! When you assume the presidency of an established university you will find a number of vice-presidents already in place. If you did not reach an understanding with the board about the existing vice-presidents before you accepted the position, you have made a serious mistake. All the vice-presidents should serve at your pleasure. This is not at all to advocate that the new president should make a clean sweep. You may very well want to keep some or all of the existing officers. But the option must be yours. If one or more members of the board suggested that you retain this or that vice-president, you should not commit to do so until you have made your own assessment. The fact that a particular vice-president has support on the board may be good or bad, depending on how the two of you get along. Any sitting vice-president who does not submit a resignation to a new president is suspect.

The matter of vice-president selection is complicated because of the custom in most universities of involving faculty and students in the process of selecting academic officers. The rules and regulations of the institution traditionally provide for the constitution of a search committee composed of some mix of faculty and students, commonly elected, perhaps with some *ex-officio* members, perhaps including regents, perhaps including alumni or other outside members. This committee conducts a national search and provides the president with a list of acceptable candidates, including both inside and outside nominations. It is up to the president to make sure that among the candidates is the individual that he or she wants. Unless there is trouble in the institution and tension between the board and the faculty, the faculty will give the new president considerable latitude in picking his or her own team. If it is necessary to replace an academic officer during the president's tenure, the matter can be more difficult. If the academic vice-president, for example, left voluntarily for reasons of health or retirement, there is not likely to be a problem unless a popular faculty member is running for the job. However, if the president finds it necessary to fire an academic vice-president who has strong faculty support, the selection of a replacement may get sticky.

During the period that you are putting your administrative team in place, you may have to make do with a less than ideal administrative structure built around the people you have and in whom you have confidence. But do not make the mistake of getting comfortable with an established management that is less than optimal. Continue to push until you have the right people in the right positions.

What vice-presidents do you need? You will surely need an academic officer, called an academic vice-president or provost, a vice-president for business affairs, and a vice-president for student affairs. You may need, depending on the size and complexity of the institution, a vice-president for research, a vice-president for graduate programs, a vice-president for administration, a vice-president for development, and a vice-president for university relations. All these positions may carry different names in different institutions. Smaller universities may combine some of the functions under one officer. Commonly, the development and external relations functions are under one vice-president. Responsibilities can be shifted around depending on the special strengths or weaknesses of a particular vice-president. What is important is the function, the workload, and how you use the vice-presidents.

You can expect grumbling about the "massive" bureaucracy. Old timers will remember when the university was run by the president, a provost, a dean of students, the director of the physical plant, and a few experienced assistants and secretaries. Those indeed were the good old days. But in those days of yesteryear the president did not have nearly as much to do and was not required to employ elaborate processes to do it. There were not as many outside agencies interfering with the university's business.

The institution was not under the heavy burden of maintaining records, accounting, reporting, and complying. Litigation was rare. The infrastructure was simpler and smaller. There was no internal audit department. There were no counseling and guidance centers, well-staffed financial aid offices, research grant and contract administration offices, research animal centers, health and safety offices, and data processing centers. For the most part, the deans took care of all that had to be done. The student health center was little more than a first aid station; it certainly was not a fully accredited hospital. Personnel policies were simple. The university's administrators could hire and fire. In these days a simple personnel action requires an elaborate process, including consultation with legal counsel. Records and meetings were closed except to those concerned with the business of operating the institution. Now they are open to everyone, including those lawyers who make a living by extorting money from the nation's public and private institutions. The massive bureaucracy and the high costs of it all stem from the legal requirements our society has elected to put on both its public and private institutions of higher education. So do not be embarrassed because you have five or six vice-presidents while your predecessor had only four. Determine the level of help that you need and build your administration accordingly.

The other key individual in your office is your executive assistant who, depending on level of experience, may be titled assistant to the president. Obviously, you need someone you can trust completely and who has the talent and energy to move paper. This is the individual who creates the image that your office has in the community. Clearly he or she must meet people well and make them feel welcome. If your assistant does not keep your schedule, he or she must be familiar with it and know where you are at all times. He or she supervises the secretarial and clerical staff and is responsible for building and maintaining a happy and efficient office that can turn out the work. The president's office must set an example. The staff must be well dressed. No matter what the current fad on campus, it does not help the institution if visitors are greeted by an unkempt individual in blue jeans. If members of the secretarial staff in your office feel that they must make some kind of "statement" by the way they dress, they do not belong in the president's office. The staff should have a sense of pride in moving forms and letters in and out of the office expeditiously. You do not want people who become sullen if asked to come early and stay late. But it is incumbent on you to recognize high-quality performance through compensation and those little extra considerations that build high morale. You can make the staff feel that they are part of a great enterprise wherein things are happening, and if you do this, they will work for you.

Once these key personnel have been identified and brought aboard, the officers along with senior staff, you must weld them into an effective management team. Organizations in which the vice-presidents aggressively defend "their turf" against intrusions by other vice-presidents do not function well. Make it clear from the outset that you will not tolerate turf battles among your staff. Keep them together in harness. Have weekly staff meetings. Attendance at these meetings should have first priority on their time, and upon your time. They should be meetings in which participation is encouraged. After your items are laid on the table and discussed, each vice-president should have the opportunity to bring up matters for discussion. If they do not take advantage of the opportunity to have a collegial discussion of their problems, you should begin to worry about them. Everyone in the meeting should have a part in bringing an item to decision and action. It may take awhile to get the level of interplay you want; you may have to ask the student affairs vice-president what he or she thinks about an academic matter or a business matter to make it clear that you want everyone's contribution. At all costs avoid the perception that among your vice-presidents there is an "in" group. Again, the "we're all in this together" approach results in productive team management. At least once a year you should take your vice-presidents and their spouses away for a two- or three-day review and planning session in which you collectively evaluate the administration's performance over the past year and make plans for the coming year. Spend some money and go to a nice place far enough away from the campus to eliminate coming and going. Make the spouses feel that they are part of it all. If you are successful, they will not resent the long hours and the late-night phone calls.

At the outset of your administration you can expect to work harder than anyone else on the team, so do not cherish the notion that you can reserve some hours of the day for deep thinking about the great issues of our time. Do that in the car or when you wake up in the middle of the night. Initially, when you assign a problem to a vice-president you will have to work the same problem until you can be confident that he or she can handle the job and come up with the right answer. As the first months go by and you develop confidence in the judgment of your vice-presidents, you can devote more time to things presidential. But if you turn your vice-presidents loose before you know how they work, you can be in a great deal of trouble at the outset of your tenure as president. For the first academic year, the president should focus on putting into place a superior management group that responds quickly, is knowledgeable and accurate, is fair and open, and is respected for its integrity. As the months pass, you can loosen the reins.

Even though you have a strong, capable vice-president for finance or business affairs, you should be knowledgeable about and stay in touch with the internal audit function. This should not be regarded as threatening by the business vice-president. You should know the director of internal audit and he or she should feel free to come directly to you if something important turns up. You should know in general the scope of the annual internal audit plan. From time to time it is a good idea to call the director of internal audit and ask point blank if there is anything that you as president should know.

One of the great myths that abound about universities is that they spend much too much money on administration. Nothing is further from the truth. A big public university may well have an annual operating budget in excess of $500 million. Compared to corporations of similar size that are so admired for the quality of their management, universities spend a very small percentage of their budget to keep the institution functioning. And for public universities the operating environment is getting tougher all the time with ever-increasing requirements for accounting, auditing, reporting, and complying. Ironically, it is the very people who put these burdens on public universities, legislators, who accuse the universities of being top heavy in administration. When it is necessary to cut the budget, they want to take the cuts out of administration. But they are never interested in reducing the administrative burden. In fact, in the same session that funds for administration are cut, some legislative staffer will dream up another report that must be filed with some state office. Unlike corporations that operate extensive management training programs, universities have never been funded so as to be able to develop management depth. Whereas corporations have two or three executives standing in line behind a senior corporate officer, in universities there is commonly no one in sight to move into an executive position should it become vacant unexpectedly. The president must keep in his or her head an inventory of faculty and administrators who have shown some aptitude for management. There will not be many of them. Management succession is a constant concern. Every time one of your vice-presidents looks pale, you will become anxious. This is even more true of deans because replacing a dean requires extensive consultation with the faculty of the college. Even if you have to use scarce discretionary funds available to the president, you should institute some modest management training program.

But a word of caution is in order about management training programs. A good many of the management programs and seminars offered by universities are conducted by management consultants or instructors from business school management departments. It would be unusual if any of these people have ever managed anything larger than a research project. Before you employ anybody or any group to bring management training to your university, make it a point to find out whether any of the instructors have ever carried significant management responsibility. If the proposed curriculum is heavy on group dynamics and interpersonal relations, you do not want it. You want your department chairs and deans to know the substance of your handbook of operating procedures. You want them to know how to fire an employee without exposing the institution to litigation and how to comply with affirmative action policies in hiring an employee. Administration at the operating levels has been enormously complicated by rules and regulations promulgated by state and federal agencies, and by court decisions, that endow employees with many more rights than anyone could possibly have imagined a few decades ago. Casual and informal relations between employees and supervisors are not advisable in this new world of employee rights. A record must be made of conversations about duties and expected performance between supervisor and employee. Under the new health and safety codes and the right-to-know rules, any unhappy employee can find a violation. What you want from your mid-level management training is practical instruction on how to cope with laws, policies, rules, and regulations designed to make efficient and effective management impossible.

The president can alleviate, in a small way, the scarcity of academic administrators, particularly minority administrators, by taking a young intern into the office for a semester or a year and exposing him or her to the full range of problems faced by the central administration of the university. Obviously, the selection of an intern must be made with great care because the individual selected will have access to a great deal of sensitive information. He or she will have to have your complete confidence. Do not be persuaded to a committee selection process. The intern program should be your program and you should make the selection.

If the internship is to be meaningful, the intern should attend all your staff meetings and be privy to administrative interactions among the vice-presidents that occur outside formal meetings. You and your vice-presidents must be willing to spend time with the intern to explain how the administration functions. After some weeks of experience, the intern can be given a special project—one of some significance—on which to study, analyze, conclude and report. A fresh look at the institution's paperwork burden is always useful and the intern can learn a great deal from examining and thinking about all the university's forms and how they are routed.

If you select a promising young minority intern it is not wise to assign to them responsibilities in minority affairs. Although the minority intern can undoubtedly give you some good advice in that area, if it is perceived that you made the selection to satisfy minority organizations on campus the intern will be cast in the role of representing a constituency and that is not the proper role for an administrative intern. It will put him or her in a very difficult position. Your objective, in this case, is to add to the pool of qualified and experienced academic administrators. The time spent by the intern in your office should be a very positive experience and should give a strong boost to his or her administrative career. If you were satisfied by the intern's performance, it is incumbent on you to make sure that your intern's next administrative position has potential for advancement. Once it is perceived that a year in the president's office leads somewhere, you will have very good people from which to choose. If the program is properly managed, these interns will be of great help to you while they are in the office and, perhaps more important, in the future. And from their side, they can learn more as a hands-on intern in the office of the president than by taking a degree in academic administration.

A survey of the number of reports that the university must file with federal and state agencies, the number of employees involved in the effort, and the cost of all this accounting, reporting, and compliance will give you some very useful numbers to share with your representative and senator. Their magnitude will shock you. Do not be optimistic about the possibility of relief from the burden. As a result of sharing this shocking information in the past, federal forms now contain a "Paper Reduction Act Notice" pursuant to 1980 legislation that provides enormously helpful information on how much time the said form requires in record keeping, learning about the law or form, and preparing and sending the form. This initiative by the bureaucracy, although a small matter in itself, demonstrates beyond question that efforts to reduce or contain government are hopeless. Do not waste time on it.

Deans are the chief academic officers of the university's schools and colleges. They are your chief operating officers. You should give them the responsibility to operate and the authority to operate. A good dean is a treasure; a bad dean is a threat to the success of your administration. As with the vice-presidents, you will find deans in place when you begin the presidency. You must get to know them well and evaluate them carefully. Remember that the dean has a very difficult job. He or she leads the faculty of a school or college and, therefore, must have the confidence of the faculty. Indeed, without that confidence, a dean cannot be effective. At the same time, the dean must be your operating officer. He or she must be part of your team. If the dean does not consider his or her school or college to be a part of the university or, put another way, if the dean is running the school or college as if it were a separate academic entity, the president has trouble. Although deans serve at the pleasure of the president, getting rid of one, particularly one who is popular with the faculty, is very difficult. But if the dean is not on your team, you must plan for and effect his or her departure as soon as possible. A hostile dean can hurt you. If you recognize the problem a dean has in walking a line between faculty and central administration, if you support the dean, and, especially if you give the dean the authority to run the school or college, it is likely that he or she will come aboard and function as part of your management group.

For the dean's part, he or she must be prepared to act as an executive and not pass all the problems up the line to you. The dean should not take credit for all the good news and blame all the bad news on the president. Beware of the dean-who-wants-to-be-president . . . soon. There will be another agenda working in that school or college.

It is important that the president and the deans see eye to eye on promotion policies. Once a year you will sit in conference with a dean and your academic vice-president to evaluate candidates for promotion. The promotion decisions on young faculty that come out of that conference will be the president's decision. Promotion should not be a matter that is decided by a vote. In the final analysis, you as president must take the responsibility for the decision to promote faculty members to a tenured position or for putting them on a one-year terminal assignment. But that decision, no matter how it is argued in conference, must be supported by the dean once it is made. The dean may be on record as supporting promotion, but once your decision is made, the dean should not abuse you for it in private. If he or she does, you will know it. If the dean is weak and recommends everyone brought up for promotion by the academic departments, leaving it to you to say "no," you need a new dean. One test of a dean is how insistent he or she is in maintaining high standards for appointment and promotion in the school or college.

Some deans will need more help than others. In some large colleges with their own sources of outside funds, the dean will be able to conduct the college's business without a great deal of help from central administration. The college may run its own continuing education program and its own development effort. You should insist on coordination with university programs in these areas, but if a college program is working well it is probably not a good idea to force centralization of the function. For the smaller schools and colleges, the president will have to provide assistance from the university's central administration in the areas of continuing education, development or fund raising, placement services, planning and budgeting.

If a deanship becomes vacant for whatever reason, you as president should be personally involved in finding a new dean. Do not leave it to the academic vice-president. If you do, the new dean will be "his" dean or "her" dean, as the case may be. Being personally involved means working carefully the composition of the dean's search committee, meeting with the committee, interviewing candidates, and of course making the final selection. It is a good idea to talk informally with members of the board about the selection of a key dean to make sure there are no problems at that end. But the final decision must be yours.

In many universities, the deans report to the vice-president for academic affairs or the provost. This makes a neater organizational table and is preferred by management experts who always want to minimize the number of people who report directly to the president. I think it is a mistake. I believe that deans should have a direct line to the president. If you operate properly, deans will soon learn that it saves time and improves chances for a successful recommendation if they first take an issue to the academic vice-president or provost. And you should make sure that the academic vice-president or provost is present at meetings with deans. Once the deans learn that their direct access to you does not cut the academic vice-president or provost out of the loop, they will not make a nuisance of themselves by calling or coming to see you about trivial matters. It strengthens the deans' position to have direct access to the president and you want strong deans. You should meet regularly with the deans in a deans' council; monthly is adequate, with special meetings as necessary. If you can make this deans' council into an effective management council, you will be a long way down the road to a successful presidency. It is also beneficial to meet with the deans in a special session at the beginning of the academic year, preferably after you have had the executive officers retreat, to discuss plans for the year. There should be a social function including spouses. This reinforces the concept of the management team. If a dean believes he or she is out there alone, your administration is the weaker for it.

You will, of course, be evaluating the performance of vice-presidents and deans on a day-to-day basis. But in these times, for the record, it is good practice to have in place a formal evaluation process whereby once a year an evaluation exercise is conducted. These evaluations provide a file to support salary increases and promotions so it will not appear to an outside reviewer that you have been whimsical, capricious, or arbitrary in your decisions. In addition, it is common for the rules and regulations of the institution to provide for a formal review of the president, his or her staff, and the deans after a term of four to six years. In some institutions, the president is given a multiyear employment contract; in others he or she serves at the pleasure of the board. Even with a contract, of course, if the board wants to replace the president it can do so, either under the terms of the contract or by making it impossible for the president to function. The existence of the contract does not guarantee the tenure of the president for the stated term. Rather, it makes it more costly for the board to fire the president in midterm. For the other officers, there is commonly no more than the expectation of annual appointments for as long as performance is satisfactory. Of course, the academic officers also hold tenured appointments as faculty members so that if they do not continue as administrative officers they have the security of a faculty position. The president, when appointed from outside the institution, is customarily offered a tenured professorship in his or her discipline. Academic departments are rarely enthusiastic about accepting an administrator into their ranks and usually take advantage of the opportunity to pry a new position out of the administration to accommodate the new president. There is usually some benefit to the department if the president is from that discipline. Thus, it is rare for an academic department to refuse outright an academic appointment to the new president if he or she is reasonably well qualified in the field. If the new president is appointed from inside the institution, these academic relationships will be already in place.

Before accepting the presidency, you should ask for and receive copies of the institution's charter, bylaws, rules, regulations, and policy memoranda. You should read them. Taken all together, these constitute the code that governs the operation of the university. You may be the first person to read these documents in years. In all probability, once you are installed you will want to commission a review and update of the rules and regulations. Revision of some of them will require board approval. Having read them, you will understand why things are done as they are in your new university. If you can eliminate some of the signatures required on documents, you may be able to speed up the flow of paper at an early date in your administration. This will get you off to a good start. Do not be so enthusiastic about streamlining the bureaucracy, however, that you move too quickly to eliminate what appear to be unnecessary written policies governing the operation of the campus. Our society has become so litigious, and both students and faculty have been endowed with so many rights, that the absence of written policies may weaken the university's case in litigation and brand you as an incompetent administrator. Policies on access to the campus and the use of its facilities are essential. There must be policies familiar to you, your vice-presidents, deans, directors, department chairs, and campus security officers on how to deal with emergencies on campus. Bomb threats are a good example. You will receive them, most likely during examination periods, and you should know in advance under what conditions you will evacuate buildings and when you will not. It is a good idea to develop these kinds of policies in consultation with the FBI and local law enforcement officials. You will probably not have to develop a policy manual from "scratch," but in conducting your review of what is in place it is a good idea to involve the university's legal counsel in the effort to make sure that you appreciate all the legal implications of the policies extant as well as any gaps in existing policies.

The president's working day and evening will be spent in meetings, on the telephone, and at a podium. What kind of record should you keep of all this daily verbiage? I believe that you should keep all the notes and texts of the remarks, speeches, and addresses that you give. It will be a valuable information file for the historian. It will also remind you of what you said to a particular group in previous years. When you are misquoted in the newspaper or when what you said is taken out of context, the existence of a written or tape record of what you actually said will help keep them honest next time. There are mixed opinions about keeping minutes or tape records of meetings. In any litigation all the records will be subpoenaed by the plaintiff's attorneys, who will pore over them to find some phrases that can be woven into a theory of conspiracy. Some administrators who have had this experience believe strongly that you should keep no official written records of meetings and no personal notes pertaining to the business transacted. However, if you follow this principle, you may find your case damaged by conflicting testimony from faulty memories. The court proceedings will be two or three years after the fact. Attorneys, judges, and juries who do not lead the kind of high-pressure executive life that you do will be astounded or, in the case of the plaintiff's counsel, will pretend incredulity because you cannot remember the details of a promotion conference held three years ago. If you are running a fair and honest management, you are well advised to keep complete records of the business conducted. Written records are preferred over tapes. The informal and conversational asides so characteristic of tape records are not helpful. Read the record before it goes into the file so you are not subsequently embarrassed by errors and omissions.

After having been in the office for some months you will become aware of comments about your management style. Your style may be labeled "hands on" or "laid back," "collegial" or "aloof," or perhaps "autocratic." You will be accused of not delegating enough authority or of delegating too much. If after meeting two or three times with a department chair who wants to argue about an issue, you refuse to change a decision, the word will spread that you are "uncompromising." For the most part these analyses of your management style will be made by people who have no idea in the world of what you are doing or why. To avoid having these uninformed views of how you do your job enshrined as the common wisdom, it is a good idea early in your administration to put your own label on how you intend to approach management, either through an interview with the local or campus newspaper or by arranging for the information to come through an interview with one of your vice-presidents. Your description of how you work will be accepted until such time as the record demonstrates that your practice does not conform to what you have announced.

If you have been attracted to the presidency of one of those institutions where final authority on faculty appointments, promotions, and salaries rests for all practical purposes with deans or faculty committees and the president is expected to do no more than ratify and recommend to the board, use the authority you do have over the budget and the appointment of academic officers and committees, as well as the prestige of the office, to build the president's authority and influence over these matters that are so vital to the institution's academic success. To the extent that you can increase the authority of the president to manage the institution you will leave it better than you found it.

Management and governance issues will be touched upon in succeeding sections of this Primer as necessary to develop other topics. Some repetition is unavoidable and may even be desirable so that the reader may consult chapters independently without having to refer to this chapter for background.

CHAPTER 3

Committees

THERE IS no university without a generous endowment of standing
and *ad hoc* committees to assist the administration in carrying out management responsibilities. The university committee can be enormously useful to the president. For example, within a university the only acceptable
excuse for a delay in decision on the part of the president is that the matter
is under study by a faculty committee or a faculty-student committee. Review and study by a committee permits administrators to be fully informed
about an issue before a decision is made. Or, put another way, it permits
issues to age or season appropriately before action is initiated. Problems
arise when a committee goes beyond its charge and considers matters that
are none of its business, or when a committee ignores the word "advisory"
in its name and charge and informs the president of its decision instead of
its recommendation.

Standing committees of the university are those that have a continuing function year after year; they remain in existence as long as that function is considered necessary. The members change from year to year, preferably through staggered terms to provide continuity. Typically, there will
be twenty to thirty standing committees, which may be grouped into
committees dealing with faculty affairs, student affairs, and institutional
policy or the operation of the institution. Among the faculty committees
will be a rules committee, a committee on academic freedom, a grievance
committee, and various other committees on welfare, travel to scientific
and scholarly meetings, and those other faculty issues of a perennial nature. The student committees will include financial aid, discipline policies,
academic probation and reinstatement, orientation, recreation, health, and
housing and dining halls.

It is the institutional standing committees focused on administrative
matters that have the most interaction with the president and his or her

staff. They are concerned with admissions and registration, the academic calendar, commencement and other academic ceremonies, educational policy, campus buildings, the library, and the important area of parking and traffic. Depending on the institution, there may be other standing committees dealing with international programs, teaching assistants, recruitment and retention of minority students, care of laboratory animals, research on human subjects, intellectual property rights, energy conservation, research grants and contracts, equal opportunity, occupational health and safety, and teacher education. The standing committee on intercollegiate athletics will be discussed separately. If there is not a committee on committees, there should be. This is a committee that reviews the institution's committee structure and makes recommendations on membership. It is important because it is through the committee on committees that the president can exert some influence on the makeup of university committees. Each school or college of the university will also have an array of standing committees to assist the dean in his or her administrative duties. Indeed, they may be equal in number to the university's standing committees. As a general rule, however, there will be five to ten of them.

Many of these standing committees have rather mundane housekeeping functions that are important to the operation of the institution. They perform a useful, noncontroversial service and do not require much of the president's time. For example, once the president has decided on how commencement ceremonies are to be conducted and the appropriate committee is given an experienced chair, the committee can proceed annually to make the arrangements and publish the programs.

Building committees from time to time are charged with having misplaced priorities because faculty members who are not on the committee do not understand why their departments do not have as high a priority for new quarters as departments whose faculty are on the committee. It is a good idea if a number of the members of that committee, including the chair, are from departments that occupy recently constructed buildings. It permits the committee to take a broad, institutional view of the problem.

The committee that deals with faculty travel or, as it is commonly labeled, the committee on attendance at meetings of learned societies may have as one of its responsibilities the allocation of a pool of travel money to send faculty members to national meetings. Since there is never enough money to meet all the requests, the president can expect to receive annual resolutions from the committee calling for more travel money. If you as president do not have any more travel money, you may be accused of misplaced priorities.

The committee on equal opportunity is strongly supported in principle by all faculty members until such time as the committee finds fault with the recruiting practices of a particular department. Notwithstanding a strong commitment to the principles of affirmative action, the faculty of an academic department will fight to the death to protect their traditional right to chose their own colleagues. If a department is not making progress in recruiting minority and women faculty members, the president will have to take action. The first move should be through the committee on equal opportunity. It will be helpful if it is a strong, respected committee with an accomplished and diplomatic chair.

The committee on intercollegiate athletics may be a single integrated committee or there may be two committees, one for men's intercollegiate athletics and one for women's intercollegiate athletics. This very important committee(s) oversees a business that bears little or no relation to the mission of a university. It is a prestigious committee and membership on it is much sought after. There are commonly "perks" for its faculty members, including invitations to banquets, tickets, travel to out-of-town games, privileged parking close to the stadium, and access to the press box. The president must be able to rely on this committee. If it does not do its job, the president is in serious trouble with the National Collegiate Athletic Association and the board of regents. If it does its job too well, the president is in serious trouble with influential alumni and the board of regents.

Ad hoc committees, as distinguished from standing committees, are designed to deal with specific problems with the hope that both the problem and the committee will go away after a decent interval of committee study and the issuance of a final report. It is the *ad hoc* committee that looks into deficiencies in the learning environment or faculty morale. The *ad hoc* committee is, of course, the device by which the president buys time to deal with a potentially nasty situation, defuses a fast-breaking and potentially explosive situation, and, from time to time, brings together a group of able faculty, staff, and students to work a difficult problem that requires a task-force approach. If not overused, the *ad hoc* committee can be a valuable management tool. It must have a clear charge and strong membership. Having once created an *ad hoc* committee, the president is well advised not to ignore its recommendations.

The search committee, formed to assist the president in identifying candidates for academic positions where the advice of faculty and students is appropriate, is an *ad hoc* committee that requires close attention from the president. A search committee procedure will always apply to the selection of provosts, academic vice-presidents, and vice-presidents for student affairs; it may apply to research vice-presidents; it will not apply to vice-presidents for business affairs, administration, or development and external affairs; it will always apply to deans. Because the search committee includes elected faculty and student members, the process of constituting the committee takes considerable time. The committee will then organize and begin deliberations. It is rare if a list of candidates for the president's consideration can be produced in less than a semester. It commonly requires at least an academic year. The press will complicate matters by demanding lists of the candidates under consideration. In the meantime, the president appoints an "acting" officer. If the man or woman you want for the job is on campus, you can appoint him or her in an acting capacity and hope that the excellence of the choice will become evident to the university community, and that the desired individual will make the committee's list. If it does not, you can ask the committee for more names. If the name still does not make the list, you and your candidate should recognize that without the committee's blessing there is little chance that the acting vice-president could be effective in the position. So, you begin a new search. Depending on the nature of the impasse, you may want to make some new appointments to the committee. In any case, search committees seem to function much better if, in addition to the elected faculty and student members, the president adds some distinguished friends of the university who are prominent in business, the arts, or public affairs and who can bring experience and wisdom to the selection process.

Standing committees and *ad hoc* committees of the university may be composed entirely of faculty members; they may have a mixed membership of faculty and staff; they may include student members. A fundamental rule of good administration is that all committees should be advisory to the president and that all committee appointments should be made by the president. There are exceptions, of course. Some special committees are created to discharge a particular function rather than to advise and make recommendations. Committees created to select the recipients of scholarships, fellowships, or other awards are an example. The president is well advised to enjoy the protection of a committee that stands between him or her and these decisions. Committees may also be created to advise officers of the administration other than the president.

You as president must maintain control over the institution's committees. Great care must be exercised in making appointments to the standing and *ad hoc* committees. Their leadership and makeup, that is to say who serves on them, will in no small measure determine whether the president leads a happy or dismal life. Nevertheless, you must avoid a blatant display of presidential authority. The device that is commonly used to protect the president against charges that the university's committees have been staffed (stacked, stuffed, packed, or loaded) with friends, adulators, and sycophants is the aforementioned committee on committees. This is a committee whose members are elected by the faculty and that each year reviews committee staffing needs and submits to the president a panel of three or so names for each vacancy. The president then selects, except in rare or extraordinary cases, one of the individuals on the list. In this way, the new committee member selected by the president is also blessed by the faculty. This system does not always ensure friendly or rational committees, but on balance it is the best game going for the administration. If the appointment is to a very important committee and if there is no acceptable nomination from the committee on committees, the president can request that the committee on committees supply additional names. It is not a good idea to request additional names too often, but in a crisis it is acceptable. If the president has looked to his or her relationships with key members of the faculty, informal conversation with influential members of the committee on committees can usually produce committees that will work with the president rather than take an obstructionist or hostile position.

In discharging its advisory function with regard to committee membership, the committee on committees, ideally, will consider the charge to the committee in question and the individuals most knowledgeable about the subject and most effective in getting things done. It may recommend, for example, that the committee on academic probation and reinstatement include the academic vice-president, one faculty member from each college, one graduate student, and two undergraduate students. That is a reasonable recommendation, but it raises the issue of the appointment of students to university committees. There are some university committees whereon student members are invaluable. These are committees that advise about or otherwise concern themselves with university services. On other committees, such as the example cited, student members provide the student constituency with an appropriate vote on policy matters that directly affect student life and at the same time give the president some designated individuals with whom he or she can communicate about decisions on individual cases about which the student newspaper will be misinformed. No one but a student can give you reliable information on how the library serves students. Student members of the library committee can and will tell you if the policies of the director of libraries are designed to protect books against students or to put books into the hands of students as quickly and efficiently as possible. Only students on the admissions committee can tell you if the registrar hates students and is determined to exclude as many as possible from matriculation or holds out a warm hand of welcome and tries to help entering students with their problems. But on other kinds of committees students do not have a great deal to offer. The committee that deals with new program priorities, for example, will receive little help from student members unless they are truly uniquely qualified. Few students are able to apply sage judgment on how the university should order its program priorities.

There are faculty members who in their passion to be popular with students vigorously support student membership on all university committees and failing all other argument will hold that service on university committees is a desirable learning experience for students. The president should resist this argument. In its classes, the university offers learning experiences sufficient to tax all serious students. The university's committees are part of the management structure and membership on them should be designed with that purpose in mind. They do not exist to teach students how committees function.

We have discussed the standing and *ad hoc* committees of the university that report to the president. The general faculty of the institution will have its own committees, elected by the general faculty according to its bylaws. These committees are charged by the general faculty and indeed may be self-charging. A very special kind of general faculty committee is the faculty senate or faculty council discussed briefly in a previous reference. This is a legislative body that represents and acts for the larger body of the general faculty. The presiding officer is usually elected from the membership of the senate. The senate will have its own retinue of committees, standing and *ad hoc*, and some of them may have the same function as the university committees that report to the president. So . . . in the typical university, there are committees within committees and governments within governments and it is the president's responsibility to bring all of these helpful people into a productive working relationship. If you as president are skillful and adroit in this task of coordination, you may achieve a degree of harmony within the structure, but you will never be able to explain to the board of regents why you cannot "get things done in a reasonable length of time." In a university, getting it done within an academic year *is* a reasonable length of time.

Some universities have a separate faculty body, commonly called a council or assembly, to deal with graduate education. They may also have a graduate faculty separate and distinct from the general faculty but, at the senior level, composed of the same people. The younger faculty members, after their scholarly reputation is assured, are advanced to membership in the graduate faculty. Like the faculty senate, the graduate council is elected, in this case by the graduate faculty. It legislates and makes recommendations to the president on the graduate academic programs. It is also greatly concerned with research leaves and research grants for the graduate faculty. Even though the faculty senate and the graduate council may have many of the same members, the natural contentiousness of faculty makes it unlikely that these two deliberative bodies will always agree on academic policy. The existence of two faculty legislative bodies may on the face of it appear wasteful of time and effort, but in reality it commonly works to the president's advantage, not precisely in the mode of divide and conquer, but because it spreads faculty authority over the academic program into two forums rather than having it all concentrated in one legislative body. The separate graduate council is more commonly a feature of universities that are developing graduate programs; mature universities have largely done away with the separation of a graduate as contrasted to a general faculty. They do not employ young faculty who are not fully qualified to instruct graduate students. If you find yourself president of an academically mature university in which the distinction between graduate and regular faculty is still retained, it is a good idea to propose and submit a plan to eliminate the distinction. It will be well received by junior faculty.

Upon receipt of a committee report the president will immediately write to the chair of the committee, thank the committee for its hard work, diligence, and thoughtful consideration of the complex issues involved, remark on the committee's perception, and promise to respond in detail to the committee's recommendations as soon as the president's staff has an opportunity to study and review the report. You must also make a few comments that will demonstrate that you have looked at the report. If you can get this letter off within a few days of receiving the report you will astound the academic community with your administrative skill. It will be amazing to them that the report has come directly to you without dying in some assistant's office, that you have found it on your desk, that you have actually read it, and that you have taken the time and had the courtesy to respond to the committee. Incidentally, it is important to send a copy of your letter to the chair to all members of the committee because the chair will not distribute your letter (he or she will not have time) and thus the membership will be deprived of the evidence of your remarkable administrative skill. Of course, to achieve this high level of administrative performance, you must make sure that the report does not die in some assistant's office.

If the report is not what the president hoped to receive, it can be sent back to the committee with comments and a request for further study. However, to avoid the appearance of rejection of the report by the administration, the president should invite the committee to meet with him or her. This gives the committee members a sense that their work is important and it gives the president a chance to make some new friends. The president may even spring for a luncheon so that assistant professor Roe can remark casually to his departmental colleagues, "I had lunch with the president yesterday, and he said . . ." If the president has the support, or even the passive acceptance, of a majority of the university committees, the chances for a presidential tenure as long as three or four years are greatly enhanced.

Having achieved this reputation for paying attention to what committees have to say and being on top of the university's business, the president will send the committee report to the appropriate vice-president and spend a few moments talking generally about the report at the next staff meeting. At this point you should let the vice-presidents and other officers assembled know how you rate the importance of the issue. If it is a "hot one," for example, involving parking where there is no solution that will satisfy everyone or anyone, it is best to resolve the matter as best you can in the summer when the faculty is largely absent and the student body is reduced in number. By the time they all return it will be a "done deal" and old news. But how to deal with the report in November when it comes across your desk?

One way to handle it is to have a vice-president prepare a detailed response and then set up a series of meetings with the committee to outline and discuss the principal issues. If there is an impasse between what the faculty want and what the administration can provide, as is generally the case, the president, stressing the importance of these matters to the entire university community, can send the report to another committee with some broad and vague purview over university affairs. The committee on the academic environment is always a good one because it is concerned with just about everything that takes place on campus. This committee will debate the matter until spring. You can bet on it. An alternative is to involve the faculty senate. Even though their authority may be expressly limited to academic matters, the senate will take the position that everything that happens within the institution affects the academic environment. Once in the faculty senate, the committee report is effectively on the shelf for another year. If it shows signs of moving along, the president can arrange for some questions from the floor so as to generate prolonged debate.

It is a happy occasion when the president receives a report with clear, well-reasoned recommendations that can be implemented without bankrupting the institution or radically altering its mission. The committee that produces such a report should be recognized by the president in some public forum and given full credit for solving a tough problem. Of course, for most problems the solution is obvious to the president and committee consideration is unnecessary. However, the solution advanced by the president will be much more palatable if it can be ascribed to a respected faculty committee. If at all possible the president should arrange for his or her decision to track a committee recommendation. It proves that the faculty does indeed have input into the decision-making process. There are occasions when a friendly committee can be led to the right recommendations. However, this is a risky procedure and should be eschewed in all but very serious situations.

However tempted, the president is advised not to suggest that this or that matter is none of the faculty's business. The president is always eager to have faculty input. Always. The inherent problem with committee recommendations is that at best they are a consensus of the members' views.

It would be rare indeed if every member of a faculty committee reviewed the same data and came to the same conclusion. More likely, there will be some members who are completely correct in their analysis and judgment and others who are completely wrong. Thus the committee recommendation, unless the chair is unusually capable and persuasive, will be half right or half wrong, as the case may be. Even with a very good chair, there may be a minority report. None of the preceding discussion of dealing with committee reports should be construed as suggesting that the president should accept and implement recommendations that are clearly faulty. The committees are advisory, or should be, and the president must have the courage to reject bad advice.

Most faculty members, if they have been around for a few years, serve on a number of departmental, college, and university committees. Some are important, some are not, but all take time. It is difficult for a faculty member, particularly one who is not tenured, to refuse to serve on a committee because service to the university is one of the criteria evaluated for promotion and salary advancement. And considering that at least some committees are essential to the functioning of the institution, committee service is properly part of what a faculty member does to earn his or her salary. Thus, the president should be appropriately appreciative of the long hours of faculty time that go into committee service. The president may well have to defend this expenditure of faculty time before the board and, in the case of the public institution, before the legislature. Some state legislators who have little knowledge of how a university functions do not believe that committee service is a legitimate part of a faculty member's work load. They take the position that the legislature appropriates funds to pay faculty members to teach, not waste hours and hours serving on committees. Of course, when they make these statements they are usually in committee. One might point out that legislators are elected and paid to pass laws, not serve on committees. However, it is not a good idea to point this out, notwithstanding the fact that the analogy has some merit. So, in every session, those speaking for the university administration explain why it is necessary for faculty to serve on committees and why such service is an appropriate part of their work load; legislators make caustic remarks; no one's mind is changed; and another irritation is introduced between representatives of the academy and representatives of the public.

Legislatures that control funding for public universities tend to be insensitive to the difference between undergraduate and graduate education. They have little or no appreciation for the amount of time faculty members must spend working individually with graduate students on their research and on their thesis and dissertation problems. They will not understand that research is an integral part of graduate education. One test of a president's ability is how successful he or she is in securing reduced teaching loads and research support for faculty involved in graduate education. The faculty will be frustrated at the institution's inability to communicate to the legislature what is so obvious—that a professor cannot do a good job of teaching three organized courses per semester and also give the proper amount of time to his or her graduate students. Legislators, particularly legislators from rural districts, will be convinced that a faculty member who only has to spend three hours a week in class for each of three courses is not working full time, and they will not be sympathetic to the proposal to reduce the load to two courses or six hours per week of organized instruction to permit more attention to the graduate program. The president can present numbers on how many hours are spent in preparation for class, in grading tests and editing papers, in serving on important committees, and in scholarship and research, only to be told that the faculty member should not be wasting time on that stuff anyway. He or she should be teaching! One way to put the issue in terms that can be understood in the state house is to cast the work load of a legislator in terms of only the hours spent on the floor of the house or senate and ignore the many hours spent on committee assignments, committee hearings, dealing with constituents, and preparing legislation. The analogy between the off-the-floor work done by a legislator and the out-of-classroom work done by a faculty member is good enough to be persuasive. This is an area where the burden of the public university president is much heavier than for a colleague in a private institution.

Chairing an academic committee is an art learned only after many years of living and working with faculty members. The president who has come up through the academic ranks will likely be adept in the art. Although most of that labor is behind the university president, there may be times when it is a good idea for you to chair an important *ad hoc* committee. For the president who has come into the university from the corporate or public service world, there are a few simple rules that must be followed. The boardroom procedure that moves business quickly according to the agenda with the phrase, "without objection, it is approved," has no place in the conduct of the business of a faculty committee.

The first basic rule is that a committee meeting should never be scheduled before four o'clock in the afternoon. The second rule is to permit, indeed encourage, all committee members to talk as long as they want on any subject. The agenda makes a handy sheet for doodling during these flights of rhetoric. The agenda is not a guide to the business of the meeting and should never be used to rule out-of-order those who want to complain about the repressive actions of this or that dean, the low state of faculty morale, or the president's lack of leadership. The person in the chair listens with unbelievable patience, and with restraint and good humor, recognizing everyone, with a gentle push here and a slight turn there, until, close to five o'clock, most of the members of the committee leave. Business can then be addressed and expeditiously completed in the last fifteen or twenty minutes by those with whom the chair has quietly caucused in advance of the meeting. If the meeting has been scheduled too early, there is a risk that the orators will run down and the chair will be faced with doing business with the full committee membership. The third basic rule is to permit all members of the committee to rewrite the minutes so that what he or she said during the meeting does not appear as foolish as it was. Of course, this means that the minutes do not come out until the semester after the meeting was held. The rewritten minutes contain little of what was discussed at the meeting; rather, they are a series of essays that represent what the committee members wish they had said. But, since minutes of committee meetings are rarely read by anyone, and since it all happened a long time ago, it does not matter. The fourth rule of academic committee chairship is to give the final report of the committee a chance to age. Take plenty of time to make sure that all affected constituencies in the university have a chance to read and comment on a first draft. Unlike the minutes that are never read, the final report is always read. It will be the product of the chair with more or less editorial help from other committee members. By the time the chair has circulated several drafts of the report, most of the committee members will have lost interest in whatever the committee was addressing. In the event there is an obstinate committee member who will not let go and does not agree with the chair, the opportunity for a minority report should be offered to the dissident. This requires work and may put an end to the controversy. If not, the minority report may cause a minor stir among a small group of chronic dissidents, but it should be manageable.

It should not concern the president that standing committees, *ad hoc* committees, committees of the general faculty, committees of the faculty senate, and committees of the graduate assembly, not to mention committees of the student government, may be dealing with the same issues at the same time. This is entirely normal. If fact, this kind of drawn-out, duplicative, multiple consideration and reconsideration of issues may give the president time to manage the affairs of the university. Indeed, on top of all of the existing committees, the president is well advised to create one or two *ad hoc* committees to consider very broad, tenuous issues, such as the campus learning environment, academic innovation, or directions and priorities, and to put on these committees some of his or her severest critics. This will keep them busy. The purpose is not so much to co-opt critics but to educate them so they will have some basis for distinguishing between what is desirable and what is possible, always a very difficult task for faculty members. Perspicacious faculty may refuse the president's call to serve on such committees because they do not want to be subject to the discipline of knowing what is possible. These *ad hoc* committees may soak up some of the energies of young Turks who would otherwise be loudly deploring an uncaring and inhumane administration. Do not be surprised if some excellent ideas come out of these committees, ideas that may make your reputation as a president with vision.

The exception is the committee on academic priorities. If membership is balanced among the schools and colleges of the university, as it must be, there will never be any hard choices made on priorities. The report will say that in the considered judgment of the committee everything is equally important and all should have the highest priority. Just accept the report with appropriate presidential gratitude. Everyone knows that you will have to make the tough choices and take the heat on priorities.

University committees, along with absentminded professors, are the subject of apocryphal anecdotes and snide humor both inside and outside the institution. The common wisdom is that when an academic problem confounds the administrators a committee is formed, and that academics spend their time in committees in long, tedious debates over trivia. There is enough truth in the characterizations to perpetuate them. But for the president, although a little humor might be permitted in this area, managing the university's multitude of committees is a very serious business. An important committee with a determined and capable chair can be a formidable force in support of the president, or in opposition.

CHAPTER 4

The Campus and Its Facilities

THE CAMPUS is the place where the community of teachers and scholars that is the university is located. Even though the terms "campus" and "university" are used interchangeably in casual conversation, the president should always keep in mind the comprehensive, even intellectual, connotation of "university" as against the more geographic "campus." The campus is the real estate. The university is the people, the programs, and the real estate. The term "learning environment" will be popular with the faculty and it is a good idea to have a committee on the learning environment as a statement to the high priority you place on the values and facilities necessary to the pursuit of learning.

The campus of a university may be several hundred acres of rolling, wooded terrain adjacent to a charming village and adorned by ivy-covered, architecturally pleasing stone or brick buildings, or it may be some blocks in a dense, crowded, noisy urban area occupied by early- or mid-twentieth century office buildings. The campus may consist of contiguous property or it may include parcels of land some miles apart. Not uncommonly, universities operate field or research stations long distances from the main campus. These may include astronomical observatories, marine laboratories, zoological, biological, or botanical stations, or inner-city centers for sociological research. These off-campus facilities are obviously built and maintained to permit faculty and students access to special environments necessary for scientific, engineering, or social science investigations.

Many universities have been the recipients of gifts of real estate far from the campus, which, if the university has accepted a covenant that prohibits sale, tax all the creativity of the president to find some beneficial use to which they can be put. As president, you are well advised to politely refuse gifts of real estate that are encumbered with provisions that restrict the use or sale of the property. You may find yourself with an expensive white elephant that consumes resources badly needed to support and maintain the campus. Of course, it may not be easy to find a gracious way to tell a would-be donor who has been generous with the university in the past that you do not want the family farm and that maintaining it in perpetuity as a nature sanctuary or pioneer village would put too heavy a financial burden on the institution. If, on balance, refusing the gift would cost more in the long run than accepting it, try to persuade the donor to provide an endowment to maintain and operate the property.

You will learn a great deal by investigating the history of the campus. How was the land acquired originally? Was it a gift or purchase? Was it dedicated for a university by action of a governmental body? Was the land set aside by a state constitution? To what extent was the original campus expanded by subsequent acquisitions? A good way to start is to walk around the campus and look at the statues; read the inscriptions on the plaques displayed just inside or just outside the buildings. If there are no plaques, someone has missed an opportunity to recognize individuals who have played a prominent role in building the campus and you should make a note to put appropriate plaques in place. In conducting research on the history of the campus, you may run across some skeletons that you need to be informed about as well as some long-smoldering resentments. If the land was acquired by gift or bequest years ago, you should make inquiry about the family of the deceased donor and the attitudes of his or her descendants toward the university. If the donor is living, you will, of course, arrange to meet him or her to determine if the university has complied with its commitments and to evaluate the possibilities for additional benefactions.

The faculty and staff that are permanently assigned to off-campus facilities or who spend long periods in residence away from the main campus commonly develop a feeling of isolation . . . that they are out of the mainstream of campus life. They are. There are steps the president can take to overcome the isolation and make sure that the faculty and professional staff are involved in activities of appropriate academic departments. Faculty who are resident at off-campus facilities can be brought to the campus periodically for a semester assignment, funds can be provided to encourage visits to the off-campus facility by student groups and campus-based faculty, and with current technology video links can be established. You should make a point of visiting all these off-campus facilities early in your presidency and give the resident staff an opportunity to talk to you about their problems and aspirations.

As president, you are the chief planning officer and have the responsibility for looking down the road at the university as it will exist one or two decades hence. Is the campus adequate for a reasonable expansion of the institution? If not, you will need to institute a land acquisition plan.

Your successor will bless you for your vision. Depending on the environment in which the university is located, it may indeed take ten years or more to acquire key tracts of land.

But, while history may praise you for acquiring at a reasonable price land to accommodate the university's future growth, you and your institution may, depending on current land use on the tracts you are seeking to purchase, be severely criticized. If you are president of a private university and work to acquire land anonymously through a private broker, paying market price and blocking up acreage over the long term, it is less likely that the action will be subject to attack by property owners or neighborhood associations. On the other hand, if you are president of a public institution and can, when all else fails, use the power of eminent domain to acquire property, you may find yourself embroiled in political battles and have to deal with hostile legislators or city council members who find political advantage in defending neighborhood political associations. Considering what the university brings to the community in which it is located, it is difficult to understand how the political leadership can subordinate the long-term interest of the many to the short-term interest of the few, but it happens. In considering any land acquisition plan you should be forewarned that there may be political repercussions from what is in the university's view a prudent long-term program.

If your university is a relatively new institution, your research will probably disclose that there was a controversy over the selection of the campus site. Those who made the selection will have been accused of conflicts of interest, conspiracies to enrich themselves and their friends, and disregard for the larger social interest. Failing any proof of conspiracies, the criticism is likely to have come from special interest groups who wanted to use the establishment of a new university to solve another problem, such as urban renewal or economic development of a particular area. Building a new university in a slum may indeed improve the slum, but it does not result in the kind of campus attractive to students, even students from the blighted area. As president of a new university you will inherit the legacy of the conflicts inherent in its establishment. So you need to know the history.

Through owning a large tract of land, whether rural, urban, or suburban, you will have neighbors. Because you operate facilities on the land, you will affect the lives of your neighbors. Because large numbers of people travel to and from the campus each day, your university will impact the public transportation system that is built and maintained by public entities. The university will not pay taxes to the local and state governments that construct and maintain the highways, roads, and bus lines. Local government officials will be very much aware that the university does not contribute directly to their tax revenues and will remind you of it when you have a request of them that involves resurfacing or widening a road, improvements or expansion in the delivery of electric power to the campus, or a simple change in zoning. Before entering into any such discussions with local government officials, you should be well prepared on the contribution that the university makes to the local economy. Know how many jobs the university provides, how much money it introduces into the economy, and how many times in the past the university has generously provided easements to the city or county to facilitate their projects. Be prepared also to comment on the intangible benefits that the university brings to the area. Local citizens will attend cultural events sponsored by the university; they will use the university library and athletic facilities. If there are no university programs that encourage this kind of interaction with the town, you should by all means initiate such programs.

The university should be an active participant in community affairs, not an inwardly focused city inside a masonry or cultural wall. It is a very good idea to set up a formal university-town council to provide for communication and exchange between the academic community and the larger society. University towns and cities where the institution has been in place for many years take the university and all that it brings for granted and have little appreciation for what a precious asset it is. You may have to remind them. Those among the city leadership involved in trying to attract new clean industries to the area will be aware of how important the university is to corporate officials searching for a new plant site, but unfortunately they will have little influence on city officials obstructing the university over a zoning issue. You may be so aggravated by small-minded, unappreciative city officials that you consider the possibility of moving the university to a new site. If, because of an extraordinary appreciation of the value of your campus as real estate, that is a realistic option, you will certainly get the attention of the city leadership. But the reality is that for nearly all institutions a combination of sunk costs and tradition means that you are stuck where you are.

Although the faculty will take every opportunity to make the point that "bricks and mortar" are not important . . . that the university is a teacher and his students (they will not be as sensitive as you about the need to specify both genders) . . . you will have to worry a good deal about the bricks and mortar. If you do not, a faculty committee will quickly point out to you that the net assignable square feet per student at your university is well below the norm necessary for excellence and, as a result, "faculty morale is at an all-time low." You should have a five- or ten-year building plan and well-established priorities for new buildings. The faculty, through the faculty building committee, should have put a stamp of approval on the plan. You should also secure board approval. Not uncommonly, some negotiation will be necessary to resolve conflicts between the board of regents' list of priorities and what the faculty believes to be of most importance. The faculty will support new buildings for classrooms and faculty offices. They will not be enthusiastic about the desire of the board to build new athletic facilities. But since the board has to provide the money for all new structures, it is not too difficult to negotiate an accommodation. The difficulty arises when one or two strong, opinionated regents pursue a personal project that in the eyes of the faculty is of low priority, or no priority at all, and that through the exercise of regental prerogative to advance their project a project dear to faculty and students is delayed or canceled. You will need the help of other board members to deal with this kind of problem and, in dealing with it, you may very well alienate a regent and find your support on the board diminished. It happens.

The net-assignable square feet per full-time equivalent student is a statistic that may or may not be useful to you. If you have more than the 125 square feet given by the various governmental offices and national associations that collect such numbers as "average" or "adequate" for a research university, it is a good idea to be vague about what you have, to observe that such statistics do not mean very much, or to launch into a boring analysis of the differences among classroom space, laboratory space, libraries, and athletic facilities. If you have less space than what is currently considered optimum for a stimulating learning environment, you may find it useful to quote the statistic to regents and legislators to justify requests for new buildings. Unless your institution has suffered a sharp decline in enrollment so that the buildings are half empty, or unless you have just completed a major building program, you are likely to be below the optimum. But if you use your space intelligently, and if classes start early and finish late, you can do very nicely with less than the number that is published as the national average for your kind of institution. Of course, the faculty will insist that the university is hopelessly crowded, that the learning environment is thereby adversely affected, and that, therefore, "faculty morale is at an all-time low." What this means is that the faculty do not want to start early and finish late; they all want to teach between 9:00 and 11:00 A.M. In the final analysis, information flowing from your own operations will tell you whether or not you need additional space, and, failing a capital budget sufficient to support a building program, you can devise other means to use the space you have to maximum advantage.

As president, it is your responsibility to make sure that the campus works, that is to say, that traffic flows, that vehicles are parked, that the roofs do not leak, that the buildings are adequately heated, cooled, and cleaned, that laboratories are equipped, that there are books in the library that can actually be made available to students and faculty, that there are work stations to access computers, and that there is proper concern for safety and security. Although it is a very good idea for you to take the time to inspect the campus in detail and to visit all the buildings to get a first-hand view of the campus condition, you obviously cannot be involved in the operation of what is commonly called "the physical plant" on a day-to-day basis. You need a vice-president or director who really knows this business. In a large university, the vice-president for business affairs will have the responsibility for buildings and grounds and the director of the physical plant will report to that vice-president. In a small university, the director of the physical plant may report directly to the president. You should know that this is a tough and thankless job. The director of the physical plant will never be able to satisfy the faculty on the small-scale maintenance and remodeling projects that directly affect their office and classroom operations. The faculty will be exasperated at the length of time it takes to complete these minor jobs. If the maintenance staff is unionized, the difficulties are compounded and your director will have to be able to handle contract negotiations. All in all, the director of the physical plant must be an individual blessed with abundant good nature, unusual patience and understanding, a good dose of parsimony, great ingenuity, and the "can do" attitude of the World War II Seabees. The director of the physical plant will have to endure an assault on the buildings and grounds by thousands of young people with little or no respect for property. His or her budget will always lag the reality that every year utility and maintenance costs will rise while the buildings are getting older.

Maintenance of buildings and grounds may sound like a routine, low-level matter that is not worthy of the president's personal attention. Not so. You should keep a watchful eye on the condition and appearance of the campus. When the campus becomes shabby, the people look shabby, and overall performance becomes shabby. When financial resources are limited, and they always are, and budgets are tight, and they always are, the temptation is to cut funds for maintenance. Do not do it! If you do, you will never be able to catch up. In the budget preparation process you should establish a minimum for campus maintenance and stay with it. In the long run, it is better to cut staff in other areas, to delay capital projects, and to trim academic programs than to reduce your maintenance budget below that amount necessary to keep the buildings clean, the roofs patched, cracked and broken glass replaced, peeling walls repainted, the pavements intact, the grass cut, and the trees pruned.

Of course, every time you build a new structure the maintenance budget increases. Raising the funds for construction is only the beginning. A new classroom building will have elaborate multimedia facilities that require trained operators. A new laboratory building will include an array of sophisticated equipment and shops that require highly trained technicians. Do not be taken in by the cost estimates presented in dollars per square foot of construction. You need to know the costs of *operating* the building before you approve the plans to construct it. Nothing makes a president look more foolish than a beautiful new building filled with sophisticated equipment and no money in sight to staff it and make it all work. It is better to build a classroom building without the latest in multimedia marvels than to have the equipment stand idle as a monument to poor planning.

Campus security is the responsibility of the chief of the university security force. Commonly he or she will report to the vice-president for business affairs or perhaps to the director of the physical plant. This individual has to be able to withstand as many slings and arrows as the president, albeit of a different kind. The chief must maintain equanimity in the face of bomb threats (most common during examinations), rapes, assaults, thefts, drug abuse, student demonstrations, and outraged students whose cars have been towed away from loading zones. Gone is the kindly old watchman of yesteryear who rounded up a stray dog now and then and wiped the vomit off a young freshman after a first drunk. Today university security officers must deal professionally with the full spectrum of crime. This means they must be trained. A university, particularly a big, urban university is a city in itself with all that implies in the latter part of the twentieth century. Moreover, it is a city inhabited largely by young people. Young people are energetic and have strong passions. They are not deliberative and controlled in their behavior. Since they are not, your police officers must be. You should meet with your chief of police at regular intervals to get a firsthand impression of the campus mood.

Another dimension has been added to the campus security problem by legislation and case law that includes individuals with psychological problems as "handicapped" and affords them the rights of a protected class. In addition, yesterday's vagrants are today's homeless and because of their enhanced political status the police are not able to deny them access to parks, streets, sidewalks, and other public property. The campus is both a magnet and a refuge for individuals who behave and dress in bizarre ways and who live on the fringe of the academic community. The incidence of petty thievery, robbery, drug trafficking, and rape is high on the margin of campuses. The best that you will be able to do is to keep it on the margin, and without the cooperation of city and county law enforcement agencies you will be hard pressed to do that. Your police force must be professional enough to be included in the federal-state-local law enforcement network. It is a good idea for you as president to ask unofficially for an outside evaluation of your university's security force.

Jokes will be made about parking on campus. Feel free to smile or even chuckle about parking problems but . . . it is no joke. If you are newly arrived to the campus for which you as president will be responsible, make the time to take more than a cursory look at parking lots and garages, access and egress, and ask the appropriate vice-president for data on the number of parking spaces available, the number reserved for faculty, staff, handicapped, visitors, car pools, motorcycles, and bicycles, and the current fee structure. It will also be worth your while to read the last two or three annual reports of the committee on traffic and parking.

The relationship between parking and the academic mission of the university and its effect on the learning environment may not be immediately apparent to those outside the academic community, but rest assured it is a fundamental element in maintaining that sense of community necessary for a happy and productive campus. If the administration does not provide reserved parking spaces for faculty and staff at low fees close to their offices, it will be clear to faculty and staff that the administration does not care about them. Morale suffers. If you have the chance to build a brand new university, you should start out with the parking system and design the buildings around it. Unfortunately, few of us have that opportunity and you will have to rationalize the system as best you can. Call in a consultant. Possibly great improvements can be made by a redesign of existing parking facilities. But beware of the transportation experts on the faculty. They will be thinking far into the future and will propose an elaborate and expensive system of moving sidewalks or "people carriers" to take the place of the automobile—that is, everybody's automobile but their own. They will want to close the entire campus to vehicular traffic. Remember that, as attractive as these visionary schemes might seem, you as the chief executive are stuck with the automobile for the next several decades and you had better plan for its continued use.

One of the delightful inconsistencies within the academic community is that those faculty members who are most critical of our materialistic society and who have dedicated themselves to protecting the environment against people will resent being assigned parking places more than a few steps from their offices. Do not expect faculty members who spend a good part of the summer backpacking in the mountains to backpack from a distant parking lot to their offices. Not uncommonly, these same faculty members have large families, drive nine-passenger station wagons or vans, and will not be content with space for a compact car. They must be convinced that the university cares about them and the only thing that will convince them is a full-size parking space close to their office.

Places for official visitors close to important university buildings are also critical. They must be protected against the territorial ambitions of on-campus constituencies. If, for example, members of the press or media visit the campus to cover a story and have to walk several blocks or the equivalent, they will be very angry and, whatever the story, the university will be portrayed as "unresponsive" or "insensitive" to public needs.

On a very few campuses, all of the buildings are of the same architectural style and the result is a harmonious unity of buildings and grounds. However, this is so rare that if you encounter the phenomenon you should inquire as to how it came about. It will almost surely be limited to very new universities or to private universities that have more control over their architects than do the public institutions. To an architect, the suggestion that he or she should build a structure that resembles one designed by another architect is an insult to his or her creative genius. Thus, old campuses that have over the years fallen into the hands of a succession of architects show at best a charming diversity and at worst an offensive conglomeration of closely spaced aesthetically incompatible styles and materials. You as president will have to make the best of your "learning environment." It is to be hoped that as part of your legacy for the future you will be able to stifle the creative genius of the architects employed by the board of regents and avoid adding further insult to the appearance of the campus.

Your long-range plan should, of course, focus the activities that involve great numbers of students and faculty in an easily accessible area where students can have a fighting chance to change classes within the time allotted to get from one class to another. Activities that involve fewer people should logically be located outside the high-density area. Thus, classrooms, laboratories, libraries, faculty offices, and student service facilities, including the student center or student union, should be central; dormitories, dining halls, recreational and athletic facilities should be on or adjacent to the campus if at all possible; research centers and institutes can be peripheral. On crowded, expanding campuses you will in all probability have to move at least some students by buses. You should never think that you have solved the space problem. Periodically, at meetings of the executive officers you should lay the problem on the table and ask for creative ideas on how the space problem can be dealt with more effectively.

Looking down the road, you may have to deal with plans to raze an old, tradition-filled building in the middle of the high-activity part of the campus. When this plan surfaces you will hear from alumni that have not shown any interest in the institution for years. There may be a great clamor to "save Old Main." You may have to save it. But in saving it, you must get commitments to an alternative plan, including donations to finance the alternative. That will be a test of the affection for "Old Main." Use the leverage while you have it.

The kinds of buildings basic to the operation of the campus have been mentioned in one context or another. They include classroom buildings, laboratories, auditoriums, theaters, office buildings, library buildings, computer center, gymnasiums, and other athletic facilities, including a stadium, intramural fields, swimming pools, and tracks, dormitories, dining halls, health center, museums, research animal center, alumni center, power plant (if you generate your own power), physical plant buildings and shops, and, of course, supporting service buildings and warehouses. On some campuses there have been constructed in recent years large structures variously called special events buildings, convocation centers, or arenas. They are modern versions of the old field houses. These structures are very useful in that they seat large numbers of people in a controlled environment. In addition to basketball games, they will permit you to hold such large and important campus ceremonies as commencements, convocations, and inaugurations out of the weather. Better to have rock concerts in such a facility where they can be policed than in your stadium where three quarters of a million dollars worth of artificial turf can be destroyed in a few hours. If you do not have such a structure on the campus or on the drawing board, you are well advised to begin the process of planning and constructing one. The faculty will not give it a high priority but, once built, everyone on campus, faculty included, will wonder how you ever did without it.

Student housing presents a perennial problem. You cannot operate dormitories at a loss for very long, and yet the rates must be below available commercial housing if the dormitories are to have a good occupancy rate. You should be able to set the rates at a level sufficient to defray costs of operation, including debt service, and maintain a reserve for major maintenance and improvements, and at the same time offer an attractive rate to the students. Of course, even with an attractive rate, the current student enthusiasm may favor off-campus housing over dormitory living. There is no way to predict the fads of the moment. How much student housing do you need? The answer depends on the nature of the institution. For urban universities whose students are largely commuters, student housing is not a big problem. If capital resources are available, a limited number of beds for out-of-town freshmen is desirable. It also aids in recruiting good graduate students if the university owns apartments that can be made available as family student housing. Family student housing used to be called married student housing, but it is no longer certain that students with families are married and it is probably not a good idea for the university to look too closely into the validity of the marriage contract. For the more traditional university, it is advisable to operate university housing at a level to accommodate at least 15 to 20 percent of the student body, with preference given to freshman or transfer students. It will save you a great deal of grief if university policy requires that students must be *bona fide* full-time students in good academic standing to be eligible for university housing. If such a policy is not in place, you will have students taking only one course enjoying the low rent and collegial atmosphere of university housing year after year.

Some of the buildings on campus will be named in honor of distinguished individuals connected in some way with the history of the institution, through either service to it or generous donations. Buildings that have not yet been named are an important asset for use in fund raising. Make an inventory of important buildings that do not yet carry an individual's name and sit down with your development officer to try to match a building with potential donors. If you receive a proposal to name a building in honor of a faculty member, dean, former president, regent, or popular political figure who is not yet deceased, be very, very careful. Since it may be difficult to stand against a strong wave of sentiment, you should have in place a protective policy of the board of regents that prohibits naming a building for an individual who has not been dead at least five years. You can always ask the board to make an exception to the policy if you really want to do so. But when a building is named in honor of a living individual there is always the risk that the university will be embarrassed by having a building that carries the name of someone who, to the great surprise of everyone, has just been indicted for some serious offense.

It is the people who occupy the campus that make universities such interesting places. There is of course a marked difference between the populations of small, rural liberal arts campuses and those of the big, public urban universities. Although both populations will be composed largely of young people, there will be more older students on the campuses of the big, public urban campuses. With some exceptions, students and faculty alike demonstrate a great diversity in physical appearance, dress, and behavior. Indeed, it would be difficult on some campuses to distinguish the people there from those to be seen on a busy day in the Los Angeles International Airport. Campuses today are multiracial. Dress ranges from conservative to bizarre. Some wear clothes; some wear costumes to "make a statement." Some of the faculty and most of the professional staff wear the conservative attire of the business and professional world that exists off the campus. Some individuals are clearly women and others are plainly men. But there are some whose sex is distinguishable only after close observation of form and movement. Among the men, facial hair is probably more common than in the larger society. Faculty tend to be older than the students, but this is not an infallible test.

It was not always thus. Before the 1960s the two groups that comprised the dominant campus population were in themselves remarkably homogeneous in appearance. The students, with very few exceptions, were young, clean, and well groomed. Depending on the self-imposed student dress conventions of the year, the young women wore dresses, skirts, blouses, socks, saddle shoes, or loafers. The young men wore neat slacks and shirts, commonly with sweaters or sport jackets. The faculty, mostly male, wore coats and ties. Frayed collars indicating genteel poverty were common, as were leather patches on elbows and fragrant pipes. Except in certain institutions, African American and Hispanic American students and faculty were rare; foreign students were not common. The radical social changes of the 1960s that began on the campuses brought as a visible challenge to the established dress norms of society a style of dress suggesting desperate poverty—dirty ragged clothing, dirty bare feet, and long shaggy hair. These styles were to varying degrees emulated by those faculty seeking to identify with students. Beads and other ostentatious jewelry appeared on both sexes. Even the dress of the staff was debased and office workers appeared in jeans and leather sandals. Any attempt by the administration to impose dress standards was resisted. And, as is always the case, people behaved and performed the way they looked. The level of performance in the classroom and on the job declined. University campuses have come a long way back from those troubled times. The appearance of both students and faculty has improved. The best-dressed students and faculty are African American and Hispanic American, probably because, in general, they are more familiar with poverty than are Anglo students and, therefore, are not motivated to assume its trappings.

Although you, as president, should not attempt to enforce any kind of dress code over the campus as a whole, you should insist that within the executive offices of the institution the staff should dress in a professional way. The people who work in your office should look and act as do the people working in a corporate office. It will set a good example.

In the modern world you must have in place written policies, approved by your board, on the use and operation of the campus. There must be a designated free speech area, or area where demonstrations are permitted, so located as not to interfere with normal instructional activities. There must be policies that govern the placement of vending machines, signs and other advertising, food stands, and booths for various kinds of solicitations. You need policies on the use of the university mail. A policy on the use of university buildings and other facilities is essential. Your police force and other campus administrators should have a written policy on how to deal with emergencies, including bomb threats, fire, or health emergencies. In short, everything that you can imagine as occurring on campus should be covered by a written policy. The existence of such a policy manual may or may not help in dealing with a bad situation. It is absolutely certain, however, that in the absence of such a policy manual you will be branded as an incompetent administrator. During and after the investigation of an unfortunate event that occurred on campus, the existence of a policy manual will prove that whoever was culpable should have known what to do and that will be some protection during the ensuing litigation.

Many of your facilities will be attractive to off-campus organizations that will seek to use them for their own purposes. The field house, convocation center, or arena may be the finest indoor facility capable of handling large crowds in the area. Your stadium may be requested for regional athletic meets. Your auditoriums, theaters, and concert halls will be sought by community arts organizations. Many of those petitioning for permission to use university facilities will be charitable groups whose purpose is worthy. The campus grounds with its broad walkways, parks, and plazas will be a magnet for peddlers and vending machine salespersons. Obviously, the institution has to promulgate policies to control the use of its campus and facilities.

If you are president of a private institution, a practical and equitable policy, with appropriate guidelines, that gives the university first call on its facilities, permits outside groups to use designated facilities for educational, charitable, and public service functions, sets a fee for use sufficient to recover all the university's costs, and reserves to the president the final decision on questionable activities is satisfactory and presents no great management problems.

It is the president of a public institution who has the problem. The president cannot, under law, pick and choose among the individuals and organizations that may seek to use campus facilities. Your policies and guidelines must be very carefully crafted so that, even though the institution is public, the campus is not open to just any organization that makes application. The priority of university functions and events over requests for use of facilities by other organizations is, of course, "a given," as is the necessity of a fee to cover the institution's direct and indirect costs. You should not, no matter how great the pressure, permit campus facilities to be used for political fund raisers. These events are not consistent with the purpose of the institution and, of course, if you permit one, you must permit all. Candidates for public office may, of course, be invited to speak on campus by student organizations, faculty groups, or the president, and, inevitably, pledge and contributions cards may be passed out by supporters at such events. However, that is not the same as renting a university hall to the committee to re-elect the local representative or senator. If you permit a charitable organization, such as the American Cancer Society, to hold a benefit on campus, you have no basis for denying the same privilege to any other Section 501(c)3 organization, and there are many that you do not want on your campus. In the interests of good community relations, you do not want to deny the use of your facilities to all community organizations. What to do? The best solution is to adopt the rule that qualifying organizations can use your facilities but cannot make a profit or take any money home from the event. You should seek the help of the university attorney in drafting the qualifications. In this way you can host the chamber of commerce banquet but deny the organization that wants to have a dinner to raise money to support a campaign to advance their position on some controversial issue. There may be some grousing and grumbling about these restrictive rules, but once the community gets used to them, if they are administered fairly and equitably, they will be accepted.

The problems of peddlers and vending machines can be dealt with by designating areas of the campus where they can operate and establishing that except where designated the campus is off limits. Such a policy has been tested in court and will stand for public as well as private universities.

If your tenure as president is five or more years, you will have an opportunity to leave your mark on the campus. Consult with a landscape architect to determine if there are inexpensive ways to dress up the grounds. There are prospective donors who will be intrigued with fountains and statuary. Lily pads, frogs, and turtles are always nice. Make sure that there are attractive signs to identify the buildings. Put benches under the trees and in shady areas. There may be a good deal of university history tucked away in storage that can be showcased in the lobbies of appropriate buildings. Recondition the portraits of your predecessors and hang them in the administration building. They and their descendants will appreciate that. Visitors like to see old books and manuscripts. Where are the old chapel bells? You can do a great deal to improve the image of the university by brightening up the campus and it will not cost very much.

CHAPTER 5

The Faculty

"THE FACULTY is the heart and soul of the university." You will hear this sentiment expressed in these words or other words very like them on frequent occasions. Unlike many other well-established academic articles of faith, this one stands up under critical examination. It is true. A university can be no better than its faculty. If you as president can leave the faculty stronger than you found it, you will have served the institution well. The only way to improve the quality of the faculty is through the rigorous application of high standards in the selection of new faculty and in establishment of equally rigorous standards for promotion and the awarding of tenure. In the promotion and tenure process the president has the final authority to make the decision. Use it. Do not democratize the process and promote faculty members by counting the votes of advisory committees or of your academic officers. Promotion is one of the few areas of academic decision where the president can have the final word. If you are president of one of those few institutions where the final decision on promotion and tenure rests with a dean or a faculty committee, your ability to improve the faculty is limited. You should work to build your authority and influence over the decision process through your budget and appointment powers.

In the selection of new faculty you can have only an indirect influence. Department faculties, department chairs, and deans will present a candidate for your approval. But although you have little to do with the selection process, you are responsible for the quality of the faculty upon which the academic reputation of the university depends. Thus, you must use all the power of your office to make sure that department chairs and deans support actively the policies you have promulgated relating to criteria for the hiring of new faculty. If a dean brings to you an appointment form with all the necessary endorsements, you had better have a very good reason for refusing to approve the candidate. An appointment that has gone as far as your office is regarded as a "done deal" by the department faculty and chair when the dean signs off on it. If at that point your decision is negative, the dean loses credibility with his or her faculty and a serious management problem emerges. Clearly, your relations with the deans should be such that they will surface an appointment early on an informal basis to get your reaction to it, and thus avoid any surprises when the final paperwork comes to your office.

If you have come to the presidency from the academic world you will know that the quality of faculty is measured subjectively. There is no quantitative system that will produce a useful and reproducible number that will be of help to you. This is very frustrating to the representatives of state and federal agencies who come to the university to make sure that you are hiring and promoting according to racial and sex quotas that are called goals. The fact that you do not have a point system for evaluating faculty members will be taken as prima facie evidence that you are in some subtle and devious way discriminating. Of course, that is what you are doing—discriminating, or trying to, among superior faculty members, very good faculty members, and faculty members who are merely adequate or satisfactory. That is still legal and proper, notwithstanding the inability of compliance bureaucrats to understand the academic criteria for hiring and promotion.

External to the university, the faculty will be ranked by the judgments of peers in other academic institutions. The judgments may be formalized through a methodology employed by a national academic organization, or they may be informal judgments made by the leading scientists, social scientists, humanists, or professionals in a particular field. There are published surveys of academic departments and academic programs that provide national ratings. Even though the survey may lag the reality by a number of years, these surveys and the ratings that emerge from them, if authorized and published by a respected and prestigious organization, are accepted in the academic world. For example, it will be accepted, with some reservations and caveats, that the graduate program in your linguistics department is ranked fourteenth among the top twenty graduate linguistics programs in the nation. Your faculty will insist that they are better than that; other institutional faculties in that field will suggest, reluctantly, of course, that with the retirement of professor so-and-so your university has slipped. But you can be confident enough of the ranking to announce in a public forum that your linguistics program is fourteenth in the nation and cite the national survey as confirmation.

What is being evaluated, of course, is the faculty in the program in question. The new building and computer laboratory, along with your extensive library resources, will be considered "a plus," but the evaluation rests on the faculty. The faculty in turn are evaluated on their contribution to scholarship in the area and the contributions made to scholarship in the area by their students. The academic colleagues making these judgments about the quality of scholarship, located in distant universities, will have read the scholarly papers and books published, but they will have no way of knowing much about the quality of graduate teaching in the department and certainly will know nothing about the quality of undergraduate teaching. These national rankings of academic programs are really a ranking of the record of publications that have come from the faculty in the program. They are useful, but only if you know how they are derived. A faculty member whose publications have been well received by his or her peers earns a national reputation in the field and this in turn results in appointments to prestigious committees, boards, and commissions. These appointments, together with invitations to speak and lecture around the world, take this successful faculty member off campus frequently. Depending on the field, opportunities to serve as a consultant put more demands on the busy professor. But all of this activity builds the reputation of your university. The problems are to make sure that teaching duties are not neglected and to fight off attempts by other universities to recruit your star.

Internally, in addition to the quality of scholarship, other criteria are used to evaluate a faculty member. Here is where the quality of teaching is important in making judgments on salary increases and promotion. Teaching performance can be fairly rated by evaluations made by students and colleagues in the department. The use of forms filled out by students that purport to evaluate the quality of classroom performance is much criticized by faculty who will assert that the students do not know enough to make fair judgments, that students will always give higher ratings to "vaudevillians" or performers, and that instructors in certain required dull courses necessary to give students the basic concepts and vocabulary will always be rated lower than those in more fun courses. There is some truth in these criticisms but you can be sure that students can always distinguish between a good teacher and a bad teacher. They will be able to make a fair comparison among their instructors. They will know who is prepared and who is not. As a student advances in the university he or she will become more accomplished at being a student and his or her evaluations will be worth more. So, in promotion conferences use evaluations by students, but use them advisedly.

Another part of the equation for evaluating faculty is service to the institution. Someone has to serve on all those committees. Someone has to advise students. Someone has to work registration. Faculty members who are always too busy for these pedestrian, but necessary, assignments are not doing their share and should be evaluated accordingly.

The demand for a faculty member is a measure of the esteem in which he or she is held outside the institution. Are there invitations to speak or lecture from prestigious universities or professional organizations? Do government agencies seek advice from your faculty member? Has he or she been elected to the presidency of the most prestigious society in the discipline or to membership in one of the national academies? Do publishers attempt to persuade your faculty member to undertake to write books in his or her field? In the sciences and professions your best faculty will have opportunities to take on consulting work. This poses a problem because you want them to engage in consulting work . . . up to a point. It makes them better teachers and provides contacts that assist in placing graduate students. However, you do not want them to be off consulting to such an extent that they neglect their university duties. Most institutions have a policy in place that permits consulting activities up to about one day per week with the clear understanding that university duties take precedent. You are well advised not to attempt to draft this policy with any great specificity. You cannot equate the activities of a professor of engineering who is consulting for a particular corporation with the time spent by a professor of humanities writing a book for a publishing house from which he or she will perhaps receive royalties, or compare either of them with a professor of music who is performing for a fee with a national symphony orchestra or opera company. Faculty members who abuse the opportunities for outside employment are soon known to their colleagues. This peer pressure together with an able department chair can put a stop to the abuse more effectively than you can. Give the department a chance to resolve the problem in house. If the abuse continues, you have the power of the budget. Use that rather than draft a tight policy on outside employment that infuriates faculty and staff alike. A faculty that is constructively engaged outside the institution through publishing, consulting, and performing will do a great deal of good for the university and those kinds of activities should be considered positively in the promotion conference.

In summary then, a faculty member is evaluated on the full spectrum of his or her contribution through scholarly publications, teaching, and service to the university. Of course, in areas of the fine arts where performance is the test of success, the quality of performance as judged by peers takes the place of scholarly publications. Professional schools will put a slightly different emphasis on their evaluations, depending on the field. In nursing, for example, clinical expertise counts for a great deal.

Having dealt in a very general way with measures of quality, we shall examine that increasingly controversial academic condition known as "tenure" and then turn to a discussion of process.

In academic institutions, tenure is a condition of employment under which a faculty member enjoys the prospect of continuing employment unless the institution can show good cause to terminate the employment. It is not a guarantee of a lifetime job. It is not analogous to tenure in the federal judiciary where impeachment is necessary to terminate the appointment. A tenured faculty member can be dismissed if the institution can show good cause under its rules and regulations.

Tenure should not be awarded for a satisfactory, adequate, or good performance. It should be awarded only in recognition of superior performance. Once a faculty member is promoted to tenure, there is every prospect that he or she will be employed for another twenty-five or thirty years. That is a major investment by the institution. The president has a fiduciary obligation to use the institution's funds to the best advantage. The president cannot afford to make many mistakes in awarding tenure. If you are wrong too often, you will leave the institution worse than you found it. Of course over a period of years people change. The bright young faculty member with so much promise who was an "easy promote" may become an alcoholic, or may be found guilty of some felonious offense. It is not difficult for the institution to show cause in straightforward cases of non-performance or malfeasance.

Although you should judge each case on its merits and take the most humane position warranted by the facts, the president must not hesitate to move to dismiss tenured faculty members when it is clearly in the best interest of the university to do so. Just make sure you have a persuasive case. It will be scrutinized first by committees with a profaculty bias that will be moved to make every excuse for outrageous behavior. If you persist, it is not unlikely that the case will move from a faculty grievance proceeding to a court of law. Do not move to break tenure without a strong case; do not be afraid to dismiss a tenured professor if the reasons to do so are compelling.

What is much more difficult than the open-and-shut case is the case of a faculty member who just stops performing at an acceptable level, one who continues to meet classes and goes through the motions but whose performance is unacceptable. His or her colleagues will be the first to know. The department chair will have the individual at the bottom of the list for salary increases. Teaching evaluations by students will show a lazy, boring, unprepared instructor just passing his or her days and drawing a salary. These cases of burnout are the reason that the tenure system is under attack from outside the university. In the public arena, legislative committees and higher education regulatory agencies are advocating multi-year contracts instead of tenure. In the private sector, outside advisory committees are pressing for a way to weed out academic deadwood.

Unless the conduct of the faculty member is impermissably outrageous or constitutes a danger to students such that he or she should be removed from the classroom immediately, you should, working through the dean and department chair build a record of the university's attempts to assist the faculty member in solving the problem(s). Memoranda to the file on conversations warning the faculty member about his or her conduct and offering suggestions on how to correct the improper behavior, as well as copies of written admonitions and warnings, are necessary to sustain a decision to terminate employment, if indeed that is the final solution.

Although the issue is not clear-cut, I believe that you as president should resist any attempt to abolish the tenure system, no matter how much you might be provoked by those few faculty members who abuse the system. The deadwood is the price that the academic world pays for the tenure system and in my opinion it is a price that should be paid. There is a great deal you can do to move out the nonperforming faculty member without abolishing the tenure system.

The tenure system is necessary for the protection of the academic freedom of the individual faculty member. Equally important, it is necessary for the protection of the intellectual independence of the university. Tenure is much like the constitution. The constitution is not called upon for protection in good times when society is tranquil and working toward common purposes. But it is absolutely essential in times when political passions are running strong. Tenure insulates both the individual and the institution from arbitrary and capricious administration and from the political fads and trends of the moment. There have been many more times throughout history when constitutions were needed than when they were not needed, and so it is with tenure.

We are living in a time when the national state is growing more and more powerful. The principal threat to the intellectual independence of universities will in the future come not from the political right or the political left but rather from attempts by the federal bureaucracy to dictate the form and content of curricula and to control the right of the university to hire and promote based on merit. All this will, of course, be a benign exercise of authority under legislation directed toward what is viewed as a desirable social purpose. Without tenure, universities will have lost a weapon needed in the battle for intellectual freedom. Tenure has been much abused by a few. It is incumbent on the president to challenge the tenure of those who abuse the freedom it provides. That will stop a good deal of the abuse. But the cost of the abuse is small considering the value of the system to the maintenance of an intellectually free university and a free society.

Early in your presidency you should meet with the deans and make clear to them your standards for recruiting and promoting faculty. So that all department chairmen get the message, and the same message, it is a good idea to put the policies in writing as an administrative memorandum.

The university attorney should review the policies because invariably a faculty member who was not promoted will challenge the fairness or appropriateness of the criteria set forth in the policy statement. Some deans will not get the message and will continue business as usual. The first time you refuse to approve an appointment or the first time one of the dean's recommended candidates is not promoted it will become clear that times have changed.

Recruiting for new faculty begins at the department level. The department that has vacant positions will initiate the search, either through a faculty search committee or the department chair acting for the faculty. The department will schedule interviews and make its decision. What was once a very informal collegial process involving telephone conversations with friends to discuss the new crop of Ph.D.'s and a first look at the annual meeting of the national association has been formalized through affirmative action requirements that all faculty positions be advertised in appropriate publications, and through scrutiny by the institution's affirmative action officer. Departments have grudgingly accepted the reality that they must establish applicant pools and make a good faith effort to ensure that women and minority candidates are included.

The president is not involved in the recruiting and hiring of assistant professors. You have to depend on your deans to keep a sharp eye on department practices and call your attention to any failure to comply with institutional policies. A good dean will recognize warning signs, as for example, a department chair who hires excessively from his or her alma mater, a department whose candidates all look alike, dress alike, and speak alike, or a department chair who hires only Baptists or Mormons. Deans must know their departments well enough to spot concentrations of advocates for a particular political ideology. While it is no longer illegal or undesirable to hire homosexuals, it is certainly undesirable for a homosexual department chair to hire homosexuals because they are homosexuals. Ideological groups like to nest in comfortable university homes and carry out their evangelical mission at the expense of the university's academic programs.

The president will have an after-the-fact look at a department's choices after a few years when they come up for promotion. If they do not show up well in the promotion conference, it is reflection on the dean and department chair. It means they were not paying attention to what you told them about adhering to rigorous standards in making appointments. However, making a mistake on a nontenured faculty member is not as serious as going wrong on a senior appointment. Assistant professors are on annual appointments until they are up for promotion to tenure, no later than the sixth year of their employment. You are not obliged to give a poor performer a full six years. In fact, it is good practice to terminate an assistant professor who is a clear disappointment as early as the department is willing to admit their disappointment.

The president should get into the process of recruiting senior, tenured faculty, but in a sensitive way. The president who dares to suggest outright a candidate to a dean or department chair will arouse suspicion and hostility for interfering with the department's right to select their own colleagues. The candidate will be forever tainted as the faculty member whom the president tried to hire. If the president refuses to approve the recommendation of the department and dean that a candidate be hired, the same charge of interference is brought and the cry of outrage is equally loud . . . unless the president can produce evidence that the candidate is guilty of a grievous academic crime, such as falsifying credentials, plagiarism, or political conservatism. If you as president know of an attractive, high-quality prospect, that individual should be introduced into the recruiting process by someone else and you should show no interest in or enthusiasm about his or her qualifications.

The best way for a president to get into the process of recruiting senior faculty is to make it clear to the deans that you want to interview all candidates for a tenured position. Of course the demands on your time and travel schedules will not permit you to see all of them, but see all that you can fit into your schedule. There is a great deal at stake. Mistakes in making nontenured appointments can be rectified in a year or two; mistakes in making tenured appointments can damage the institution for decades. You cannot in good conscience leave the appointment of senior faculty solely in the hands of the deans. Over time, you may develop more confidence in the judgment of some deans than in others, but even in the case of a recommendation from a dean with sound judgment it is beneficial to stay in the loop. The candidate will be pleased that the president wants to see him or her, and that may tip the decision of a much-sought-after faculty member in favor of your institution. The deans should be pleased that you have the interest to help them in their recruiting efforts. If a dean does not seem eager to take advantage of your assistance, it suggests that he or she is more interested in turf than in building a great institution. Deans may, against their better judgment, yield to pressure from a strong department chair or from a department faculty committee. A traveling dean may not even see the candidate. The fact that the president wants to see all candidates for a tenured position will strengthen the hand of the dean and make sure that the dean takes the process seriously. It is certainly in the institutional interest to avoid appointment to a tenured position of faculty members who are poor teachers, indifferent scholars, full-time consultants, otherwise distinguished individuals who see the university as a place to initiate a comfortable retirement, or political activists who seek to use the institution to advance their own ideological agenda.

Again considering what is at stake, it is entirely reasonable for the president to take the position that all candidates for tenured positions come for a semester or a year as a visiting professor. During the period of the visiting appointment the faculty can get to know the candidate and the candidate can determine whether your institution is the place where he or she wants to build a career. On occasion it will be alleged that a candidate simply will not come without tenure and that the president's intransigence is standing between the department and the chance to bring in a real star. You must, of course, judge each case on its merits. You should not be prevented from doing what you want to do by your own policy. But remember that this exceptional candidate is leaving some institution or some employment. Make a few phone calls. You might turn up some information that has not been considered by the department that is pushing so hard for a quick decision on an initial tenured appointment. You may find out that the "star" is attempting to separate from a spouse to take up cohabitation with a graduate student. Beware of the candidate who insists on bringing along an indispensable research assistant. Find someone who has a close personal friend at the candidate's institution and find out what you can about personal relationships. An undesirable pattern of behavior at one institution is likely to be repeated at another. The candidate that you really want will be the one to insist on a visiting appointment. From the point of view of the real "star," it is your institution that will be on trial.

Most university presidents will have had a great deal of practice in reading and evaluating the candidate's curriculum vitae. Assessing educational and professional history and accomplishments is straightforward. Evaluating the scholarly research is more difficult and requires the assistance of experts in the field. Always make sure that there are no unexplained gaps in the chronological record, that is to say, that there are no years unaccounted for in the postsecondary school history. A chronological gap commonly reflects a period of activity or inactivity that does not reflect well on the candidate. Note how long it took the candidate to complete the terminal degree in his or her field. Look for perturbations in publication activity. Look for changes in the field of interest. Your review of the curriculum vitae is a point of departure for the interview and for your own personal investigation of the candidate.

Improving the quality of the faculty through successful recruiting is, of course, only a part of the program. The other part is improving the quality of the faculty already employed by the university. Department chairs and deans have the major role to play. They must evaluate the performance of their faculty in the classroom, with graduate students, and in service to the department and institution. They must evaluate the quality of their scholarly work and their productivity. If a young faculty member is having difficulty in the classroom but is otherwise a very promising scholar, the department should see to it that he or she gets some help in improving teaching effectiveness. Most large universities have established centers for improving teaching effectiveness.

How well the deans and department chairs are doing this job will become clear to the president during the annual promotion conferences. Although the process may carry different names at different institutions, once a year the president and his or her academic officers receive from the deans their recommendations for promotion or termination of faculty members. The recommendations from the deans are accompanied by extensive files containing the recommendations from departmental and college committees and from department chairs, together with full justifications supporting the recommendations. Personnel files on the faculty members up for consideration should also be available. After the president and appropriate vice-presidents have reviewed all this material, a conference is scheduled with each dean to discuss the recommendations. The conference includes the president, the academic vice-president or provost, the dean or vice-president with responsibility for the graduate program, the dean of the school or college whose recommendations are under consideration, and anyone else the president believes can contribute to the hard decisions that have to be made.

You are well advised to keep the conference small. You should also structure the process so that all recommendations come in at the same time . . . once a year. If you are so unwise as to entertain recommendations for promotion throughout the year, or even twice a year, you will not be able to provide the even review and decision process that the candidates deserve. This cannot be a casual, on-going exercise. If you permit an unstructured approach to faculty promotion you will be in serious trouble. The timing is important. Customarily, the reviews and conference are held in late fall so that the faculty members under consideration will have the decision early enough in the new year to make their plans. Most universities observe a convention that they will not offer positions beginning in the following fall semester to faculty at other institutions after May 1. Thus, faculty members who will not be promoted to a tenured position at your university will have the spring to seek another position. In a big university, there will be seventy-five to one hundred promotion decisions to be made every year. To do the job right, the president should block out ten days to two weeks of time in the late fall to study all the recommendations and documentation and conduct the conferences.

In the conference, you must make sure that the environment is not adversarial with the dean against the officers of central administration. This is another endeavor where the "we're all in this together" attitude should be set by the president. After the dean presents his or her recommendation on an individual candidate, there should be a free exchange of comments, questions, and answers among the participants. After the full record of an individual's contributions has been examined and after the personnel files have been consulted to verify this or that statement made by the various recommending bodies, the president requests the sense of the conference. For assistant professors the question is to promote to associate professor with tenure, to hold for review next year, or to place on a terminal one-year appointment. For associate professors the question is to promote to professor, hold for review next year, or deny. Although the opinions of all the participants should be clearly expressed, the president should not take a vote. The final decision rests with the president. Since some faculty members who were not promoted will undoubtedly appeal and may indeed go to court alleging that the decision was based on racism or sexism, you are advised to take and retain such notes as will bring back to your mind the reasoning that lead you to the decision that you made. But bear in mind that they will be introduced into the record in any court proceeding that derives from the promotion conference.

You should also be mindful that the decisions you are making will affect the careers of those faculty under consideration. Consideration must be deliberate and thorough and must be on the merits. But bear in mind also that you are the steward of the university's resources and, however much you might be inclined to agonize over the distress your decision to terminate causes a young assistant professor, your duty is to protect and defend the quality of the enterprise. Indeed, in public institutions you are the public's trustee charged with the proper use of public resources to advance the mission of the university. If you do not have the courage to make tough, unpopular decisions, you are in the wrong business.

The decision is clear in the case where all the recommending entities (department chair, department advisory committee, college advisory committee, dean, and your academic officers) are in agreement. It is never difficult to distinguish between superior and unsatisfactory. The problem comes in those cases where the recommendations are not unanimous and you must draw the line between superior performance and very good performance. Here it helps to know the people who are making the recommendations and how they weigh the elements that make up the record. For example, the department will put more emphasis on teaching and departmental service; the college committee will weigh scholarship more heavily. If the candidate shows great promise but the record for promotion is not quite made, you are well advised to hold the decision for a year, instructing the dean to confer with the faculty member about strengthening his or her performance in certain areas. If a book is about to be published, hold the decision until it is out and has been reviewed. You may want to take the matter under advisement for a week or so while you talk personally with people in other institutions who are familiar with the candidate's work. Of course, if the candidate is an assistant professor in the sixth year of appointment you will not, under the rules of the American Association of University Professors to which most institutions subscribe, be able to avoid a decision. This is a good argument for taking a hard look at candidates in the fifth year of service. If the dean does not bring the candidate to the conference in the fifth year, ask that the candidate be reviewed. Your academic vice-president or provost should be on top of this issue.

Some deans will bring up everyone recommended by the departmental chairs. Those deans are not doing their job. Other deans will err on the other side and be overly conservative in making recommendations. Their judgment is questionable. You should after a year or two know how your deans approach the promotion conference.

Some faculty will be jointly appointed in two departments or give a great deal of time and energy to interdisciplinary programs. If you do not look out for those very valuable people no one else will. The departments will be concerned almost exclusively with their full-time people. It is a good idea as a regular item of business to compile a list of those faculty who render service outside their departments and give them special consideration. If you do not do this or figure out some other way to keep track of these people, no nontenured faculty member who is worried about promotion will devote any time to interdisciplinary programs.

Even though you have clear institutional policies directed toward the recruiting and promotion of minority faculty and women, the departments will be very conservative in recommending them for promotion. The reality is that minority faculty credentials tend to be weaker and their record of performance less impressive than that of their peers. Because of financial problems, they might have had to attend less prestigious regional colleges and universities; commonly they held a job while attending school; commonly their primary and secondary education did not prepare them adequately to meet the academic standards of a first-class institution of higher education. You must look at the records of these faculty members with understanding of what it has taken to bring them to where they are. Time will take care of this problem but right now you have to take care of it. If a minority faculty member or woman faculty member shows a potential for growth and has worked hard and constructively, you are fully justified in taking a risk and promoting him or her, notwithstanding recommendations to the contrary. This is an area where you must lead. On the other hand, if a minority or female faculty member is making a career exploiting the civil rights legislation and has been behaving in a way to set the stage for litigation, be prepared to make the appropriate decision and go to court.

Some young faculty members who are performing well but not well enough to be promoted react very strongly to a negative decision. Their egos will not permit them to accept the fact that their record is not sufficient to justify promotion, so they conclude there must be other, sinister reasons why they were not promoted. Not uncommonly they will weave elaborate theories of conspiracy based on personal relations with colleagues in the department or the department chair. Minority faculty will charge racism; women faculty members will charge sexism. Their charges must, of course, be fully investigated to determine if there indeed were reasons other than performance that led to a negative recommendation. The investigation must be fair and impartial. There is no shortage of plaintiff's attorneys to bring suit against the university. But if you have done your job properly, there is little prospect that they will succeed. Do not be surprised, however, at how far a wounded ego will go to avoid facing up to failures in performance.

The president should work to maintain good relations with the faculty. If you give them a good, honest, efficient administration you will have their respect. The great majority of the faculty are dedicated, hardworking, creative, intelligent men and women. If you provide the facilities and resources and stay out of the way, they will do a job that will be a credit to the institution and they will not attempt to get into your business and help you manage the institution. However, you will be disappointed if you think that people who choose the academic life and dedicate themselves to teaching and scholarship are more noble than the average citizen and free of the flaws that are found in the individuals that make up the larger society. You will encounter self-dealing, venality, and hypocrisy among the members of your faculty.

Some faculty will be very critical of the president. Do not take it personally. It is not you as an individual but rather the position of president that offends them. They resent authority and particularly the fact that you receive a salary higher than theirs. There are faculty who believe that, because they have a Ph.D. degree and are recognized as expert in a field of knowledge, society has an obligation to support them at a relatively high level and that they have no obligation whatsoever to society or its institutions. They resent the fact that a businessman who owns and operates a number of laundries has an income that is higher than theirs, lives in a bigger house, and drives a more expensive automobile. They see the businessman as uncultured and illiterate and not entitled to receive such a reward for his labors. They have no appreciation of the risks he took to start his business and the long, anxious hours he put in to make it a success. They are indeed very much antibusiness. A faculty member who is a recognized expert in a narrow field of knowledge is accustomed to attention when he or she speaks. Certainly, he or she commands attention in the classroom. Unfortunately, it seems to be a very easy step from being an acknowledged and respected authority in an academic discipline to the self-delusion that you are expert in all fields and should be listened to as intently when you discourse on the foreign policy of the United States as when you talk about your field of expertise.

You will find, therefore, that, despite your efforts to build a better university, there will be a group of faculty who will be your constant critics. They will write critical articles in the campus newspaper decrying your lack of leadership and deploring the sorry state of faculty morale; if they can interest the local daily newspaper in what they have to say, they will exploit that forum as well as local television. The challenge is to be so good at your job that they are disarmed and will have little credibility on the campus. They will be well known to their colleagues. In all probability they criticized your predecessor. From time to time you will have to make a tough, unpopular decision that will provide them with ammunition. This comes with the territory. If you have the respect and confidence of the majority of the faculty, your critics will not be able to do a great deal of damage. Over time, you might be able to win some of them over by asking for their advice. Appoint them to committees. From time to time there may even be substance in their criticism. It always pays to consider the other point of view.

Your university will be unusual if the faculty does not include individuals persuaded to a political ideology that is a good distance to the left or right of center. The left-leaning faculty will be the more numerous and for the most part will be resident in the departments of political science or government, economics, and sociology, but they may also occur throughout the departments that make up the liberal arts, fine arts, and humanities, and perhaps in the school of public affairs and in the law school. They will range from dedicated, hard-line Marxists, now very much on the defensive as a consequence of world events, to those who eschew identification as communists or socialists but advocate more government intervention in and control of the economic, social, and political affairs of the nation and the world. Some will be very vocal, highly visible faculty members who in speeches, articles, and books attack the established order. They will propose alternatives to capitalism and free market economies. Some will be well-reasoned scholarly articles advocating central planning for the economy; some will be extreme and bizarre asserting, for example, that private property is a conspiracy against the poor. Among your very liberal and left-leaning faculty there will be very popular teachers who consistently win teaching awards. Students are inclined to be very much taken with gadflies and rebels who challenge authority and advance concepts that shock their parents. Since a high level of liberal "noise" is common in universities, it does not present a problem for the president within the academic community. It is difficult to find a country with a central planned economy that is not having severe problems and that reality has dampened the enthusiasm of the more rational advocates of government intervention.

Faculty members to the right of center will be few and most probably resident in the business and engineering schools. They will not be as visible or noisy as their colleagues on the left—unless they are outraged about what they perceive as a "moral issue." Their concern will be focused on society's apparently limitless tolerance of what they regard as criminal and immoral behavior and upon the intrusion of government into business and economic activity.

The influence of the more extreme faculty members, those who feel they must make some kind of statement through a bizarre appearance as well as their arguments, is constrained through their own silliness. You should treat the radical faculty with benign tolerance. After all, there are really very few of them; they just seem numerous. Do not attempt to isolate them; they will isolate themselves. You will have to take particular care in evaluating them for salary increases and promotion because if they do not measure up to standards they will be quick to charge discrimination based on their political views. If, on the merits, a promotion decision on one of these faculty members comes down as negative, be sure you can make the case. Do not let your own political views influence a promotion decision one way or the other.

It is, of course, in the world external to the university that the actions and antics of radical faculty members cause a problem for the president. You will be on the defensive. You will take the position with angry alumni, donors, public officials, and other constituents that universities are by their very nature places where a multitude of ideas and opinions are considered and examined by students, and that there must be intellectual freedom of expression on campus if the university is to perform its function. If pressed, you can explain the protections given by the constitution and the courts to faculty in the exercise of academic freedom. And, in general, the press has educated the public to understand and appreciate just why the president and the board of regents cannot and should not fire a professor who is leading a movement to impeach the governor. Although individual legislators may be piqued by a faculty criticism of his or her favorite piece of legislation, state legislatures as a whole have come to understand better the nature of universities and why it is not wise to attack the university for views expressed by a faculty member.

However, this still leaves the president to deal with a distressed parent whose young son or daughter has fallen under the spell of an angry young professor who represents himself or herself as the champion of the poor, homeless, and oppressed and has encouraged the son or daughter to join a picket line outside their father's place of business. These kinds of problems must be handled with all the tact and diplomacy that you can muster. And while they take up the president's time, they will not do the institution a great deal of damage in the long run. It is when the president is out seeking money from wealthy individuals, foundations, and corporations that the activities of liberal and radical faculty members can present a serious problem. You may have to explain to the president of a corporation just why the company should contribute $100,000 to a capital funds drive when one of your economics professors known for antibusiness views has published an article calling for government regulation of that company's business. This increasingly common problem will be discussed in the chapter on development.

Very soon after taking the president's chair you should review the policy on faculty leaves because the faculty will seek your support for improvements. In private universities a traditional policy providing for sabbatical leaves is probably in place, and that is well and good. In the public sector in many states, legislators have not been enthusiastic about giving a year's paid vacation to faculty who in their opinion do not work very hard anyway. So public universities that have not been able to institutionalize sabbaticals have, depending on their ability to make funds available, adopted policies to award faculty development leaves or research leaves at appropriate intervals to deserving faculty. It is very important to faculty who have had years of heavy teaching duties to have time to study, pursue scholarship, and develop new courses. It is in the best interests of the institution for you to support the most generous leave policy that you can fund and defend in the political arena. In the sciences and engineering it has become common to give young faculty members time early in their careers to establish research programs, through either reduced teaching loads or a semester leave. This is important if you are to recruit and retain able young scientists and engineers.

The president should not remain aloof from the faculty, but the demands of the job make the president's time a very valuable commodity. You will not have time for sociable chats with faculty members who stop by the office. Formal contacts with the faculty occur through the councils, senates, and committees discussed in the section on management and governance. Throughout the year, the president is involved with the faculty in campus ceremonies, such as commencement, honor's day, scholarship banquets, and receptions in honor of distinguished academic visitors. At least once a year, the president should address the faculty on the state of the university. Traditionally, this is done at the annual meeting of the general faculty. However, also traditionally, the faculty do not attend this meeting in very large numbers. You should put your remarks on the state of the institution into a written text. The "President's Address to the General Faculty" can thus be given wide circulation both on and off the campus, and no one reading it will know that only thirty-seven faculty members turned out to hear the president. You might increase faculty interest in the annual meeting of the general faculty by using the occasion to make teaching awards to outstanding teachers or to otherwise recognize publicly those faculty members who have received honors and awards throughout the year.

The best way to maintain friendly and cordial relations with the faculty is to entertain them in the president's home. You should plan a series of dinners or other social events over the academic year. Certainly, early in the fall semester you will want to have a reception for the new faculty. There will probably be an organized retired faculty and staff association for which you can arrange a dinner. If there is no formal organization for the retired faculty and staff, you should consider organizing one. The emeritus faculty are a gold mine of information on university history and tradition. You should know these people. They will want to help you. Honor the holders of endowed chairs and professorships with a dinner. After the results of the promotion conference have been communicated to the candidates, you might recognize those who were promoted by having a dinner for them, the department chairs, and deans. Throughout the year visitors will come to campus. Depending on the occasion, it will be appropriate to invite certain members of the faculty to luncheon or dinner. At the end of the year, sit down with your director of special events and determine if there is any particular group of faculty you have missed. These continuing social obligations are very wearing. You will not have many free evenings. But never underestimate how important these occasions are to a successful presidency. They are part of the job. If you do not enjoy them, pretend that you do. There are ways to be relaxed and gracious even standing in a receiving line for the better part of an hour after a grueling day. Work on it. The faculty and its quality, attitude, and support of the institution and its programs are what distinguish a first-class university from a run-of-the-mill institution.

CHAPTER 6

The Curriculum

W HAT IS taught at your university and how it is taught are properly the business of the faculty. It would be unusual if the faculty's prime responsibility for the academic program of the institution was not defined in the rules and regulations of the university. When it is taught and where it is taught, that is to say, course scheduling, are in the president's domain but as a practical matter the departments, schools, and colleges play the major role in building the course schedule. To exercise the faculty responsibility for the academic program, you will find in place departmental, school, college, faculty senate, and university standing committees engaged in reviewing and approving, or recommending approval for, new courses and programs, as well as the elimination of existing ones. It is up to the department chairs, the deans, and the academic vice-president or provost to stay on top of this process and make sure that this edifice of faculty committees is functioning as it should. Because faculty members are excessively tolerant of their colleagues, there is always the danger that an aggressive faculty member will propose a new course that reflects his or her personal academic interest but has little relevance to existing programs, and that his or her colleagues will acquiesce rather than deny the request and take on the burden of endless arguments and appeals. If the curriculum oversight and review bodies working at various levels within the organization are carefully constituted, these efforts by some faculty members to do their own thing at the expense of a coherent program will be minimized. The president should not have to be involved in arguments over initiating or eliminating courses. This is yet another very good example of why the president must be able, directly or indirectly, to manage the university's committees.

But notwithstanding the responsibility delegated to the faculty in the design, development, and implementation of the university's curriculum, the president must play a leadership role in addressing the major curriculum issues before the institution. This takes skill. You do not want to intrude in the faculty's business. That will be resented and resisted. The faculty prerogative in matters curricular is jealously guarded. But as president you must take the lead and speak both internally and externally on curriculum issues. In view of the national interest in the quality and relevance of university education, you will have to be informed about the issues and you will have to develop positions on them. In your public addresses you are advised to avoid surprising the faculty with the positions that you take. You would not want a group of distinguished faculty from your own institution repudiating the recommendations you have just made at a national meeting.

Your interest in the curriculum should be manifest at the institutional level. The positions you take will, of course, reflect your own educational philosophy. The curriculum at your university puts its stamp on your students and its intellectual effects are carried into the world by your graduates. Are they what you want them to be? This is the fundamental question.

The logical place to begin your evaluation of the university's curriculum is through a review of the history of curriculum development at the institution. How have the general education requirements and the degree programs evolved over the years? What happened in the 1960s when students were seeking "relevance"? Did the faculty cave in and reduce or eliminate established required courses in basic disciplines? Have there been recent revisions to repair the damage? It is a good idea to read recent reports of accrediting agencies that have sent teams to evaluate your institution's programs. Once you have the background of how your institution's curriculum has come to its present condition, you should schedule a session with your academic officers and the deans to learn what they think about the general education requirements and the academic programs currently offered by the various departments.

Your principal interest, of course, is in the general education requirements, also known in some institutions as the required core curriculum. You can leave degree programs to the deans and department chairs unless graduates from some of your programs are being shunned by recruiters or are failing to measure up to national norms.

No matter what their major or area of concentration might be, you will want all the graduates of your university to have shared a common intellectual experience and to have demonstrated a minimum level of academic achievement. The general education requirements or core curriculum should develop in your undergraduate students a proficiency in the use of the English language and some knowledge of and ability to use another language, or several. Upon completion of a baccalaureate degree, a student should have an enhanced ability to listen, speak, read, write, calculate, think, reason, solve problems, create, and adapt to a changing environment. He or she should have a sophistication in mathematics sufficient to understand numerical analysis and to be able to evaluate the floods of data that purport to describe the condition of the economy and the environment. The digital processes that drive computers should be understood, at least in a general way.

Your graduates should have a knowledge of the history and development of human civilization over time, the elements of culture, and how we as a society have come to where we are. An understanding of inquiry and the methods of science is essential. The graduating senior should have an appreciation of the liberal and fine arts and their importance in determining the human condition.

The student should know what he or she does in the process of thinking. An understanding of cognition and how to bring the mind to bear on the analysis and solution of problems is fundamental to the constructive use of the mind.

It is to be hoped that the student appreciates the essential role of ethical standards and values in a healthy, productive society.

If a student has creative talents, your institution will have failed if it does not in the educational process assist the student to discover and develop those talents.

Perhaps most important, your undergraduate program should have instilled a desire to continue to learn and a knowledge of how an individual can continue the development of his or her intellectual resources.

Beyond the general education requirements, it is desirable for the student to acquire skills that will permit him or her to carry out a socially useful function.

You may find this list deficient. But whatever your educational philosophy, you should not permit academic conservatism, academic bureaucracy, faculty intransigence, or arrogant accrediting agencies to prevent you from putting in place a curriculum that develops your students' intellectual abilities and provides them with an intellectual experience that prepares them to go forward. It may take some years to effect the revisions that you want, and you may not get everything, but your leadership in this all-important area of the university enterprise is essential.

How to do it? There will be great debates about the body of knowledge and skills that should be common to all students. The faculty may not agree with your vision as presented to them. How many hours should be required in the basic disciplines? How can the institution ensure that all students develop a minimum competence in writing? In mathematics? The liberal arts faculty will insist on more courses in the humanities, social sciences, and fine arts; the professional schools will support more liberal arts courses in principle but in practice will resist because of pressure from accrediting agencies that must approve the professional programs. All of the existing courses are necessary, they will argue, and if the professional schools have to add more liberal arts courses, their baccalaureate degree programs will have to be extended to five years.

You have a ministerial role in curriculum matters at this level, arbitrating informally among faculty groups and administrators and supporting the faculty in conflicts with external bodies. Accrediting agencies are independent, single-mission agencies that can become arbitrary and overbearing. You can calm these waters. State coordinating board bureaucrats may attempt to extend their authority over degree programs into course offerings and even course content. This, of course, must be vigorously resisted and may require action by you at the highest political levels. The faculty should appreciate your support and defense of their traditional academic authority over academic programs, course offerings, and course content. But whether they will or not depends on how well you handle these sensitive matters. You want your university to be a leader in what is commonly referred to as curriculum reform.

Whether reform is called for or not, the president must steer a course between radical and bizarre curriculum experiments and resistance to any change because of a deadly conservatism. And steering the faculty is never easy. Do not be discouraged if it takes two or three years to guide curriculum changes through the faculty approval process. Universities are themselves among the most refractory of bureaucracies. The way to start the process of change or reform is to bring the deans into agreement and then appoint your most respected and influential faculty members to an *ad hoc* committee or task force to work it all out. Of course, the chair and a majority of the members must be in agreement with what you want to accomplish. Your academic vice-president or provost will play a key role in developing the strategy and articulating the administration's views. If he or she is not enthusiastic about and committed to curriculum reform it probably will not happen. Students also have a role to play in the process. They can be most helpful working through councils at the school and college level and through university committees on which they have representation. There should be student representation on the curriculum task force to balance faculty conservatism.

In addition to the president's leadership in effecting constructive change in the curriculum, the president is also the guardian of the curriculum. You must be alert to efforts of politically motivated and cause-oriented groups of faculty to initiate new academic programs that deal with social and political phenomena of current interest. Recent years have seen the rise of programs (indeed, in some universities, departments) of African American studies, Mexican American studies, ethnic studies, women's studies, and gay and lesbian studies. Proposals to initiate such programs will, after much debate and with many changes and modifications, in all probability reach your desk with an endorsement, or qualified endorsement, by the faculty. However individual faculty members might feel personally about the academic worth and merit of such programs, few will risk standing in opposition and being publicly vilified as racist, sexist, or conservative.

When a request to establish such a new academic program comes to you carrying the faculty stamp of approval, it will not come as a surprise. You will have observed it working through the academic bureaucracy and in all probability you will have determined your position on it. You should proceed very deliberately, no matter how much political momentum it carries for early approval and implementation. As president you cannot, and should not, stand against the social changes occurring in the larger society. It is appropriate for universities to study the social and political phenomena of our time. The question for the president is—how?

In their enthusiasm, the faculty proponents of "bold" or "cutting edge" programs will favor creation of a new academic department or departments to establish the program firmly in the academic structure of the university. But, if you have paid attention to the membership of your committees, it is unlikely that the faculty recommendation that comes to you will recommend the creation of a new department. More than likely, the faculty will recommend that these new programs of study be incorporated within existing departments, coordinated by an interdisciplinary committee, or perhaps supported by a new center with a modest budget to fund curriculum development and research. Even liberal causes cannot easily overcome basic faculty conservatism when it comes to altering the structure of schools and colleges. This will all cost money but can be an acceptable solution if the new courses offered require the same level and quality of student performance as is required in established degree programs. You cannot allow courses in ethnic studies, women's studies, or any other kind of studies to be nothing but a forum for activists to advocate causes, criticize the established order, attack traditional social values, or proselytize. You owe it to your students to make sure that these programs lead somewhere and are not just an easy path to a degree.

Although there will be a great deal of noise from frustrated activists deprived of a department of their very own, the majority of the faculty will support an approach that establishes new and innovative programs while preserving the structure and integrity of the university. Academics recognize full well that if their appointments are in traditional discipline-oriented departments salary advancement and promotion are more secure than if they are assigned to an interdisciplinary program or center. Students recognize that they have better prospects for employment if their degree is in, say, sociology rather than ethnic studies. Those pushing for departmental status for such programs will be loud but few in number.

In summary, the university should be open and flexible enough to accommodate in its curriculum the social and political realities of the times, but in a way that protects and preserves the integrity of the academic process and does not debase academic standards. With these guiding principles, the president has the opportunity to be creative, particularly if he or she has access to some funds that can be directed in support of innovative new programs in the social sciences. But, be careful. You may have more trouble with the board of regents than with the faculty or students in dealing with these issues.

CHAPTER 7

Students, Student Activities, and Student Services

PUT AS simply and directly as possible, the mission of the university is to develop the human resources of society. The students are the humans that the university is attempting to develop . . . intellectually. Until recently, students were the fortunate beneficiaries of a generous and wise society that created, maintained, and operated universities to enhance the human condition. The students were presented with a great opportunity to develop their minds and learn skills. The cost to them was less than the capital and operating costs required to build and operate the institutions, and in the public institutions the cost was substantially less. Society accepted the proposition that knowledge is better than ignorance and was prepared to pay for the development and dissemination of knowledge.

However, in recent years students have been persuaded that they have a "right" to attend a university and that they are not fortunate beneficiaries but consumers in the full and current sense of the word. They expect to get what they are paying for in the same way that they expect full value when attending a movie theater. They are in general not knowledgeable about the true cost of their university education and who is paying for it. Gratitude for the opportunity to attend a university is not much in evidence on campuses today. Thus is heard the common argument that the university is for the students. It is not *for* the students, at least not in any proprietary sense. It is *for* the society that built it and operates it to carry out the social mission entrusted to it.

However, few students come to the university because they have pondered on the benefits that accrue to society from a literate, cultured, educated populace. Why do they come? Some wiser-than-average students do indeed come because they want to develop their minds and enhance their intellectual capabilities. Some come because they have decided on a specific professional or business career and know exactly what they have to do to achieve their objective. Some come because they want to prepare themselves for a career but have not yet determined which career. Some come because their families want them to get a college education and the student cannot think of anything else to do. Their friends are going to a university. A few come because they want to participate in intercollegiate athletics. Some come because they have heard that you can have a good time at the university, and they do have a very good time, but generally they do not stay very long. Some come because they have been out in the world trying to make their way in society without an education, or with an education in the wrong field. They are older and they know exactly what they want to do at the university. They want to do it quickly. They are, in general, very good students. Some students come because of financial aid programs that provide a modest income as long as they are students in good standing. Some come on a part-time basis because they want to broaden and enrich their lives. So, in terms of motives, the student body is diverse. The mix depends on the kind of university and where it is located. In a large urban university, diversity is at a maximum; in a small-town liberal arts college the student body is more homogeneous.

Putting aside the reasons and motivations that brought the students to your campus, once admitted, attending classes, and participating in university life, they begin to change—there is an awakening of the intellect. For a faculty member, and for the president, the greatest reward that comes from interactions with students is to be a part of this awakening—to see them begin to inquire, to question, and to develop an intellectual enthusiasm for learning. It comes sooner to some than to others but, sooner or later, when it comes it brings a great satisfaction to those responsible for the success of the academic process.

Most students upon entering a university are for the first time on their own in the sense that they have left home and are free of direct parental supervision. Most of them remain financially dependent to a degree. Older students, of course, are an exception to the rule. But, experienced or inexperienced, supported by the family or paying their own way, our society has decreed that eighteen-year-olds are adults. As a consequence, the university no longer stands *in loco parentis*. The institution does not have in any significant degree the authority to control behavior of students over and above application of the laws that apply to everyone else. You can suspend or expel students for violations of rules and regulations, but more and more commonly students fight such suspensions or expulsions in court and if they do not succeed in overturning the sanctions at the very least they delay their implementation.

But although students are independent adults and behave as such, they need and demand a good deal of looking after. The organized efforts to care for students are usually called student support services or just student services. They are administered by a vice-president for student affairs or a dean of students. In large universities these service and support functions are structured into centers and offices headed by directors; in small institutions they are managed from the office of the dean of students. They include housing and food, health care, registration and admissions, counseling and guidance, testing and career placement, and learning skills. In some institutions the university pays part or all of the cost of a student ombudsman and a students' attorney. Where there is a large number of international students, the university operates an international office. Services for handicapped students commonly are institutionalized. There is a growing need for universities to operate child care facilities. In addition to centers and offices that serve in direct support of student needs, there are student-oriented activities over which the institution exercises at least some degree of oversight and for which the institution pays most or all of the cost. These include the student union or student center, the university band, and student publications. If the university has a department of journalism the student newspaper may be a product that competes in production quality with a metropolitan daily, albeit with an immature editorial policy, and has a similar capital investment in plant and equipment. The university may hold a license for a student-operated radio station. The university, depending on the environment in which it operates, may find it necessary to operate a transportation system for students. In cooperation with the military, the institution may be home to an ROTC program.

The university also provides for student organizations and these flourish on all campuses. Students with like interests will come together and register as a student organization. The act of registration requires a statement of purpose and, when that is approved, results in the appointment of a university sponsor, usually a faculty member, and access to university facilities. In a big university there may be as many as five hundred student organizations, including clubs built around various sports, scholarly and professional societies, political groups, hobby groups, religious organizations, associations for foreign students, honor societies, and student service organizations. One of the first things the president should do is look over the directory of student organizations. It will give you a quick overview of student life on campus. Of course, students are not obliged to submit an organization for university approval by registering it. They may form an organization off campus and forego the privilege of using university meeting rooms, telephones, and other facilities. Indeed, some of these off-campus organizations may come to your attention through unauthorized use of the university's name. Anyone can print stationery and list a telephone.

In applying to become a registered student organization, the group must submit a statement of purpose. You may think that, if the president of the university does not approve of the purpose of the organization, registration can be denied. Not so. In these times when tolerance of any and all social activity or behavior save what is officially considered criminal is considered to be a virtue, the university cannot pass on the merits of the proposed organization's purpose without taking on litigation it cannot win. Only if the actions or activities of the organization are clearly inimical to the educational purpose of the institution can the president be reasonably confident that a decision to refuse to register or to deregister is sustainable. Of course, very few organizations with a purpose that is basically inimical will so state. An activist animal rights group will hardly admit that their purpose is to break into your research animal facility and release the animals. The purpose will be put forward in language that cannot be challenged. The inimical action will have to be proved before the organization can be deregistered. In reviewing the list of student organizations you will probably find a gay and lesbian student organization under some name. Some members of the board of regents, conservative politicians, alumni, and society at large may be of the opinion that such an organization is *de facto* inimical not only to the university but to the larger society as well. But universities have fought this issue in the federal courts and lost. When new appointees to the board of regents express outrage that such an organization exists on campus, give the federal judiciary full credit. The new regents probably will not appreciate a lecture from you on tolerance and human rights within the university community. But as they serve on the board, they will learn.

Membership in student organizations should be restricted to *bona fide* students in good standing, faculty members, and staff. You can make this rule stick. It will keep the professional paid organizers and demonstrators out of the leadership of certain student organizations that have a political purpose or are organized to promote a radical social agenda. It will not solve the problem, but it will help.

All university organizations must accept and conform to university policies. Universities have declared that they do not discriminate on the basis of race, color, national origin, religion, sex, age, veteran status, or handicap. Some have added "sexual preference" or words to that effect. Those organizations that do not accept such a policy against discrimination, or that do not want to subject themselves to university authority, may elect to function as off-campus organizations.

On some campuses these include some fraternities and sororities of the old "Greek system" that cherish the freedom to select their members without having to demonstrate conformance with university policies on discrimination, hazing, insurance, or financial accountability. On some campuses the university has moved to deregister certain organizations because of liabilities connected with their activities. Whether or not these organizations are independent and off-campus, they can get the institution into trouble when their members, your students, are seriously injured during hazing connected with initiation rites or through problems arising from alcohol abuse. Because of the university's inability to control directly the activities of independent, off-campus organizations, state laws have been passed to prevent hazing. However, if your vice-president for student affairs or dean of students is worth his or her salt, a good deal of pressure can be brought on these organizations, perhaps through an interfraternity council, to make them conduct themselves properly. Although some of the older alumni may remember fraternity hazing fondly as a rite of manhood, society will no longer tolerate the risks it presents.

There are student organizations that have a high visibility and represent the university at public functions, such as intercollegiate athletic events. Student service organizations and cheerleaders are a good example. They have by tradition certain privileges. In the public eye, they will have official status and it will be assumed that the university sponsors them and is responsible for their conduct. No matter what their official status within the institution, these organizations require more oversight than most student organizations because they can get you into trouble. It may be a good idea to separate them from the legion of conventional student organizations and consider them as a special kind of sponsored student organization. As a *quid pro quo*, the organization receives special status and privileges in return for accepting closer oversight and guidance. Cheerleaders are a case in point. Talented students try out for the squad and are evaluated by a panel of judges. Selection is based on merit. But if you are president of a big, public university and the selection process does not produce any African American, Hispanic American, or Asian American cheerleaders you have a problem. In such a situation there are larger and more important issues than just how many points a judge has awarded this or that candidate. You should intervene, preferably covertly, but overtly if you run into opposition, to make sure that the university is appropriately represented before the tens of thousands of people who crowd the stadium.

It is a good idea for you as president to review the relationships between sororities and fraternities and the university to avoid surprises. You may find that the fraternity house is built on university land under a lease that you may not want to renew. There may be other organizations that have enjoyed a long-term "sweetheart" relationship with the university that it is not in the best interest of the institution to continue. You will learn a great deal by prying into these matters, but you may not make many friends.

Students are in general young. This means they are for the most part healthy and energetic. No matter how rigorous the academic standards at your university, studying and class assignments will not absorb as much of this human energy as you would like. Part of the solution to the problem of dissipating student energy in a constructive way lies in well-organized and well-equipped recreational and intramural athletic programs. These will enjoy a high level of participation by the student body. These programs not only will burn up a great deal of excess young animal energy but also are in themselves educational. Those participating learn that after an individual has perspired heavily he or she feels good. This used to be part of common wisdom when everyone perspired as a result of working or simply because it was hot. Now, however, with the decline in the common experience of physical labor, and with the marvelous systems of climate control that maintain living, working, and traveling environments at comfortable temperatures, many young people rarely perspire and indeed have come to equate perspiring with bleeding to death. University athletic programs teach that sweat washes off and that you can feel good without taking a drug.

Intercollegiate athletic programs, as distinct from recreational and intramural athletic programs, are business operations that have less and less impact on student life. They present a management problem that will be discussed subsequently.

Not all students will be interested in campus cultural events but they are an important element in education outside the classroom. You should make sure that the cultural entertainment program is adequately funded and that university facilities are available to it. You and your spouse should from time to time make a practice of showing up at these cultural events.

Rather than review the administration and management of all student services, discussion will be focused on issues of greatest sensitivity and those with the potential for causing the most trouble.

Students will never be enthusiastic about the food in the university's dining halls. You can expect a level of "noise" in the form of complaining letters, telephone calls, and articles in the student newspaper. Obviously, you should not be involved directly in responding to them unless the complaints originate from someone who merits special attention. Your vice-president for student affairs should make sure that whoever is receiving the complaints is smart enough to send up the line those that need the attention of a senior officer or of the president. However, if the "noise level" rises suddenly, the matter needs your attention. If you have a student ombudsman, he or she will have a feel for the problem. It is up to your vice-president for student affairs to make sure that the food service is managed by an experienced, capable in-house administrator or a good outside contractor. The same applies to the dormitories. Experienced, capable management is very important. In reviewing the budgets for these non-academic enterprises, make sure that you maintain adequate reserves for repair and renovation. The fact that a roof needs to be replaced should not come as a surprise to anyone. When it does need to be replaced, you should be able to do it out of a reserve for that purpose without doing violence to your operating budget. To build and maintain adequate reserves you need to set fees high enough to support current operations and maintain appropriate reserve accounts. The students will complain about the fees. After all, they will be gone when the new roof is needed, so why should they pay the bills for posterity? The answer is that someone who went before paid for them.

Living in a dormitory will be a new experience for most students newly admitted to the university. It should be a positive experience and assist the student in finding his or her place in the institution's social environment. It is to be hoped that your university will have enough capacity to accommodate all the new freshmen who seek to live in a dormitory. When large numbers of young students from different environments, many of them free for the first time from parental supervision, come together in a dormitory it is a very exciting time for them. To prevent chaos, the university must impose some discipline.

Rules and regulations on dormitory conduct should be carefully reviewed with legal staff to make sure that the controls you propose and the penalties for their violation are permissible under law. You can be sure they will be tested. Rules for dormitory living should be based on common sense and they should be enforceable. It does no good to promulgate rules that you are unable or unwilling to enforce. There should be tough penalties for behavior that poses a threat to health and life, such as possession of fire arms or possession and use of drugs in university housing. People who set fires in university dormitories and apartments are not just pranksters. On the other hand, your rules should not be drawn so tightly that youthful exuberance that may cause no more damage than a late-night disturbance draws a suspension or expulsion. After you have a reading on your vice-president for student affairs, ask him or her to review the rules and regulations to see if they are consistent with the commonsense guideline.

Student health centers range all the way from a nurses' station through an outpatient clinic to a fully accredited hospital. If your university is in an isolated, rural setting you will need more; if it is in or close to an urban area with a full-service hospital, you can get by with less. The days when epidemics would race through a student body sending hundreds to the health center appear to be past us. A student health fee high enough to pay the costs of a campus hospital will be a great burden on the students and will be vigorously criticized and resisted. After all, students are young and healthy. They are rarely sick and do not want to pay for people who are sick. But if the fee is not high enough to permit the health center to pay its way, the heavy burden will fall on the university. You must seek a balance between what it would be nice to have and what you and the students can afford. The best solution is to provide health insurance for students through some reputable carrier and offer an outpatient facility on campus with staff and equipment commensurate with the size of the student body. Rely on a local hospital as much as is consistent with the level of care it offers. It is not likely that you can provide on campus the quality of medical care necessary to deal with the traumas of skiing accidents or the complications of drug abuse. City and county hospitals are better equipped. Hospitals in the area will in all probability be pleased to discuss with you some contractual arrangement that will be beneficial to the hospital and to the institution.

Soon after you take the president's chair, ask the appropriate vice-president to provide you with some numbers on the performance of your admissions office. Pay particular attention to the turnaround time. With the automated systems currently available, there is no excuse for weeks to elapse between inquiry and answer or between application and decision. If it takes longer than forty-eight hours to move the appropriate paper out of your admissions office, you may need a new director of admissions. Of course, there may be categories of applications that are held for a good reason and for which the office cannot make a fast decision. The office can, however, provide a fast response explaining the reason for the delay. The office of admissions is for many the front door of the university. It deserves your personal attention to make sure that both attitude and performance are what they should be and can be. Nothing makes a better impression on potential students and their parents than a university that provides a quick and understandable response to letter and telephone inquiries. Look over the application forms, brochures, and catalogs that are sent by the admissions office. It may be time with the advent of a new administration to rework them. The director of admissions should also be evaluated on his or her ability to furnish the president with accurate data in the desired form in a timely manner.

Some decades ago, students who felt the need for counseling went to the dean of students or a local member of the clergy or called home to talk to Mom or Dad. In today's environment, however, unless your institution is very small, the dean's office cannot provide the professionalism needed. The counseling and guidance function should be institutionalized. If you do not have qualified staff with all the appropriate credentials doing this job, you are exposing yourself and the institution to an unacceptable risk. If a depressed student takes his or her own life, there will be very properly an investigation into the circumstances. Very likely, the student will have sought help and have been a client of your counseling center. If the record of just what kind of help the deceased student received from the university will not stand up under professional review, the institution is in trouble. Find out who is running this operation and what his or her professional competence is. Of course, the great majority of the cases will not be life threatening or even clinical. They will require a staff who can offer good common sense to a student who is having difficulty coping with the world of the university.

Tests to measure academic potential and performance have come under criticism from those who perform poorly on them. They criticize the test rather than address the weaknesses and inadequacies that caused the poor performance. Although this is perhaps an understandable human response, the university's merit-based academic programs would be severely and adversely impacted were the institution to be denied the use of tests. The director of the testing and placement center, under whatever name it functions on your campus, should be well versed in the public debate on the use of tests that is in progress and be in a position to defend articulately the case for testing and to provide you with up-to-date statistics on the subject. The attack on testing strikes at the heart of the university's ability to evaluate academic potential and performance and it must be effectively countered.

Most universities are not in the business of remediation. At least they do not want to be and are reluctant to admit it if they are. In the past, if a student was unable to do university-level work, he or she was advised to go to a less demanding institution or try to improve academic skills at a junior or community college. In recent years, however, universities have institutionalized a tutoring function in the form of a learning skills center. There is a significant difference between operation of a center to provide help to students who literally do not know how to be students and the offering of remedial courses that duplicate what a student was supposed to have mastered in high school. The president is well advised to support the learning skills center but resist the offering of remedial courses. It subverts the university's mission to expect the institution to divert scarce resources to take on the mission of a failed system of public secondary education. It is up to the larger society to correct the failures of the elementary and secondary system of education. Unfortunately, public universities do not everywhere have the option as to whether to undertake remedial education or not. State legislatures, in their desire to improve the retention of poorly performing students, have in some states put the burden of remediation on the public universities instead of on the student, the high schools, and the community colleges where it belongs. In this case, the problem for the president is to make sure that the function of remediation is structured as a separate enterprise and does not vitiate the regular departmental course offerings. High standards of academic performance must be maintained and it must be understood both inside and outside the institution that they will be maintained.

It is a very good idea to establish within the office of the dean of students, possibly in cooperation with the students' association, a student ombudsman. The ombudsman should be a mature, experienced student, selected by the students, who can help resolve problems between students and university officialdom. Of course, you do not want a student with a mission who views his or her role as adversarial. You want a mediator. This should be a salaried position. The president can learn a great deal about how the institution is performing by reviewing once or twice a year a summary of the cases before the ombudsman. In fact, the president should meet each semester with the ombudsman to receive a report on the problems students are having with the university bureaucracy. A cluster of repeat complaints may indicate that one or two individuals are in the wrong job and are giving some office of the university a very bad name.

The function of a students' attorney is to represent students in civil conflicts with apartment managers and other businesses that serve students. It should be clearly understood that the students' attorney will not file suit against the university. You do not need to pay anyone to file suits against you; there will be enough plaintiffs' attorneys available to perform this function. In large universities the position of students' attorney will be jointly funded by the students' association and the administration. Needless to say, the selection of the individual for the position of students' attorney will be a test of the president's ability to evaluate prospective candidates. The students need a good, solid, well-prepared attorney who will work hard to pursue vigorously a large number of small, routine cases. A posturing activist who uses the position as a platform for radical activism will not serve the student interest.

The student union or student center is an important focus for student life on campus. The president's main concern is to make sure that the director of the union is competent and that the service provided by the union is commensurate with the union fee charged. Take the time to walk through the union from time to time to make sure it is being properly maintained. Familiarize yourself with the union's programs. Have a luncheon there when it is convenient. In your conversations with students inquire as to their perceptions of the union and to what extent they make use of it. Performance of the student union should be one of the questions considered in your meetings with the student ombudsman. Students who pay a union fee will have a legitimate grievance if the union is not well managed.

Most universities have a band. Students who are so inclined try out for membership. Membership is considered to be both an educational experience and an enjoyable extracurricular activity. Student members will not be exclusively from the music department but will come from all the departments, schools, and colleges of the university. The band will perform at various university ceremonies and at athletic events and will also be in demand for parades and concerts off the campus. Clearly, you want the band to be a credit to the university. If you lose a football game, it will be some consolation if your band outperformed that of the rival institution. So, it is important for the university's image to have a first-class band director, someone who is at the same time technically competent, good with the students, and respected by his or her colleagues in the music department. In all probability the director will hold an academic appointment in the department. It is equally probable that the faculty of the music department will not consider the responsibilities of the band director and the work connected with the band as "scholarly." Consequently, if you have a very good band director who holds a nontenured position as an assistant professor in the department, you must be prepared for a problem if the faculty resists his or her promotion to a tenured position. The president is well advised to stay ahead of this problem. Good band directors are very hard to find and you do not want to lose one over a squabble with the music department faculty. If you are recruiting a new band director, involve the department and make sure the individual is of the caliber who can be promoted to a tenured faculty position. If the director is already employed when you become president, find out through the dean if there is likely to be a problem. If you are fortunate enough to have a very good band director it is to your advantage to get the problem behind you and make sure that he or she is on the dean's list of recommendations for promotion. If the dean is unwilling to override a reluctant faculty, bearing in mind that the contribution the director makes outside the department is important to the institution, and if a reasonable record of academic performance is there, promote the band director. Do not let a myopic music faculty run off a good band director.

Student publications add life, color, and excitement to the campus but they will test you. If you have a department or school of journalism, the student newspaper, as a laboratory newspaper, will be an integral part of the instructional program. But even without an academic program in journalism there is no way to avoid having a student newspaper. In fact, notwithstanding the problems that stem from a student newspaper, you would not really want to be president of a university that did not have one. You may even have an underground student newspaper in addition to the established newspaper. There may be an array of student magazines and newsletters as well.

Your problems come from the fact that, under the banner of "freedom of the press" and court decisions that have extended First Amendment protection to the most childish and sophomoric student publications, students push the limits of tolerance as far as they can. Any attempt to control the content of student publications will bring cries of "censorship!" The best that you can do is to support an array of editorial boards and advisory committees to bring the pressure of common sense to the enterprise. You will probably have some leverage through the budget, but this is not the case in all institutions. If the problem is gratuitous obscenity, the advertisers and the student body itself will in time bring it under control. If the current student editor is a political radical, you will have to endure the consequences until his or her term expires. This is a very good reason to limit the term of editors of student newspapers to one year. A well-produced student newspaper is the equal in appearance to a metropolitan daily. Because it looks so professional, it is not obvious to the reader that the editorial content is the product of young students whose views of the current scene are neither informed, balanced, nor tempered by experience.

It is a good idea to insist that your interviews with reporters from the student newspaper, or any reporters for that matter, be taped. If, as is all too likely, the interview as published contains wild distortions of what you said, there will be a record upon which the reporter can be called to account. If you have reason to believe that the paper is deliberately printing lies and distortions, use all the power of your office to put a stop to it. Ethical behavior is no more prevalent in the student body than in the larger society. The university should seek to build ethical values in its students, and student publications should certainly be included in the effort. Student investigative reporters who are convinced that their cause is just and noble will not hesitate to skew the facts and use information selectively in writing a story to advance their position on an issue. Indeed, why should they when the working press sets the example? If they are called to account in their student days perhaps they will carry the lesson into their subsequent professional career.

If you inherit an already established student-operated radio station, you can privately curse whatever president initially approved its license, but unless you can demonstrate flagrant abuses you will not be able to close it down. The same kind of foolishness and nonsense that characterizes student newspapers will go out over the airwaves under the university's name. Although it takes an affirmative action to subscribe to or pick up a newspaper, those listening to a radio do not have to make much of an effort to be exposed to a student radio program. Thus, the number of complaints you receive will be from a bigger audience. However, if it gets too bad, you may be able to get some help from the Federal Communications Commission. Check into how the station is administered and who is responsible for programming. Without running the risk of being accused of heavy-handed censorship, you can probably set up a board of responsible faculty and students to exercise oversight for operations and programming.

It is difficult to explain to regents, outraged alumni, and state officials why the president cannot immediately bring under control a student newspaper or radio station that has run amok, either by removing the editor or program director or by suspending publication. But even at the risk of being labeled "weak" or "indecisive," you are well advised to be deliberate and go slow on dealing with a student newspaper or student radio station problem. No matter how bizarre or outrageous the student behavior is, the working press and media will rally to their cause. The local newspapers will editorialize against you. Seek legal counsel and make sure the board of regents understands the consequences and is not surprised at the furor that will result when you remove an irresponsible student editor or eliminate objectionable copy prior to publication. Go by the book and do not attempt a solution that you are not "big enough" to implement. One approach is to convene a committee of the leading publishers and editors in the region and ask them for advice and counsel on how to deal with the situation. If you can bring them together as peacemakers it will isolate the student editor and make it possible for you to solve the problem without provoking the local media.

During the 1960s, ROTC programs were a focus for antiwar protestors and general student hostility. Anyone wearing a uniform on campus was a potential target for abuse. Those days are behind us and on most campuses the ROTC is considered a desirable program that offers financial support for students participating in it. Beyond the direct benefits to participating students, there is the tradition that in our democratic society an officer corps with a significant civilian component is preferable to a military caste made up entirely of service academy graduates. Because of the military's own budget limitations it is difficult to get a new program authorized and indeed you may well be faced with losing an ROTC program through retrenchments on the part of the services. As president, you should support the program and include a commissioning ceremony in your annual commencement activities. If at all possible you should attend the functions and reviews that occur during the academic year. Include officers who direct the ROTC program in invitations to official occasions that occur throughout the academic year. Entertain them from time to time so that when the program is reviewed by the military you will be perceived as a president who is strongly supportive of the program and your university will receive high marks. The students who depend on ROTC support will thank you. Make sure that your congressional delegation knows that you are enthusiastic about the program and what it brings to the university.

At most universities, a student must maintain a minimum grade-point average to remain enrolled. Failure to do so results in scholastic probation and, if performance continues below the minimum, scholastic dismissal. The institution will have in place rules, regulations, and procedures governing probation, dismissal, and readmittance. You should be familiar with them because, in the appeal process from the decisions of committees, deans, and vice-presidents, the president will be the court of last resort. You should not get into the process, however, until the case comes to you as the last step in the appeal. In addition to academic difficulties, students may get into trouble through violations of federal, state, or local laws or through violations of the university's rules and regulations. Universities generally have rules prohibiting the possession of firearms on campus; conduct that interferes with or disrupts the normal operations of the institution; conduct that endangers the health and safety of other students, faculty, staff, or visitors; damage to university property; illegal sale or use of drugs; unauthorized possession or use of alcoholic beverages; unauthorized possession of keys to university facilities; conduct designed to incite lawless action or riot; and such other conduct or actions that may be specified because of conditions extant at a particular institution at a particular time.

Students that violate federal, state, or local laws can and should be arrested and prosecuted in the appropriate court. Failure to do so in a case that may appear trivial may come back to haunt you in more serious cases. Selective prosecution will get you into trouble. Since the university will in many places be a city within a city, your police force should have good relations with municipal, county, and state law enforcement authorities. The university may very well have to call for help in emergencies. You can expect local courts with elected judges to be very unenthusiastic about dealing with misdemeanor cases involving student misbehavior. Do not be surprised or disappointed if they enjoin you against disciplining the offending students, grant long delays in bringing the culprits to trial, and then send them on their way with an admonition. In a system where judges are elected and students are enfranchised at the university rather than where they reside, the university cannot expect to get much help from the courts. About all that you can do internally to enforce the university's rules and regulations, whether or not there has been violation of law, is to suspend or expel a student. You should review the institution's procedures to make sure that the student has the right of due process. You can be reasonably sure that within the last twenty years the university's rules and regulations have been tested in court for their constitutionality and rewritten when they have been found to be flawed. However, to be sure that your rules and regulations are current and compatible with existing law, you should inquire as to when they were last reviewed and amended.

If a group of students has engaged in organized disruptive behavior under the banner of protesting an alleged injustice or insensitivity on the part of the administration, the president's response must be deliberate, measured, and firm. Above all it must be firm. If students break into a dean's office, or into your office, and occupy it to force the university to accommodate to this or that demand, they should be removed, arrested, and jailed. The quicker you can act to remove them the less television time they will have to posture about alleged injustice. You and your chief of security should have a plan in place to deal with this kind of situation. If the protestors can be moved from the university facilities they have occupied before the television crews arrive, you will have won the day. Of course, such decisive action will not be popular on campus. There will be allegations of police brutality. You will be accused of overreacting and being insensitive or worse. The student newspaper will rail against the use of force and complain about the administration's failure to negotiate what will be represented as perfectly legitimate demands. But the disruptive activity will have been dealt with expeditiously and the academic community will respect you for it. The merits of the students' action can be argued by their attorney in court rather than through a bullhorn out your office window. Most important for the near future, students who observe their activist fellows in the toils of legal and disciplinary proceedings will have less enthusiasm for a similar adventure.

The president will interact with students through the normal conduct of the business of the president's office. He or she will meet from time to time with the officers of student government and other student organizations that have occasion to schedule meetings with the president. There will be scholarship banquets, breakfasts, lunches and dinners with student organizations, honors ceremonies, and commencement. You should do as much of this as time permits. But the normal business of the job brings you into contact with a select group of students—students who have excelled academically, students who are active in student organizations, and students who have been elected by their peers to represent them in some capacity. Most of the students you will meet carry responsibility to advocate some position. If you as president want to talk about the university with the "average" student, you will have to meet with students who are not officers in a student organization. Ask your dean of students to pick groups of students at random, the computer can give you a good random sample, and invite them to your office for an afternoon coffee once or twice a semester. You will be very pleased at how much you can learn through a frank and open conversation with this mixed group of students. You may not like everything you learn, but this kind of exchange will give you information you cannot get in any other way.

You will also be amazed at how little students know about the university. It will be very unusual if any student knows much about the institution's budget or can explain the tenure system. After ascertaining through some informal conversation what kind of group the computer has produced, ask a few provocative questions. Have any of you ever had a really bad teacher? Do any of you belong to a student organization? You don't? Why not? Have any of you ever consulted the students' attorney? What kind of service did you get? These kinds of questions and the answers you get will start a flow of information that will help you to do your job better. Find out how many of the group are on scholarship. Ask minority students what kinds of problems they have encountered. Ask older women students what provisions they make for the care of their children. Ask the whole group if they would be willing to tax themselves to provide child care facilities. After you host such groups two or three times and it becomes known that you investigate and take action as a result of what you learn, these afternoon sessions will be very well received. You are cautioned, however, to find out at the outset if the random process has produced a reporter from the student newspaper or an officer from the student association. It is also a good idea to have a few of your academic officers present to assist in answering questions put to you by the students.

As president, you will be much in demand by student organizations. It will enhance the organization's prestige if you accept an invitation to speak to the group. You will receive invitations to breakfasts, luncheons, and dinners. Student groups will seek appointments with you in the president's office. After a time, and after you have wasted some hours attending trivial functions, your executive assistant will be able to screen the many invitations and select those that you should try to accept. Do as much of this as you can. However, no matter how great an effort you make to be available to students and to attend student affairs, you will be able to accept only a small fraction of the invitations that come into the president's office. As a result, you will be accused of being remote or aloof, and of not caring about students. You must set your own priorities on the use of your time and not be persuaded by these cries for attention.

This chapter has focused on the management problems that spring from students and their activities. When plagued by these problems, the university president who has been in the classroom and who has supervised graduate students will remember the pleasures of teaching and guiding students and will be able to keep the vexations in perspective. The university president who has come from the corporate or public service world and who has not known the satisfaction that comes from constructive interaction with students may find student editors and activist student leaders difficult to tolerate. You should remember then that the students are the university's core business. The academic process adds value to its human products. Everything else that goes on in a university is peripheral to the core business—the students. Some presidents, in order to stay in close contact with students, from time to time will teach a course. This is a very good thing to do . . . if . . . the enormous pressures on your time will permit you to do the kind of job that will give you a high student evaluation of your performance. But no instructor, much less the president of the institution, should walk into a classroom unprepared. If you cannot take the time to deliver a superior performance as a teacher it is better not to indulge yourself by teaching a course.

Years after you have left the presidency you will encounter men and women who will say, "I graduated from the university in _____ and you signed my diploma!" They will be glad to see you and eager to share their memories of experiences they had at the institution during your presidency. This is one of the rewards of the job that you get as a kind of deferred compensation.

CHAPTER 8

Research and Scholarship

UNIVERSITIES ARE in the knowledge business—generating it, transmitting it, and disseminating it. Society accepts as given the proposition that knowledge is better than ignorance, although from time to time some members of society seem determined to perpetuate a state of ignorance as long as possible. The major part of the knowledge that the faculty transmits and disseminates through teaching and publication comes from the accumulated store of human knowledge. They are passing it on. However, some of the knowledge that is transmitted and disseminated is new knowledge produced by the faculty through research and scholarship. Some of this new knowledge is useful; a very small part of it may be of such fundamental importance that it has the potential to transform society. Moreover, the process of investigation and inquiry in which the faculty is engaged is as important as the knowledge produced from it. The students involved in the process, for the most part graduate students, learn how to do research and this is the most important part of their learning experience. In the various kinds of intellectual and experimental activities necessary to the discovery and production of new knowledge, a great deal of the accumulated body of knowledge possessed by the human race is rediscovered and regenerated. But the process of rediscovering and regenerating it is the best kind of educational experience and the verification of knowledge already in the public realm is in many ways a comforting as well as enlightening process. In other words, the process does not have to generate new knowledge to be successful in an educational sense.

The progressive, competitive developed or industrialized nations in the world are heavily engaged in research for economic and national security reasons. You can buy the knowledge product of research or you can steal it, but what you cannot buy or steal is the capacity to do research. This capacity to do research is what universities give to their society and, indeed, is one of the main reasons why societies support such costly and expensive institutions as universities. You can perhaps buy or steal the people who have the capacity to do research, but if you want them to continue to do it, you must provide the facilities, the laboratories, libraries, computer centers, graduate students, colleagues, and overall intellectual environment that make it all possible. In short, you must provide them with a university. Information, knowledge, and wisdom are closely related commodities. Information becomes knowledge when you know what it means. Knowledge becomes wisdom when you know how to use it.

It is possible, of course, to conduct research in institutions other than universities. Corporations and national laboratories are engaged in research, both in the United States and abroad. But in the United States, national policy has been and is to support research in universities through a flow of federal dollars in the form of research grants and contracts. It is a policy that has served the nation well and there seems to be no likelihood that the policy will be changed in the near future.

Universities and their faculties pursue knowledge for its own sake. The human race, or at least some of its members, have learned that knowledge is in and of itself good whether or not there is a use to which it can be put or an application in which it can be used. However, those that support universities are not always certain that their money should be spent pursuing knowledge for its own sake. They want the institution to develop knowledge, to do research, that will be useful in solving society's problems. So universities, particularly public universities, have "sold" the research they do as necessary for the continued health and economic prosperity of the state and nation. While this argument has been successful in convincing state legislators and officials to support university budgets, it has the result of raising expectations that, when they are not met in the short term, cause a basically sound argument to lose its force. Universities should not have economic development as part of their mission. If universities carry out their mission of developing the human resource and generating new knowledge, then economic development will follow and can be directed and encouraged by organizations formed for that specific purpose. Mr./Madam president, you should resist any attempt to cast your university as a chamber of commerce, an economic development agency, or a contract research institute. Although you may accept private and government research contracts, and they are important to the university enterprise, they are not *central* to your mission. If they become that important, you are a research institute rather than a university. You must find and maintain the balance.

Some critics of universities decry the faculty's involvement in research, taking the position that the faculty is paid to teach and should be in the classroom. The critics complain that the classrooms are left in the hands of graduate student teaching assistants and junior faculty while the senior faculty pursue their own interests. Commonly, it is alleged that the graduate students working as teaching assistants do not speak English. Research, the critics say, is something that a faculty member does to avoid teaching, and the implication is that it is a selfish desire to escape from the job the faculty member was hired to do that leads him or her into research.

As president you must be familiar with all the arguments pro and con, and you must also be able to present persuasively the case for research. Although there will be some exceptions, you will be able to demonstrate that faculty engaged in research receive higher teaching evaluations than those who are not so occupied. It should not be surprising that the faculty member who is intellectually alive and engaged in inquiry is a more stimulating lecturer than one who is offering other people's work, more or less as a loudspeaker. You should have at your finger tips statistics on the number of senior faculty who teach lower-division courses. If you do not like the statistics, you had better review teaching loads and get together with the deans to make sure that senior faculty are indeed bearing their share of the undergraduate teaching responsibility.

The common misapprehension that faculty involved in research do a poor job of teaching, and vice versa, must be addressed and those that hold it should be disabused. If some faculty on your campus are called "research professors" it suggests that you have a research faculty and a nonresearch faculty. The president should abolish the title and make clear that all faculty are expected to be engaged in research and scholarship.

You should also make sure that graduate students engaged as teaching assistants have passed an examination in English. It is a good idea to distinguish through title and salary among graduate students hired to teach. Younger, less experienced graduate students should assist regular faculty members but should not have responsibility for a class. If a graduate student is to be given responsibility for a course, he or she should be an experienced, mature student, well advanced in meeting the requirements for the Ph.D. degree, and, indeed, academically the equal of faculty teaching at community colleges and in many predominantly undergraduate institutions.

Since the quality of your faculty will be judged in the academic world on the quality of their research and scholarship, and since the quality of research and scholarship is one of the criteria on which a faculty member is evaluated for promotion and salary increases, you as president should encourage the faculty to pursue research and scholarship and promulgate university policies to facilitate that activity. You should make funds available to support faculty travel to meetings of learned societies so they can present the results of their work and be judged on its merits. You should maintain a research fund to provide the faculty with modest research support on a merit review basis. This is important for young faculty who have not yet built a reputation that will make them successful in the national competition for federal research funds. You should help them to get started. You should make it possible for a faculty member to get some relief from teaching duties to do research. A half-time research assignment for a semester every few years is a good way to support the effort. If you have a sabbatical program, so much the better, but seven years is a long time for a young faculty member to defer a focused effort on research. As a faculty member develops a successful research program, he or she will attract graduate students and begin to make a contribution to the preparation of master's and doctoral candidates. The faculty member will have significant responsibilities in supervising graduate students and, if it is done well, it will consume a great deal of his or her time.

Research in universities is done by faculty members who function as independent principal investigators and as an organized activity carried out in centers, institutes, laboratories, and bureaus. In the first instance, the faculty member prepares a proposal and directs it to the appropriate funding agency. In universities with a large volume of contract and grant funds going to faculty as principal investigators, the institution maintains an office staffed to assist faculty members in the labor of preparing proposals in the correct form and administering them subsequent to an award. This office will be informed about the requirements of the various funding agencies and how overhead rates are to be calculated. To make sure that some enterprising faculty member does not commit the university to do something it is not prepared to do, university policy should require that all proposals clear through a central office where all the necessary signatures can be obtained and verified. Although funding agencies receive proposals from individuals and evaluate them on the merits, the grant or contract is made to the institution rather than the individual. The grant or contract may move with the individual, but while the recipient is at a particular institution, that institution and its officers are the responsible parties.

You as president should review the research administration system at your university to make sure it is functioning efficiently. If this office makes many mistakes or misses filing and reporting deadlines, faculty morale will indeed be adversely affected, and for good reason. The faculty will already be unhappy because such a large piece of their grant goes to the university for overhead. They will consider it as "their" money and will point out that "their" overhead more than pays "their" salary. They will consider the overhead to the university as more than the reasonable cost of utilities, janitorial service, security, and other obvious direct costs. They will not know the cost of the building in which their laboratory is housed. The fact is that if the institution does not get a fair overhead rate it cannot accept research grants and contracts for very long. It costs money to do research. The president should have enough facts and figures at his or her finger tips to be able to articulate the university's position on what it costs the institution when a grant or contract is awarded to it. Some funding agencies will attempt to negotiate a lower overhead rate than the federal auditing agency allows. Some foundations will refuse to pay certain overhead items. If you take a hard line you may have to deal with a very angry faculty member who did not get important research funded because of the university's "mean and greedy" posture. You should be reasonably flexible on overhead in special cases and accept the fact that some projects that should be pursued will not pay their way.

The organized research activities carried on through centers, institutes, laboratories, or bureaus are ongoing activities. The research unit will have a budget line and a permanent core staff. The larger ones will be administered by a director and include several principal investigators. Although such research activities commonly receive funding from the university, they will generate many times the university contribution from outside grant and contract funds.

Between the individual principal investigator with a single project grant or contract and the large well-staffed research institute administering a number of grants and contracts, the president may find a flourishing free enterprise zone that needs a good deal of attention. For example, in reviewing the mail you might notice a piece of official university stationery that carries a subhead identifying the source of the correspondence as the "Human Resources Laboratory" and identifying one of the professors in the Department of Sociology as "Director." You will not have heard of this laboratory previously and you will not find it listed in the university directory. Neither will you find it listed in the budget. You ask your vice-president for research about this laboratory. He or she has never heard of it but in a week or so reports back as follows. Professor Diehler, who is listed as "Director," is indeed on the university payroll but he was, of course, in Washington and no one knew where he could be reached. The chair of the sociology department knew nothing about the laboratory. After a number of telephone calls to various faculty and administrators, someone remembered that Professor Diehler recently received a $17,000 grant from the Small Business Administration to support the research of two graduate students to survey community attitudes on individually owned drive-in groceries as compared to drive-in grocery chains. Returned from Washington, Professor Diehler announces that he created the "Laboratory" by the simple expedient of printing the stationery. He explains that he needs the "Laboratory" as an official vehicle so he will be able to compete effectively for federal research funds. He makes a point of the fact that he paid for the stationery with grant funds and insists that he

thought that the university policy memoranda dealing with official stationery and creation of research units did not apply to him because university
funds were not involved. When reminded that the grant was to the university rather than to him personally, he complains about the excessive
overhead being charged by the institution. When informed that he does
not have the authority to create research units, he makes it clear that he
resents the administration interfering with his research and observes that
it is because of this kind of harassment that "faculty morale on campus is
at an all-time low."

The easy response from the administration is to approve, after the
fact, the creation of the "Human Resources Laboratory" and congratulate
Professor Diehler on his grant. But if you do not keep a firm hand on
organized research activities within the institution, you will be astonished
and dismayed by the rapid proliferation of centers, institutes, laboratories,
bureaus, and editorial offices that no one will know anything about until
you receive a request for budget support when federal funding is cut back
or abolished, you receive a request for remodeling of office space for a
center no one ever heard of, or the self-appointed director of a nonexistent
center requests a reduced teaching load because of heavy administrative
responsibilities. Shortly after the stationery is printed in violation of university policy, the laboratory begins to publish and distribute a newsletter.
If the costs cannot be defrayed by the grant, they will be artfully concealed
in the departmental maintenance and operations budget. The classroom
that suddenly disappeared from the inventory and course schedule is now
to be found behind a sign reading "Human Resources Laboratory, Professor B. F. Diehler, Director." The embarrassment becomes acute when a
state legislator calls to request a report issued by a unit of the university of
which no one in the president's office has ever heard. Do not be too quick
to say, "It's not one of ours!" The chances are it is.

Editorial offices present a special problem because many scholarly
journals, prestigious and widely respected but nevertheless on the brink of
bankruptcy, exist through a kind of symbiotic relationship with universities known as the rotating editorship. The editorship passes among faculty
members at different institutions at either regular or irregular intervals
depending on the financial capability of the university to sustain the
honor. The chair of the department of the fortunate university selected as
the new home for the prestigious journal will speak eloquently to the distinction conferred upon the faculty member selected as editor, his or her
department, and the university and then request relief from teaching duties for the new editor and additional funds and space to support and
house the operation as the university's contribution. Thus, the university
enters the editorial and publishing business until the honor is passed to
another university.

It is difficult for the president to defend the institution against one of these parasitic journal obligations. You might as well be resigned to carry one or more of them for a few years as part of the scholarly burden and gain as many points as possible by doing so. To refuse is to turn one's back on scholarship, be a man or woman of little vision, be content with mediocrity, miss the whole purpose of a great university, throw away an opportunity to develop real excellence, and, of course, bring "faculty morale to an all-time low." You are well advised, however, not to make a commitment of space. Find a few dollars in the budget for secretarial help, approve a course-load reduction for the editor, but hold the line on space. If you allocate space to the journal, the enterprise within a year will be back for more and be solidly entrenched. On the other hand, if the faculty member who has been honored with the editorship is forced to conduct the work and enjoy the honor in his or her own office, he or she will be delighted in just a few years to see the distinction pass to a colleague at another institution.

Bearing in mind that the research enterprise in a university can get out of hand very easily, you should make a careful review of how the function is administered soon after you take the president's chair. Although the deans have an important role to play in overseeing research in their schools and colleges, you should insist on maintaining a research management office in central administration. It should report through a strong vice-president, knowledgeable about research and able to deal effectively with faculty entrepreneurs. Where there is a large amount of contract and grant money flowing into a number of departments and organized research units, there is a great potential for abuses. Someone with a good nose for fraud should be monitoring expenditures from contract and grant funds lest the institution be embarrassed by a bad audit. If a principal investigator is subcontracting extensively it is a good idea to check on the organizations receiving the contracts. The money may be going to a wife or relative as president of the company providing the service. Travel expenses paid from contract and grant funds should be reviewed carefully. An auditor may find that grant funds are being used for personal entertaining.

Purchases of scientific equipment have a potential for causing trouble in public institutions. The principal investigator, usually for very good reason, will insist on the purchase of a specific piece of equipment manufactured by a certain company. This may put the university in conflict with a state purchasing commission that by state law requires equipment purchases to be put out for bid. There are usually provisions for exceptions if the institution certifies that a particular model from a particular manufacturer is the only equipment that will do the job. But proving up the exception may be so time consuming that the principal investigator will have taken his or her grant to another institution by the time the purchase is authorized. You will not get much help from the turf-protective bureaucrats in the state purchasing office, so you will have to work through political channels to simplify purchasing procedures for scientific equipment used in research. The loss of a star investigator to another institution because it took six months to buy a piece of equipment for his or her laboratory will get the attention of the state leadership if the matter is presented properly.

In administering the research enterprise in a university a certain amount of bureaucracy and paper work is essential if the president is to stay on top of what is going on among the entrepreneurial faculty. This is the place where a series of administrative policy memoranda, however pettifogging they may appear, may be the only way to rein in the fast movers. Circulated to deans, directors, chairs, and other administrative officials and regularly revised and brought up to date, these memoranda provide a written, authoritative set of "dos," "don'ts," and "how tos" that establish at least minimal consistency in what the various departments and offices of the university do and how they do it. With such a book of policy memoranda on the desk, no administrator can make a convincing case for being ignorant. For example, to maintain control over the official stationery of the university both as to how it looks and what it says, the president issues a policy memorandum on the subject of official university stationery. It will require approval by the president's office of all purchase vouchers issued to pay for university stationery. The business office will route to a designated individual in the president's office all such purchase vouchers. That individual will sound the alarm when a new, unauthorized research or editorial office first appears. A call to the dean or department chair will remind the faculty entrepreneur that any request to establish a new center or office must go through channels and receive approvals as specified in administrative policy memorandum no. 88–29 on organized research and scholarly activities. With much complaining about harassment, the request will then come forward to be reviewed properly and dealt with on the merits. While an expert is designing a state-of-the-art management information system for the university you will at least have in place a mundane mechanism that works.

Once a year the president should sit down with appropriate members of his or her staff and review the research activities on campus. You should evaluate the quality of the research in progress, the levels of activity, and the success in generating outside funds. This will tell you in what fields of research the university is a strong, respected player, and where it is weak. It is an excellent move to eliminate research units that are inactive. That will send out a message that you are serious about research management on campus. You should also be interested in the involvement of students in the various organized research units and the extent to which the units are supporting master's theses and doctoral dissertations. Once a reporting and reviewing system and schedule have been established, the information can be analyzed by your office of institutional studies and distributed as appropriate.

Nationally, the "score" on research is measured in the number of dollars received by a university from outside funding agencies that make awards by a merit review system. It is a competitive system in which the best proposals are funded. If the amount of money your university is receiving is increasing you are on the right track. Of course, your faculty cannot generate competitive proposals if you do not have the facilities and equipment necessary to support the proposed research. And you will not be able to recruit and retain the quality of faculty capable of generating competitive proposals without the facilities and equipment necessary to support the research and without the quality of graduate students that such high quality faculty will expect to involve in their work. Substantial capital expenditures are necessary to get into the research business and substantial operating funds are necessary to maintain the equipment and facilities. It is this reality that has prompted some universities to attempt to obtain funds to construct research facilities directly from Congress through the appropriation process rather than through merit review by funding agencies.

Some universities, in order to cast their record of success in obtaining research funds in the best light, include monies appropriated by state and federal agencies to support agricultural and engineering experiment stations, and as other "special items," which do not come under peer or merit review. In comparing the real quality and vigor of the research enterprise on your campus with that on campuses of other universities in your class, make sure that you are comparing funds awarded through the merit review process rather than an appropriation process.

If your university does not have an established and successful research program and you are determined to build one, it will be a long process and one in which you play the pivotal role. It will be up to you, working with selected deans and faculty, to develop from government and industry the funds required to seed and build a research program. The federal government, concerned about the rich-get-richer charges made by institutions that are not receiving federal research dollars and are in districts with influential congressmen and senators, has initiated programs designed to provide a more even geographic spread for some research funding. Representatives and senators have amended bills to provide for creation of research facilities in universities that have not been successful in winning funds in the peer or merit review system. If you have or can muster the political influence to get into this game, go to it. Just be sure you do not promise to do something that you cannot do. If you use political influence to secure a research contract that requires performance beyond that which your institution can deliver, your credibility will be greatly diminished.

In recent years universities have become interested in the intellectual properties developed through the research and scholarly activities of their faculty and research staff. Most have issued new policies on patents, licenses, and intellectual property, in general providing for the faculty or staff member and the university to share in royalties or license fee revenues derived from work done or products developed by university employees on university time. Some institutions have gone further and, in return for research support, have awarded exclusive licenses to commercial organizations interested in developing a university invention into a commercial product. Without exception, however, universities have been careful to protect the right of the faculty to publish in the public domain the results of their research efforts. The only restriction has been in the nature of an agreement to delay publication for a period sufficient to allow the supporting company an opportunity for exclusive access to the information.

There is a new climate in which transfer of technology from university to the marketplace is encouraged and, although some faculty members in some institutions have expressed reservations about the commercialization of the university, faculty in general have not resisted a closer relationship with business. It is perhaps an acknowledgment that, if universities are to continue to receive the funds necessary for their operation, there has to be a broad level of support for them within the larger society, and support from business is an important part of what is billed as a new partnership among the academy, government, and industry. As president, you should review the institution's intellectual property policy and the form of the proposed and existing agreements. Are any of them producing revenue for the institution? How is that revenue being used? If possible, it should be designated for the general support of research on campus. It will be well received if you direct part or all of the revenue to a fund for the support of young faculty attempting to establish a research program. It will be most unusual if the university is receiving any substantial amount of money from royalties or licenses, but there is always the hope that a university invention might produce a very significant income for the institution. You should have policies in place to profit from that eventuality.

While most of the attention from outside the university will focus on the research being conducted in science, engineering, medicine, pharmacy, and business, the quality and quantity of the creative and scholarly research being conducted in the humanities, social sciences, and fine arts will determine how your university is regarded in the intellectual world. It is much more difficult to secure funds from outside agencies to support scholarly work in these fields than in science and engineering. But, in general, it does not cost as much to support scholarly work in the humanities as in the "hard" sciences. Because of the importance of this kind of scholarship to the academic community, you are advised to apply your efforts to support the deans of those colleges in their quest for research support and to use discretionary funds at your disposal for seed money and challenge grants to support scholarship in the humanities, social sciences, and fine arts.

The future will see a broader appreciation on the part of the larger society of the value of research and scholarship in colleges and universities that previously have not been regarded as research institutions. State legislatures are beginning to appropriate small amounts of money to support research in smaller, principally undergraduate public colleges and universities. Liberal arts colleges are becoming more active and more successful in seeking grants to support scholarly activity. Results will be seen more in faculty development and improvement than in the creation of significant new knowledge, but that is a worthy goal in itself.

CHAPTER 9

Operating the Institution

$\mathbf{A}$ BIG, comprehensive, undergraduate and graduate, research university may consist of more than fifteen schools and colleges, over fifty academic departments, 250 to 300 degree programs, 6,000 to 7,000 courses, 2,500 to 3,000 faculty members, some 4,000 academic and research assistants, and a staff in excess of 10,000 employees. The student body in one of the big universities is 40,000 to 50,000. If there is a large teaching hospital associated with the university's medical school, include that population of physicians, nurses, staff, and patients in the university community. When you add to the students, faculty, and staff their dependents and the employees of the many businesses that serve the university community, a major university is in and of itself a medium-size city. It is a very large enterprise.

A review of all of the functions that are necessary to the operation of a modern university dispels effectively romantic images of the academy as it existed in the golden age of Greece when students sat under an olive tree at the feet of their teacher. As much as the faculty may cherish those images, they are the first to complain when one of the many functions that support teaching and scholarship is not properly performed. It is critical to the success of a university president that the infrastructure supporting the educational mission of the university is well designed, well built, and operating effectively and efficiently. It has to work. To assess the quality of the infrastructure, you need to know a great deal more about a university than is within the common knowledge of the average faculty member. Indeed, preoccupied with teaching duties and research, the faculty will not care much about the complex array of functions that support their activities until one of them fails.

If you are newly come to the presidency it is unlikely that you will be fully knowledgeable about all the operations conducted in support of the institution's mission. Probably you will be more comfortable with the academic enterprise and have less personal experience with student affairs or business systems. You should face up to the gaps in your knowledge and experience and start immediately an on-the-job learning program. After all, how can you evaluate the performance of a vice-president if you do not really know what he or she is supposed to do? It is difficult to communicate with the vice-president for business affairs if you cannot read a balance sheet, an income statement, or a statement of cash flows and understand the findings of an internal audit. It is difficult to appreciate the accomplishments of the vice-president for student affairs if you are unaware of the great variety of services the university provides for students and untutored in the fundamentals of the legal framework that limits the university's actions in dealing with students. So . . . after you have assessed the state of your ignorance, ask questions, read carefully, and ask some more questions.

The word "infrastructure," the structure below, is one of those useful, inclusive but constructively ambiguous terms that in the passive sense connotes no more than a foundation, but in a more active sense connotes a kind of engine room. The infrastructure of a university, that "structure" below the departments, schools, colleges, and their academic programs, is very much an engine room. There are three parts to it—the academic affairs infrastructure, the student affairs infrastructure, and the business affairs infrastructure. The president's office, external affairs, and development constitute a superstructure. In your early days in the president's chair it will be perhaps most helpful to you, in contemplating how and why it all works, to think about the infrastructure in terms of function. It is better to organize your management by fitting administration to function than the reverse.

Budgeted units that are commonly included within the academic infrastructure include general libraries and special collections, the computer center and its satellite operations, museums and galleries, the university press, a center for laboratory animals, conference centers, and an office of institutional studies. Functions that are essential but may or may not be organized as separate units include course inventory, course scheduling, catalogs, assignment of classrooms and other academic space, research administration, and continuing education. Obviously, these are not all of equal importance; some have more potential for causing a crisis than others. If a mainframe computer crashes you have an emergency. A problem in the art museum probably will not be of such urgency as to require you to cut short a meeting in Washington.

The academic reputation of a university is directly related to the size and quality of its general libraries and special collections. Every evaluation of every academic program will include an examination of the library resources available to that program. You, as president, must be a strong defender of the library. But you should also know that (1) The university library is a bottomless pit that can absorb all the funds there are; no institution has enough money to maintain and operate a library that is satisfactory to the faculty. (2) If the administration buys books and periodicals, there is not enough money to catalog the collections and provide necessary services to library users; if the administration employs sufficient technical staff to catalog the collections and provide services, there is not enough money to buy books and periodicals . . . Hobson must have been a director of libraries. (3) There is no way to schedule library hours to satisfy everyone; some students and faculty will demand that the library be open twenty-four hours a day, but you cannot afford to do that. (4) The central or main library will be in a perpetual struggle to absorb departmental libraries; departmental libraries are self-generating and fight fiercely to survive. (5) All librarians want faculty status, including tenure.

There is no easy solution to library problems. The best you can do is to appoint sound people to the appropriate committees and hope you get support for reasonable budget recommendations, a sound acquisition policy, and operating policies that you can afford. Library automation and an on-line catalog will dampen some of the noise from advocates of departmental libraries. If library automation is not well advanced in your institution, this is a project that you should get behind and push. You can afford some departmental libraries but not very many. You should not approve faculty status for librarians for the simple reason that they are not faculty.

The director of libraries or head librarian is another one of those key appointments to which you must give close attention. Do not let the academic vice-president make that decision without your consideration and approval. University libraries are composed of a general collection that supports the instructional mission of the institution together with various special collections that support the graduate and research programs and add to the scholarly luster and distinction of the institution. It is the special collections that get the attention of scholars and the press that deals with cultural affairs. In making speeches, you may cite the number of volumes in the university's library, if indeed you are proud of the number, but it is the fact that your library houses Lord Rutherford's papers or the Sir William Jones collection that will cause people to sit up and take notice. If your director of libraries neglects the general collection and spends his or her days in pursuit of special collections, wooing book collectors and haunting book auctions over the world, the faculty and students will soon take a dim view of how the library is administered. The director of libraries should be service oriented and technically competent, particularly in the area of library automation. He or she should not be excessively protective of books but rather motivated toward putting the library's books into the hands of faculty and students as efficiently as possible. An associate librarian can function as director of special collections and in this position the bibliophile protector and conservator will do nicely. It will help if the library committee is a balanced committee with membership spread over the schools and colleges of the university and including faculty who deal with large undergraduate sections as well as those primarily involved in graduate education. The committee should also include graduate and undergraduate students. This committee will sound the alarm if the leadership of the library is inclined to spend all the library's funds acquiring rare and distinguished collections.

Most universities have found through study and experience that it is significantly cheaper and more efficient to concentrate the institution's library resources in a central or main library rather than have them spread over the campus in departmental or branch libraries. However, departmental faculties want their libraries in their buildings and can and do present persuasive arguments to justify the space, staff, and funds necessary to the support of the departmental library. Even though the institution has a long-standing policy that prohibits the establishment of departmental libraries, they have a way of just coming into being.

The departmental library begins with a few shelves of books in the departmental office. It grows through gifts of books and journals solicited from alumni and retired colleagues, complimentary copies of books from publishers, and unsolicited gifts from the heirs of professionals who are looking for someone who will help them clean out the family library. Once this unofficial departmental library reaches a size where it is transferred to the departmental conference room, it will be known within the department as "their" library. A request to build shelves in the conference room is an indication of what is happening but such requests probably would not go to anyone who would recognize them as the sign of a growing departmental library. At this point, unless all university book orders, regardless of source of funds, are routed through the main library purchasing system, departmental operating funds will be tapped to buy books. There may be requests to foundations to buy books. But if your administrative systems are working, all requests to foundations will be reviewed by your development office, and your office will be advised.

In the next phase, the departmental library flows out of the conference room into an adjoining classroom that is taken out of the classroom inventory. A work-study student or research assistant is assigned to work as a librarian. But the first time that the administration learns of the existence of a departmental library is when the department makes a request for a budget line that would make the underground library legitimate. This will test your mettle and that of your director of libraries. The main library will undoubtedly be short of staff. To add a staff member to serve as librarian for a new departmental library will not be enthusiastically received by the director of libraries. On the other hand, it is probably not a good idea to send a truck to haul the departmental collection to the main library. Nearly all of the collection will duplicate the holdings in the main library. Unless after review there is a compelling reason to authorize another departmental library, the best course is to permit the collection to remain in the department, refuse to provide any financial support in the form of staff or an acquisitions budget, and make sure it does not take any more space from the instructional program. If you cave in and give official recognition and support to one new departmental library that just grew, next year there will be two or three more.

Since the faculty is the premier group on campus, and since the senior faculty enjoys tenure, it is not surprising the librarians have organized to win what they refer to as "faculty status." But although librarians support the academic mission of the institution and although senior professional librarians may hold part-time appointments as lecturers or senior lecturers, as a group, librarians are not faculty and should not be considered as members of the faculty. There is no barrier, or should be no barrier, to librarians attaining a faculty appointment as long as they have the qualifications and experience in a field and there is need for their teaching service on a regular and continuing basis. However, few professional librarians are qualified for faculty positions and few are engaged in teaching as part of their regular duties. They are employed to work in the library. To confer faculty status upon librarians as a group would, logically, qualify other professional groups on campus . . . research professionals, computer center staff, and professionals in the business operations . . . for the same consideration. Faculty status means "tenure," and "tenure" brings a degree of independence that makes it impossible to direct an employee in the performance of duties except in a very general way. Although it is appropriate for faculty to be independent in this sense, you cannot grant the same degree of independence to other groups of professional employees without diminishing your authority to manage the institution. When an accrediting team recommends faculty status for librarians do not be persuaded; the recommendation will have been written by the library specialist on the accrediting team and will be wholly self-serving.

Computer centers are like libraries in that every university must have one and both libraries and computer centers can spend all the money there is. They are different in that, while books never become obsolete, computers become obsolete very quickly . . . just about the time they are installed. If the president spends all the money there is on the library, he or she will develop a reputation as a truly scholarly president with great vision, a president with sound academic values, and the institution will have a great library. On the other hand, if the president spends all the money there is on the computer center, his or her values will be questioned and the university may well end up with yesterday's hardware and systems that do not provide the capabilities needed. The faculty will disagree on what is needed and no two consultants will give the same advice. In reviewing the university's infrastructure, the computer center is an element where the risk of making a mistake is high and the cost of making a mistake is high.

Three kinds of computing services are necessary to a university—administrative computing, research computing, and instructional computing. Administrative computing services, commonly called data processing, support the business operations of the institution and include accounting, payroll, purchasing, personnel records, admissions and registration, the library, institutional studies, and possibly other functions, such as alumni records and the development office. It is data processing that generates the enormous volume of reports that the public university must file with state and federal agencies. The administrative system has to be up and running to process the payroll or nobody gets paid. It must be reliable. Faculty and students cannot be permitted access to this system for research or for any other reason. It must be under the control of the vice-president for business affairs. It must be a secure system.

Research computing supports independent faculty research, organized research, and the graduate program. It has a very different function from data processing. The research computers include big, powerful mainframes, minicomputers, and PC's linked in networks. Faculty and students will have access through remote job entry terminals and workstations. The whole may be linked to various national networks. It is this research computing function that will be the primary concern of the faculty computer committee, and it will be that committee that sends forward a stream of urgent requests for expensive hardware and software to maintain a state-of-the-art system. There will be members of the faculty in the sciences, engineering, and social sciences involved in modeling of complex systems who can fully utilize the capacity of the research computer center twenty-four hours a day. Thus, if the test of adequacy is to provide all the computer time that everyone wants, your system will always be, from the faculty viewpoint, inadequate.

If you are president of a major research university you will be faced with the problem of acquiring and operating a supercomputer. If you are to compete successfully in science and engineering research the need is real. Negotiations with vendors may produce an attractive arrangement that, with lease options and discounts, may avoid consuming the entire equipment budget for the next five years. If your resources are not sufficient to buy or lease a machine directly, you may be able to lease a block of time on a computer owned and operated by another university. This is not just a piece of equipment it would be nice to have; your faculty must have access to a supercomputer if your university is going to be a major player in the research game.

Instructional computing involves the use of the computer in direct support of teaching. It is used by the instructor in the classroom and by students who interact directly with the computer in classrooms equipped with banks of terminals. Over the past several decades a number of systems have been designed to support computer-assisted instruction. They have been sold as the way to improve faculty productivity and increase the quality of instruction, and labeled as "classrooms of the future." Although the jury is still out on the issue of increased productivity and quality of instruction, it is clear that the cost of installing and operating systems of computer-assisted instruction is very high. Enthusiasm on campus for "classrooms of the future" is not high. On the other hand, there is an acknowledged urgent need to provide improved access to computers for students in science and engineering for both instructional and research purposes.

The issue for the president is how to organize and deploy the institution's computational resources and how to come up with the money for the high capital costs and operating costs. It is essential that the business computing function be maintained separate and apart from the research and instructional function. The business function should report to the vice-president for business affairs; the research and instructional function should report to the academic vice-president or provost. You need a good, experienced, practical director of data processing; you need a technically expert and creative director of the academic computer center who in terms of credentials can command the respect of the faculty. It is not essential that the director of the computer center have an academic appointment but it is preferable.

Because it costs a great deal of money to acquire and operate the computers that constitute the university computer center, it stands to reason that computer time is a very valuable commodity. As president, you should make sure that the system used to allocate time on the machines is fair and equitable but at the same time does not promote frivolous use. The faculty and students would like access to the computer center to be free. That is not a good idea. Those who use the computer center should have to pay for the time, but of course, unless they have money from other sources, you will have to provide the money. The best and most commonly used system is to provide in the budgets of the academic departments and other appropriate operating units of the institution a line item for computer time and materials consumed. Initially, the amount can be based on historical usage and then it can be adjusted based on justifiable need. It will then be up to the department chair or research unit director to allocate monies for the purchase of computer time to the faculty or research scientists and to their graduate students. Since there will not be enough money to take care of all requests, there will be pressure on the faculty to include requests for funding for computer time in their grant and contract proposals to outside funding agencies, and to devote their energies to soliciting grants for computer time from other sources. The in-house rate established for use of the computer center should be set in consultation with and upon the recommendation of the faculty computer committee. Putting the system on a business basis will ensure that no one plays with the machine.

If you are president of a public university you may encounter another problem in attempting to develop and operate the computers necessary to support the business and academic operations of the institution. In some department of state government, a bureaucrat will have compiled information on how much the state is spending on data processing and how this sum has been increasing over the years. This astonishingly large number and the steep upward slope of the curve will get everyone's attention and the result will be the creation of a new authority either under existing law or through a new statute to exercise some control over the purchase and operation of computers and data processing equipment on a statewide basis. The effect upon the university will depend on the regulations promulgated under law, the degree of sophistication of the director of the new department, and the magnitude of his or her ambitions. At the very least the university will have to submit reports on its computer systems and anticipated future needs. It may be necessary to explain the difference between research instruments used by faculty and students and the data processing equipment used in support of the business operation, and argue that the research computers should not be subject to the state requirements for submission of requests to purchase or lease computers.

If you are forced to send your requests through a state approval process involving a bureaucratic chain of officials, none of whom understands that your research program on artificial intelligence and expert systems cannot function on the kind of machine adequate for printing checks, and culminating in a state purchasing policy that produces a machine based on the low bid, your faculty will be in revolt. You must resist any plan to implement a state computer network in which all state-owned computers are consolidated under a single authority. Built to serve the needs of departments of state government, such a system will not be able to meet the academic and instructional needs of the university. The university must have the degree of independence necessary to control its own destiny in designing and operating the computer system it needs to support its research and instructional mission. You must be prepared to spend whatever political capital is necessary to maintain that independence.

The university may operate an art gallery, a natural history museum, or a historical museum. The collections that make up these museums support the teaching mission of the institution and are also open to the public. In some universities these collections are spread out among the various departments of art, history, archaeology, geology, botany, and zoology; in others they are assembled in a building designed or adapted for effective display. If the collections are properly housed and accessible to the public, they support the public image of the institution as a center of learning and have a way of attracting gifts of other collections from private donors. If they are not properly housed and in fact hidden away in store rooms and closets where they can be neither seen nor used, the faculty will press for the construction of a gallery or museum. Of course, it costs money to construct and operate an art gallery or natural history museum and you will also have to expand your operating budget to include directors, curators, conservators, and those talented at preparing exhibits.

In the fine arts, you must make sure that the acquisitions budget is controlled so that a single individual cannot purchase paintings, statuary, or other works of art without the advice of a faculty committee and without the approval of the president's office. An advisory committee is also useful in making sure that exhibits are in good taste and bear some relation to the teaching program. You should have a policy that governs gifts to the university of works of art and their exhibition, including exhibits out of doors, so that you will not be surprised some morning to see gracing the grounds in a prominent place a piece of sculpture that is at best grotesquely ugly or at worst obscene, and that was accepted on behalf of the university by the chair of the art department without any consultation with you or anyone else.

Donors who want to give the university works of art can create very delicate situations. It is difficult to say "no" to a longtime friend of the institution who has been generous in other ways, but never make the mistake of obligating the institution in perpetuity to exhibiting a donated work of art and never accept a stipulation that the gift may never be sold or otherwise disposed of. You owe your successor the flexibility to deal with unforeseen circumstances. Do not accept the responsibility of putting a value on the gift or endorsing the valuation of an appraiser. Make it clear that the monetary value of the gift is between the donor and the Internal Revenue Service.

A university press can bring distinction to the institution but, even though it carries the name of your university and thus has about it an air of the academy, never forget that it is a business and must be operated like one. The university press that does not require a subsidy is a rare bird. The challenge is to keep the subsidy as low as possible and for that you need a director who is more than an editor and bibliophile. You need a man or woman who can run a business and knows how to maintain a balance between scholarly works that are appropriate to a university press but will never sell and those books that will make money.

In making the important decisions on what to publish, the director of the press will be advised by a faculty committee. The committee will be biased toward accepting manuscripts of intrinsic scholarly importance. That should come as no surprise and, indeed, it is the obligation of university presses to publish as many first-class scholarly works as they can afford. But, the more they publish, the higher the subsidy. The director of the press will need your help in maintaining the balance, and the way to help is to appoint a committee that includes enough business-oriented faculty members to restrain the enthusiasm of those members of the committee who are so overwhelmed by the quality of a scholarly treatise that they want to publish it regardless of cost. However, this faculty advisory committee should not advise on budget or financial matters. Your business officer, or someone from that office, should be assigned the responsibility for working with the professional staff of the press to solve business problems.

During budget preparation, look carefully at the budget submitted by the university press. The subsidy should be budgeted going in and not be appropriated every year after the fact to cover the operating deficit. Beware of overly ambitious book lists. Review the marketing strategy. Keep track of the inventory. If you still have three thousand copies of a book published three years ago, someone made a mistake on the size of the edition. If you have too many of these mistakes in your warehouse, it is time to ask some questions. It is also time to have a sale.

If your university does not have a press, you may receive a proposal from the faculty to establish one. You must then consider the question of whether your institution has achieved a maturity and stature sufficient for the intellectual support of an academic press. Be advised that those who want to launch a new scholarly press will commonly underestimate the cost of such a venture. Make a survey of other university presses and get as much data as you can on their operating costs. If you do not have funds to underwrite the cost of a press, you might, as an alternative, be able to negotiate a cooperative agreement with another university press that would undertake to co-publish and distribute scholarly books produced by your faculty. The agreement should provide that any volume published with the imprimature of your institution is properly reviewed and approved by a faculty committee. Such a cooperative venture will give your faculty some scholarly visibility at very substantially less cost than establishing an in-house press.

As president you will need an individual responsible directly to your office who can produce and analyze data on very short notice. In a large university, this capability may be centered in an office of institutional studies with a director and staff. This office is charged with developing, analyzing, and presenting in a timely way the data that tell you how the university is operating and how it compares nationally with other institutions. It provides the numbers that you need to support your position in making a recommendation to the board, answering a request from a legislator or bureaucrat, or making a speech to the faculty. It will be unusual if a week goes by that you do not call the director of the office of institutional studies with a request for information on faculty salaries at comparable institutions, the number of Ph.D.'s awarded to African American graduate students in the field of mathematics, which institutions pay a salary to the president of the student body, or the level of annual giving by alumni who have graduated in the last five years. It is best if you do not have to go through a vice-president or dean for access to these kinds of data. Organize this function for your convenience.

Other functions essential to the operation of the institution include maintenance of the course inventory, course scheduling, assignment of classrooms and other academic space, revision and publication of catalogs, research administration, and continuing education. Inventory, scheduling, and classroom space assignment is usually handled by an "old pro" from the registrar's office and in the modern university it is highly automated. A big, comprehensive, graduate research university may list more than six thousand courses but, of course, not all of them will be offered in one semester. On occasion, a department may seek to convert a classroom to other purposes. If a battle over space gets as far as your office, you should not be pleased about it.

Catalogs are official publications of the university and the catalog under which a student enters has been determined by law to be a contract between that student and the university in the sense that the university is bound by the terms and requirements set forth in the catalog. When students began taking disagreements over academic requirements to the courts, universities were forced to have their catalogs reviewed by legal counsel and make revisions based on advice received. Upon taking the presidency, you should confirm that the institution's catalogs have been recently reviewed by legal staff and revised as necessary. Unless you have the rare privilege of building a completely new university, the institution's catalogs will be venerable documents, modified from time to time over a period of many years, with many deletions and additions. A thorough revision and editing to make sure that all the verbiage is still needed will in all probability produce a much thinner and cleaner document. Catalogs are usually in the domain of the registrar, but if he or she has been in the job for many years it might take a directive from you to initiate a review and revision of the official catalogs.

Research administration was discussed in the chapter on research and scholarship. As university research has come to be viewed as a means to economic development and enhancement of national competitiveness in the world market place, as more attention is given to "technology transfer," and as intellectual property is seen to have great potential value for the institution, research budgets are growing and the need for sophisticated research management is imperative. The research enterprise can no longer be run from a vice-president's hip pocket.

If you have a college of natural sciences you will have research programs in the life sciences, and that means that you will have the problem of caring for laboratory animals. If your research programs are substantial, it is better to maintain a central facility for research animals rather than have them scattered around in a number of laboratories. Since the research funds will undoubtedly come from federal sources, your institution will have to meet increasingly stringent standards for the housing and care of laboratory animals. Animal rights activists are becoming more militant. You can comply with state and federal regulations more effectively and provide better security at a central facility built for laboratory animals than you can if they are kept in cages stacked in a faculty member's laboratory. You should review the institution's policies on laboratory animals and make sure they are adequate for the research programs in progress.

The president will have considerable latitude in how the institution's continuing education programs are managed. Professional schools are serious about it and indeed in professions that are certified, registered, or licensed by a state agency or professional organization a certain number of hours of continuing education may be required to maintain certification, registration, or licensure. These programs can be conducted under the authority of the dean of the professional school or college or centralized, with the cooperation of the professional school or college, in a division of continuing education under a dean or director. A division of continuing education also would be responsible for the various outreach programs, formerly known as "extension," and for offering both credit and noncredit courses ranging from courses acceptable in a regular degree program to summer programs for alumni involving travel to romantic, faraway places under the leadership of a faculty member known for studies in the classical ancient world, central American archaeology, or thirteenth-century cathedrals.

A division of continuing education with an overly ambitious dean or director can get you into a great deal of trouble. Someone in your office should read carefully all the brochures and other promotional material issued by the division. Make sure that the relationship between the university and a particular travel agency is a proper one. Have the university's attorneys look into the institution's liability as a sponsor of international excursions. A university should not have too much "hustle" in its continuing education programs.

There is little to be said about the conference centers operated by your university except to note that they should pay their way. Fees should be set at a level that permits recovery of the direct costs of the meeting as well as an appropriate share of the overhead. Of course, some meetings of particular importance to the university will have to be carried. The budget for each event should indicate the source of funds and, if the cost is to be met by other than registration fees, the source of the funds and an account number should be included in the budget so there will not be any end-of-year surprises. The president's office, the deans' offices, or grants from foundations are common sources for funds to hold conferences, symposia, seminars, and the like. University policy should require that every event have an official sponsor so that the responsibility is clearly fixed, and the policy should also make clear what university officials are authorized to sponsor an event. You are well advised not to delegate this authority below deans. If the policy and procedure for obtaining an official sponsor for a conference and scheduling the facility are not enforced you will have some very strange groups with very questionable agendas meeting in the university conference center. There is risk that the university will be embarrassed and that you will be called to account.

The student affairs infrastructure has been introduced in the chapter on students, student activities, and student services. Here again we have come a long way from the days when a dean of students stood *in loco parentis* and took care of all student academic and personal problems. The necessary student support functions have been institutionalized and professionalized.

For most students, the first contact with your university will come through the office of admissions. This is the office that is responsible for the university's relations with high schools and junior colleges, and for whatever outreach programs that you have. It receives and evaluates applications for admission and the student's credentials in support of the application. It evaluates high school credits and, in the case of transfer students and graduate students, the courses that students have taken elsewhere. It enforces the admissions policy of the university and makes the decisions to admit or deny the students who apply. This is the front door of the university, and when the student comes through it you want the experience to be pleasant. The attitude of the director of admissions and his or her staff is very important; the efficiency with which the staff processes the paper work is very important. If a student seeking admission concludes that the director of admissions and the staff are rude, unresponsive, insulting, legalistic, and determined to make it as difficult as possible to be admitted to the institution, you have a serious problem at the front door.

No matter what the provocation, the admissions office staff must be courteous, friendly, helpful, and ready to turn the other cheek. It is not easy. The student who swaggers in, demands to know why the university needs all this information, makes comments on how stupid the entire procedure is, and arrogantly claims a close friendship with a member of the board of regents is a problem for a tired, harassed, and overworked admissions counselor.

A director of admissions who knows the business will hold training sessions for the staff and make sure that during times of peak workload the stress is properly handled. The president should show a personal interest in the affairs of this office and give the director of admissions his or her personal support. The director's job is much different than it was a few decades ago; it is a much higher profile position. A great deal of attention is given to who gets into the university and who does not. There is intense competition among universities for minority students and for national merit scholars. Your director of admissions will feel the pressure and it is important that he or she feels part of the administrative team. Make a phone call now and then during the "busy" season to inquire about how things are going, and when you have a social function for senior staff be sure to include the director of admissions.

Not too many years ago, some public universities were prohibited by law from spending appropriated funds on recruiting students, and what organized recruiting went on was focused almost exclusively on recruiting athletes. Institutions with strong programs in music and the arts recruited talented students in these areas, and those with prestigious scholarships and fellowships competed for the academically superior students. But, recent years have seen changes in recruiting practices and recruiting objectives. Now, recruiting for students who are academically superior and, particularly, recruiting for talented minority students are institutionalized and a great deal of time, effort, and money is going into these programs. There are programs to identify students with academic potential in high schools and establish early contact with them to see to it that they are well advised, to provide them with information about the university, and to tailor financial aid packages for them. High school counselors who influence student decisions about colleges and universities are wooed by institutions of higher education. Alumni clubs are pressed into service to provide local support and resources for recruiting bright students, especially minority students. University presidents, deans, and other senior officials are seen more often at high schools and community colleges. Special efforts are made to bring superior high school students to the campus at the close of their junior year to expose them to the best that the university has to offer. As president, you should know about these recruiting efforts, who is directing them, how they are organized and staffed, and how much money is being expended on them. You will certainly be asked about them. To the extent that you can, you should participate in them. Although many of the recruiting programs will be run by the schools and colleges, it is a good idea for your office to exercise a general oversight to make sure that the same university message is being delivered by all recruiters.

Although you must rely on your director of admissions to administer the admissions policy of the institution, enrollment management is a function that should be controlled by you and your immediate staff. Clearly, you do not want a campus that is overcrowded and thus you should not admit more students than can be accommodated in the institution's facilities and properly instructed by the institution's faculty. But you do not want an empty campus with underutilized facilities either, particularly in view of the fact that a significant proportion of the university's revenues are derived from tuition. In addition to the total number of students enrolled in the university, you will be concerned about the makeup of the student body—the ethnic diversity, the ratio of males to females, the age profile, geographic diversity among your students and the number of foreign students, the number of students receiving financial aid, and the number of working students. You should have a profile showing the number of credit hours for which students are registered, and data on whatever other measures are necessary to give you the information to understand the character and quality of the students. With these data, you and your vice-presidents can devise an enrollment management policy to produce the kind of student body that is appropriate for your institution.

Devising and implementing an enrollment management policy are, however, two very different things. In a public university, your policy will have to take into account the realities of the social and political environment in your state. You cannot maintain an enrollment policy with admission standards so high that the sons and daughters of the average citizens of the state are denied an opportunity to matriculate. A public institution should maintain admission standards such that students who perform reasonably well in high school can come and demonstrate their ability to do university-level work. If your performance standards are high, as they should be, many students will drop out along the way. You may lose as many as 40 percent between admission and graduation. This is the price a public university must pay, and indeed should pay, for providing access to higher education for the people who pay the bills.

Although admission standards are a principal tool in managing enrollment, there are other considerations. In public institutions tuition levels will be established directly by the legislature or by the board of regents under authority delegated by the legislature. If the board sets tuition too high, there will be political repercussions that will get the board's attention. Private universities—high-prestige institutions that consistently admit only a fraction of those that apply—can obviously charge more than schools that have to recruit vigorously to maintain enrollment at a satisfactory level. But even for the high-prestige schools the market exerts a control over tuition fees. In order to attract talented minority students the prestigious private schools must be able to offer competitive scholarships, so the availability of financial aid is also a factor in establishing enrollment policy. While some high-cost private schools are fighting to maintain enrollment, low-cost public schools with good academic reputations are seeking ways to limit enrollment without discouraging the application of qualified minority students.

The point is, whether public or private, enrollment cannot be allowed to "just happen." The president should manage it so as to optimize the number of students, and the quality of students, bearing in mind the various social and political interests of the society that the university serves.

In a large university the office of the registrar will be separate from the office of the director of admissions; in smaller institutions the functions of admissions and registrar are combined. The registrar maintains the official catalog of courses and prepares official publications, such as catalogs, bulletins, and course schedules. Compilation of statistics and dissemination of reports on enrollment, class sizes, attendance, and performance are within the purview of the registrar's office. The registrar supervises and administers the process of registration, schedules classes and final examinations, collects, records, and distributes grades, maintains academic records, and issues official transcripts. In short, the registrar is a key player in the "nitty gritty" of the instructional program. Your registrar has to be able to manage an office whose functions are automated and see to it that the systems are state of the art. If your registrar has been long in the job and has not kept pace with developments in computer technology as applied to the registrar's function, you will have to move quickly to put in place an associate registrar who can apply the technology. As with the admissions office, the office of the registrar must be an efficient, responsive office that can move paper quickly.

The registrar is in contact with the faculty during registration and through the collection of grades. A good registrar will not be overly bureaucratic in dealing with the faculty and will, in most cases, be able to coax and cajole "laid back" members of the faculty to get their grades in on time so that transcripts can be prepared and issued. But when certain members of the faculty consistently miss deadlines and ignore their responsibilities to their students, the registrar will need your help. Using the authority of your office through deans and department chairs, you should support the efforts of the registrar to maintain the official approved schedules of the institution.

When in the course of registration unexpected demand for certain courses occurs, the registrar must be prepared, upon request of the department, to move quickly to open new course sections and find a place and time for them to be taught. But decisions made under the pressure of the registration process cannot be made unilaterally by a department chair, a dean, the vice-president for academic affairs, or the registrar. The department has to determine the need for another section of a course and find an instructor, the registrar has to find a time in the schedule and a room in which to teach it, and the dean and the academic vice-president have to find the money for another course section. But the biggest test of the mettle of the registrar is the add-and-drop process.

You would think that, with the sophisticated computer capabilities possessed by most universities, the institution should be able to design and operate an efficient system for registering students. And it is true that with automated systems and on-line capability registration procedures on most campuses have been much improved over the chaos that reigned some years ago. But the add-and-drop problem will test the best of systems.

It all starts when a young male student who signed up for a particular course at a particular time, say on a Monday, Wednesday, and Friday at 10:00 A.M., learns that an attractive, young female student who has caught his eye is in another section of that same course or in a completely different course on Tuesdays and Thursdays at 10:00 A.M. He drops the course for which he registered and adds the course for which the would-be object of his interest has registered. However, the attractive, young female has found out that her sorority sister who seems to be very bright has signed up for still another section or course. So the attractive, young female enters the process of adding and dropping. When about 40 percent of the student body is engaged in dropping and adding courses all within the short span of three or four days, the system is, to put it mildly, perturbed. A student body of ten thousand will generate several hundred thousand course changes during registration. In some universities a system of pre-registration whereby a student registers at the end of the spring term for the following fall gives the administration some information on the demand for various courses and assists in planning but it may exacerbate the add-and-drop problem. The probability that a student will want to change his or her schedule varies directly as the third power of the time between registration and the beginning of classes. Of course, the majority of adds-and-drops are not frivolous. Most students enter the process for good and sufficient reasons.

The problem is compounded on the institution's side by the course schedule. The catalog is a complete inventory of courses, not all of which are offered every term, while the course schedule is a menu of what the university is offering in a particular term. The course schedule is printed and distributed so that students, faculty, and administration will have an accurate listing of what is to be offered in that term. It includes the course name and number, the days and times the course is offered, the building and room number, and the instructor's name. In some institutions where registration has been automated the course schedule is on-line and available through terminals in departmental offices.

The course schedule is born anew each term, semester, or quarter. Although published in good faith, the course schedule is at least in part fiction and no one has ever construed it to be a contract between university and student. Consider how the course schedule is developed.

The faculty, through the departments, schools, and colleges, submit a schedule of the courses they want to teach in the term in question. The administration looks at the submissions with some skepticism. Sure enough, the submissions contain courses that have not "made," that is to say, have not attracted the minimum number of students necessary for many years. Most public universities have a minimum size—usually ten undergraduate or five graduate students—that is required for a course to be offered. State legislatures are not enthusiastic about paying a professor's salary for teaching two or three students. Private universities are not subject to the minimum size rule by law but rather by economic imperative. Independent study arrangements can be made for students who need a particular course that has not "made" in order to graduate, but this requires considerable extra work on the part of a faculty member. The administration questions those courses that are perennial losers and inquires why certain courses that are necessary to degree programs are not being offered. It develops that the professor who teaches a required course is on leave, involved in a research project, or on special assignment for curriculum development. But in view of the administration's concern and some student complaints, the courses necessary to complete degree programs are then added to the course schedule. But since no one knows who will teach those courses, the entry is followed by the cryptic word "staff." This is a challenge to students who immediately set out to learn who the mysterious "staff" will be.

Other students are demanding that the university offer courses that are "more relevant." These courses turn out to be "fun" courses or courses that advocate a particular ideological view or support some social cause. The students demanding them have been put up to it by a faculty member whose department has decided that such a course should not be offered. The so-called relevant courses are not relevant to any degree program offered by the university. The frustrated faculty member may accuse the administration of violating his or her academic freedom, with academic freedom in this context defined as the right to teach what the faculty member wants to teach, when he or she wants to teach it, with, of course, the university paying an appropriate salary to the faculty member.

While all this discussion is in progress, the course schedule goes to press, is printed, posted, and distributed. The faculty and students complain that the administration has distributed the schedule too late for proper academic advisement of the students. The administration blames it on last-minute changes and a delay in the printing division. As soon as the new course schedule is received, the academic departments propose to add or delete courses equal in number to about 30 or 40 percent of their entire departmental offerings. There is no particular reason why it is 30 to 40 percent, but it generally works out that way. Reasons for the changes abound. A professor scheduled to teach a particular course has unexpectedly received a grant that will take him or her to New Zealand for the semester; the room in which the course was scheduled has somehow turned into a faculty laboratory or the departmental library during the summer; the departmental faculty in a lively meeting has determined to reshape the curriculum and that particular course has been eliminated and two new courses have been added; the professor scheduled to teach the course has flatly refused to do so because the teaching assistant that he or she was depending upon has left the university; a new faculty member has joined the department and the understanding was that he or she would be able to offer a new course.

The administration, of course, resists all these changes and each is negotiated. Meanwhile, registration begins and neither students nor advisors know that a particular course has been canceled or that a new course has been added until after a student attempts to register for the canceled course or a professor tries to recruit students into a new course that does not appear on the schedule. And so the process is further perturbed. Students will call home and advise their parents that they cannot get the courses they need and probably will have to stay an extra semester. The president will hear from the parents and read in the student newspaper about all the problems of registration. The registrar will be harassed and testy. Do not criticize your registrar and suggest that he or she "shape up." This is an excellent time for you to leave town on an important visit to Washington. When you return registration will be behind you and another semester will be underway. Registration is a process you should leave to those employed to conduct it.

That is not to say, however, that the president should not know what is going on in the registration process. If there are too many problems the university will receive very bad press at the beginning of each fall term. With expanding computer capabilities and capacities, new programs are available that permit students to register by telephone through personal interaction with the institution's computer. Waiting in line is eliminated. It cuts down on friction because it is difficult for the student to argue with the computer. If your institution has the machine capability you might want to experiment with this kind of system.

You should also identify on your campus that group of courses around which most of the registration problems develop. These will include the big, lower-division service courses and certain required courses in the big professional schools, courses designed to weed out would-be majors and reduce the number of students going into the professional degree programs. In making up course schedules, departments are inclined to give first priority to the interests of their own faculty in their own majors. The university's interest in scheduling a sufficient number of service courses may be overlooked by some of the academic departments. The result is a great many angry students unable to get the courses they need for their programs. If your academic vice-president or provost has been on the campus for a few years, he or she will be familiar with the history of registration problems and should be able to anticipate and prevent these kinds of situations. But if they occur, you should intervene, preferably through the academic vice-president or provost, but directly if necessary to assert the institutional interest in the scheduling of high-demand courses. If it becomes necessary to ask some faculty member to give up a favorite departmental course with twelve students to teach a service course with sixty students, he or she should be willing to make that sacrifice for the university.

The office of student financial aid is another function that has grown in size and complexity in recent years. A great deal of money is available to students in the form of scholarships, fellowships, tuition grants, loans, and work-study funds. This is another office where you need a professional staff and a director who is both knowledgeable and a good manager. About 25 percent of your student body will be receiving some kind of financial assistance, although of course this figure varies greatly depending on what kind of institution you are leading. The point is that the number of students involved with the office of student financial aid is significant and they must be treated with courtesy and understanding by a staff that is motivated to find the money to help them rather than to find reasons to question their eligibility.

Most presidents come to the job with a degree of maturity, that is to say, they are not young, and can remember when students managed to graduate from universities that did not have counseling and guidance centers staffed with professional counselors. But social science, psychology, and psychiatry have moved up in the world and you can make a case that the world has become a much harsher place than it was. A university that does not offer counseling and guidance services to its students is guilty of a serious omission. The president's responsibility is to review the credentials of the staff of the counseling and guidance center to make sure they meet professional standards or, put another way, to make sure they know what they are doing. It is not unlikely that a "rape crisis center" or at least that function will be included within your counseling and guidance center; drug abuse will give the center a lot of business; emotional disorders will engage a good deal of the staff's time.

Counseling for students with academic and learning problems may be included within the center or it may be provided in a separate office. Testing, career planning, and placement services should be offered somewhere in the organizational structure. You should familiarize yourself with your institution's placement services because they are of interest to parents, alumni, and corporate friends of the university. You can anticipate questions about placement when you are speaking to these groups.

The student health center has the potential to be a major headache for the president. In the chapter on students you were advised to rely as much as possible on local hospitals and health insurance and to maintain a minimal health facility on campus. But even with no more than an outpatient clinic there is the potential for frightening liabilities. Campus lore will be replete with stories of students who went to the health center with a serious, life-threatening condition and were turned away by a nurse who told them to take an aspirin. Some of those stories might be true. The director of your health center and his or her staff must be able to recognize something serious when they see it and to get really sick students off campus and into a hospital with dispatch. Under no circumstances should the student health center attempt to deal with traumas from motor vehicle accidents, skiing, or assaults. Your system should be geared to fast response and efficient EMS transportation to an off-campus hospital. If you have a medical school and there is a teaching hospital adjacent or close to the campus, so much the better. If not, you should seek a contract with a local hospital. Above all, do not advertise a level and quality of care that you are not prepared to deliver.

As president of a university you will find yourself in the restaurant, hotel, and apartment house business. None of those are good businesses to be in, but your division of housing and food service will put you in them. The director of this enterprise is another one of your managers who deserves your sympathy and understanding . . . if he or she is doing the job. Students will complain about the food, the rooms, and the rates. They will produce a very high level of wear and tear on the buildings and furniture. They will violate every university rule designed to govern conduct in the dormitories so it is a good idea to have as few rules as possible and to enforce those few with penalties that catch the students' attention. The operation of the dormitories and dining halls must pay its way and provide for a prudent level of reserves. There will be years when students want to live in dormitories and there will be waiting lists; there will be years when the fad is to live off campus and you will have a high vacancy rate. You should attempt to steer a conservative middle course. Do not build too many new dormitory rooms during the times of long waiting lists and do not be too quick to convert empty dormitories to office and classroom buildings when the demand is low. If the institution has used bond proceeds to build dormitories you will have covenants to worry about and a debt service problem in the years of high vacancy rates.

International students have special problems and if you have a significant number of them the institution should operate an international house or international office so they will have a home on campus. There will be a need to offer an intensive-English course. There will be problems with visas. Political turmoil at home may cut off the flow of funds upon which the student depends. This is another student function where you need a professional director. Students from some parts of the world regard themselves as guests in the United States and behave accordingly; students from other parts of the world learn very quickly how to exploit our system and it is in their culture and traditions to do so. A hunger strike to coerce the university administration is an example. Whereas the strikers know that in their own country such a strike would have no effect on the authorities except perhaps to occasion laughter, they quickly learn that in the United States it produces TV cameras, deep humanitarian concerns, and letters to the president's office accusing you of insensitivity to the legitimate concerns of the students. The problems arising from the behavior of some foreign students are part of what an international community brings to the university. It is better to have the international students and all that comes with them than to have a parochial campus.

Student publications, the band, the student union, recreational and intramural athletics, the ombudsman, and the student attorney have been discussed in the chapter on students and there is little to add here except to reiterate that they are all important functions and must be properly administered if your presidency is to be successful. The vice-president for student affairs has a great deal to look after and must be supported in his or her efforts. One of the benefits of a weekly staff meeting is to give this vice-president a forum in which he or she can discuss problems freely with the other officers and with you. It is important that the vice-president for student affairs retain perspective and balance in the very turbulent part of the academic world where he or she works. Most of the students are young and therefore long on energy and short on wisdom. It is very comforting to a student affairs vice-president to know he or she is not standing out there alone.

The business operations of the university constitute the third essential element of the infrastructure. Although you must rely on your vice-president for business affairs to operate the business side of the enterprise, you, as president, must understand the business functions that support the institution. The functions include accounting, auditing, bookstore operations, budgeting, data processing, grant and contract administration, inventory control, legal counsel, mail service, management information service, payroll, personnel services and employee relations, physical plant operations, planning, printing, purchasing, receiving and delivery, and security. The physical plant operations include services necessary to the maintenance of buildings and grounds, telephone services, and provision of utilities. Some universities operate their own power plant, some purchase power, and some do both. Clearly, if you are in the business of producing electric power you have different problems than if you buy it.

In reviewing these functions with your business vice-president, you should examine the organizational structure that is in place. It may well have just grown up over the years without any consideration of how it might be improved. Ask about the key people in the business enterprise and get a feel for their performance and level of compensation. Are there backups for the essential managers? What kind of training programs are in place? How do you encourage the development of professionalism? Do you send promising young employees to programs where they can upgrade their skills? If part of the work force is unionized, you need to be fully informed on the contracts in place and who conducts the negotiations. If the university contracts out for any services you should find out how the contracts are awarded. If they are awarded through any process other than competitive bidding be alert to the possibility of "sweetheart" contracts that may not be in the best interests of the institution. How long have the contracts been in place? What is the quality of service? Are there any personal or family relationships involved in the awarding of the university's business to off-campus contractors?

There are several areas where the president needs to pay particular attention. What is the current status of litigation involving the university? If you have inherited any significant amount of old pending litigation, have a session with the university's attorneys and try to settle as much as possible. Satisfy yourself as to the quality of the in-house and outside counsel that represents you. You cannot afford to have second-rate legal counsel. If you are president of a public university you may find yourself required to use the state's attorney general for legal services. This can be a serious problem. Although there might be occasions when you will be moved to file suit as a plaintiff, in most litigation the university will be the defendant. The young, modestly paid lawyers on the attorney general's staff will rarely be able to stand up against the kinds of plaintiff's lawyers that will come against you. If there is a lot at stake you should attempt to get the attorney general's approval to hire outside counsel to assist his or her office.

You should also review the university's insurance policies with the vice-president for business affairs and legal counsel. Are there gaps in the coverage? Have you made the best deal on premiums? Is it time for a new assessment of risks?

If you are president of a public university, the state auditor will have the responsibility of an outside, independent auditor. If your institution is private, you should inquire as to what firm is engaged as the university's independent, outside auditor and how long it has been engaged. Although you may be satisfied with the service from the outside auditor and put a high value on the experience that the firm has had with your institution, the engagement partner should be changed every five or six years. If the relations between the engagement partner and your vice-president for business affairs are too friendly, there is a potential for problems. Make sure that the annual management letter comes directly to you and find the time to meet personally with the outside auditors to discuss it.

The president should inquire about environmental problems impacting the institution and the responsibilities of the health and safety office. Most universities involved in research handle radioactive materials. Is there a radiation safety officer and to whom does he or she report? How does the institution collect and dispose of hazardous wastes? Are there buried fuel tanks on university property? If so, how long has it been since they have been inspected? If leaks are detected, where have the fugitive hydrocarbons gone? Do the emissions from university incinerators and stacks meet prevailing environmental standards? What kind of asbestos problems do you have? If the director of your physical plant does not know the answer to that question you need a new director. Problems, indeed crises, in these areas can come up very quickly and you should know how you are organized to deal with them. Among your science and engineering faculty you will find a good deal of expertise in the recognition and solution of environmental problems. Some of your faculty will be deeply concerned about environmental degradation and professionally involved in state and national organizations working to improve the environment. Curiously enough, some of them may not be as concerned about problems stemming from operations in their own laboratories as those attributable to industrial operations. Perhaps it is because the university is seeking new knowledge to benefit humankind whereas industry is seeking only profit. Whatever the cause, the university should clean up its own backyard and that will not happen unless the president insists on it. A committee of faculty knowledgeable about environmental problems can be of help to you, and their attention to the university's efforts to reduce any adverse impact on the environment will stand between you and the faculty member who charges you with trying to shut down his or her laboratory.

The issue of campus security has been discussed in the chapter on the campus and its facilities. The chief of security most commonly reports to the vice-president for business affairs, but this is an area where reporting lines should not prevent you from dealing directly with your chief security officer. You should know the chief and be familiar with his or her training and experience. In the case of violence on campus, the president's office will become a "war room" and before taking any actions you as president must be certain that in any given situation the security forces have the capability to do what you want them to do and what the chief says they can do. If there is any doubt in your mind that the university police force is not a thoroughly professional organization, you must move immediately to professionalize it. Policies to deal with bomb threats, terrorism, and other forms of campus violence must be carefully crafted. Your chief of police should be on good terms with local, state, and federal law enforcement agencies so that in the event you need to call for help there will be a personal relationship to facilitate cooperation. In any situation where university police officers have to maintain or restore order among unruly students or intruders, they will be accused of "police brutality" and of "overreacting." It does not matter what the provocation is or how deliberate and restrained they are in dealing with it. You must have a policy and apparatus in place to investigate such incidents with a fair and impartial process that has credibility within the university community.

The news and information function does not fit readily into the academic, student, or business elements of university infrastructure. It should report either to you or to your vice-president for development and university relations, if the institution is large enough to support such an office. The director of news and information has the responsibility for informing both the internal university community and the public about the university and what it is doing. Interaction with the press and media is only a part of the job. This is a communications job in the largest sense; grinding out press releases and sending them to the newspapers will not help very much. The position demands a thorough knowledge of the academic and research programs of the university, the history of the institution, and its traditions. It requires sensitivity and creativity. In a private institution you can get away with using the term "public relations"; in a public institution the use of state funds to sell something to the public is a sensitive issue and the focus should be limited to providing information. It is, of course, a fine line. When something of interest occurs on campus it is embarrassing to the president to have a number of different "university sources" saying very different things to the press. You can do nothing about what students might say, or what members of the faculty might say. You can insist that the administration speak with a single official voice. That should be your voice or your delegate's voice. Press releases about important matters should clear through your office.

Your institution will surely have an equal employment opportunity officer and an EEO office. The EEO office is responsible for monitoring the institution's compliance with federal and state laws against discrimination and with its own internal policies to assure that individual civil rights are protected. Although you appoint this officer and he or she reports to you, you must be careful to ensure the independence of the EEO officer. The director of that office cannot be viewed as being the president's person. The office must have the capability to make an independent investigation of any and all allegations of discrimination and report the findings as the evidence justifies. It is a very difficult position. Whoever holds it can act neither as a defender of the institution nor as an advocate for the complainant. In addition, this office compiles statistics on hiring practices and the salary and promotion records of minority employees and female employees.

It is very much in your interest to have an individual in this position with an impeccable record of performance and the high credibility that is earned by superior performance. If you "park" this responsibility with an administrator who is not good enough to advance but not bad enough to fire, it will be a big mistake. When state or federal investigators from the various bureaucracies built to ensure compliance with laws designed to protect human rights and prevent unconstitutional discrimination come to campus, and they will, your EEO officer must have the stature and the data to deal with what will be in nearly all cases contrived and manufactured allegations. If the allegations are true and one of your supervisors or managers has abused an employee, you should know it before the complaint moves off campus. With the right kind of EEO office, the complainant will have taken his or her grievance there and you will have the opportunity to provide an appropriate remedy satisfactory to the injured employee and thus eliminate an appeal to off-campus authorities. When your EEO officer determines after investigation that a complaint is frivolous, you should be able to sustain that finding in subsequent administrative proceedings and in court.

Development or fund raising is an important function and is considered in a separate chapter. The operation of an intercollegiate athletics program is also discussed in a separate chapter.

You will find that the university pays dues to a large number of national, state, and local organizations ranging from the American Association of Universities (if you are a major institution) to the local chamber of commerce. Some of the dues will be paid by the president's office and some will be paid directly by a school, college, or department. You are concerned primarily with those paid by the president's office.

If you investigate these various memberships you will find that many of them came at the request of a dean or department chair and resulted from a particular program interest. Some of these people will have long departed from their position or from the institution while the dues continue to be routinely paid year after year. Someone should be paying attention to make sure that the university is receiving value from these memberships. Pruning this list will save some money. If your proposal to discontinue the university's membership in this or that organization draws only a mild protest, there is no need to continue paying the dues. At a meeting of the deans' council you might suggest that deans and department chairs should review the costs of memberships paid from their college, school, and department funds.

Some of the major national organizations are professional associations of university presidents. You will be the official representative of your university and will have the opportunity to go to meetings, to participate in conferences and symposia on important issues in higher education, and, of course, to serve on committees. You are well advised to think carefully about how much time to allocate to this kind of professional fellowship. If you find yourself attending a great many of these meetings and discussing issues about which you are already completely informed, it is time to consider frankly if perhaps by attending these meetings you are really seeking an escape from the problems on your campus. If you are happier off the campus than on, and if in your frequent absences your provost or executive vice-president seems to have no trouble making the important decisions, it may be time for you to move off campus permanently into another position. The time you spend in going to these meetings, giving and listening to papers, working on committees, participating in studies, and reviewing position papers is time you should be spending on your university. If you have ambitions to be a national leader in higher education you can best serve that ambition by making your institution the best in its class. After you have established your agenda for the university that is paying your salary, you will have earned your reputation in higher education and then you can spend time away from campus going to meetings.

No matter how advanced the automated systems on your campus might be, the institution presently operates and for the near term will operate on a flow of paper. A voluminous flow of letters, memoranda, reports, vouchers, invoices, applications and appointment forms, budget forms, acknowledgments, minutes, advertisements, solicitations, and other printed material is in constant motion into and through the university. Some of it flows in specified channels, moving from one office to another, where approvals or endorsements are added or where it is stopped through lack of approval. The president can learn a great deal about the institution by a review and consideration of the paper flow. Consider first the kinds of transactions that the various pieces of paper record or support. Ask your assistant to assemble all the approved university forms that are in current use. Then ask one of your staff to undertake a paper flow project and report to you on the status quo and what improvements might be made to eliminate either unnecessary paperwork or unnecessary stops in the flow of the paper.

After you have a grasp of the situation, sit down with the vice-presidents and ask them to take a fresh look at the forms that come through their offices and how they are handled. There will be correspondence, personnel forms, forms for the transfer of funds, forms for the preparation of the operating budget, forms for travel requests and expense reimbursement, minutes of committee meetings, legislation from the faculty deliberative bodies, and, of course, forms from state and federal agencies that must be properly routed. Track each form. How many approvals are required by university policies and administrative procedures? Should changes be made in the policies and procedures? If you are public, how many approvals are required by law and regulation? What paper do you as president have to see? You will learn a great deal from this exercise and, even if you see no opportunities for improvement and make no changes, it will have been worthwhile. The paper flow records the transaction flow and that is, after all, the basic record of how the institution operates.

Finally, you should be aware that among the considerable staff that supports your institution there will be a network of old hands, professionals in every sense, with the experience and competence to solve problems and make things function properly. Their titles will not be impressive—they will include the administrative and executive secretaries, the administrative and executive assistants, the assistants to . . . , and those called "managers." These are the people who receive the service awards at the annual recognition ceremony for staff members. They have stayed with the university in good times and bad. For them it is their career; for some it is their life. Find out who they are and make sure they are appropriately recognized and compensated. It is not difficult to identify them. Ask your assistant who to call in purchasing (or payroll, or accounting, or the budget office) when you want to get something done. There may be twenty or thirty people in this network. These are important people with a value to the university far in excess of what you pay them. If, in a chance encounter, you can call them by name and exchange a few words of personal conversation, your institution will function well.

CHAPTER 10

Budget and Planning

THE PRESIDENT must maintain control over the budgeting function and must be personally involved in building the budget. If you delegate too much authority in this area to the vice-presidents you will surely lose control of the institution. Review the policies under which the budget is developed and read carefully the budget guidelines and instructions that are sent out annually to the department heads. Budget policies must be carefully crafted to protect the administration against charges of making whimsical, capricious, or arbitrary decisions based on personal prejudice.

Each department head will be required to submit a budget through channels and following the guidelines approved by the president by a certain date. Of necessity, these guidelines will be restrictive and set limits designed to hold the requests to the same order of magnitude as the funds that are likely to be available. Upon receiving the guidelines, a number of the department heads will conclude that the guidelines cannot possibly apply to their department because of obvious, critical, and overriding needs. So they violate the guidelines. Budget requests from academic departments flow from the department chair to the dean; budget requests from other than academic departments flow through one or more administrative levels to the appropriate vice-president.

Problems in holding budget requests within guidelines will stem largely from the academic area. Conscientious deans, if they happen to be in town, will notice that some departmental budget requests do not follow the president's guidelines and will send them back to the department chair with anything from a mild inquiry to an acerbic reprimand, depending on the relative political strengths of dean and chair. This initiates a series of heated exchanges between dean and chair, interrupted during the times they are away from campus and involving "promises" made to the chair when he or she agreed to take the job. The only certain result is that the budget will not be submitted on time. As the date approaches when the president must submit a budget to the board . . . the dean is by this time traveling in Europe and the department chair is in a mountain cabin . . . the academic vice-president is directed to go ahead and make the decisions necessary to conform the budget to the guidelines. When the budget is finally approved, the faculty of the department that ignored the budget instructions will call a special meeting and in high dudgeon will accuse the administration of ignoring faculty input into the budget process. This will give you a measure of your dean. If the dean does a neat sidestep and explains to the faculty that he or she was attending an important scholarly meeting in Paris and was not consulted in the budget process, you should begin a search for a new dean. A good dean would handle the matter.

All this budget discussion will prompt the faculty senate to send forth their annual resolution calling upon the president to establish a faculty budget advisory committee to ensure that the faculty is appropriately involved in the budget process. Of course, the faculty senate does not intend that the committee be advisory. It is their position that the faculty should, through some mechanism, approve the budget prior to its adoption. The argument will be as follows: The board of regents has delegated to the faculty the authority to legislate in the area of academic policy and program and obviously the budget controls the academic programs; it is the faculty who are knowledgeable about academic programs and thus the administration should be guided by the faculty in developing the budget in the academic area. The argument is persuasive because the president should indeed be guided by the faculty through its advice on academic directions and priorities. It is also true that allocation of faculty positions, levels of faculty salaries, departmental operating budgets, library expenditures, and computer center support do affect academic program development.

But because of its collegial nature, the faculty finds it very difficult to make hard budget decisions. A faculty senate or faculty budget advisory committee will recommend strongly that the president respond positively to all the budget requests made by their colleagues. The fact that funds are inadequate will be a secondary consideration to a faculty committee. It is, after all, up to the president to provide the funds. The faculty will not make the tough decisions on allocating resources to support a plan or to recognize and reward merit. You can accurately predict that the faculty solution to budgeting will be to split up in equal amounts whatever money is available. The president must retain budget authority in the president's office. If a faculty budget advisory committee is already institutionalized, the president must have the courage not to be bound by its advice; if such a committee is not in place you do not need one. Faculty advice on academic priorities can be solicited and obtained through other mechanisms.

The place for faculty participation in building the budget is at the point of origin—the academic department's budget council.

One of the most challenging budget issues is the allocation of faculty positions. Those colleges, schools, and departments currently experiencing high enrollments will submit compelling arguments that their classes are too large for quality instruction, that they are in fact generating more semester credit hours than are reflected in their budgets, and that as a result their faculty are overworked and morale is at an all-time low. They will demand new positions to maintain an acceptable student-faculty ratio and will express concern that their program will not meet standards for accreditation if current trends continue. A review of the teaching loads in those departments is clearly in order. If the dean of the school or college is able and experienced, more often than not you will find that a large number of students are instructed in large sections, an efficient way to handle big enrollments, and that the instructors are assisted by readers, graders, and technicians, and that in fact these instructors are not carrying the burden of a higher workload than those in other departments.

The lesson here is that dividing the number of students by the number of faculty, while it produces a useful index, does not tell the entire story about faculty work loads. If one faculty member, with adequate support, instructs 200 students in one section instead of 20, it does not follow that to maintain a 20:1 student ratio the department should be authorized to hire nine more faculty members. It can just as well be argued that the department shows a commendably high level of productivity. While everyone would prefer small classes of fewer than 20 students, and many liberal arts colleges advertise small classes, the reality is that many large public universities do not have the resources to offer small classes at all levels of instruction. In those institutions the student-faculty ratio should be considered on a school, college, or university-wide basis rather than at the department level. At the lower-division level, the departments should schedule large sections so that in upper-division and graduate courses the classes can be limited to smaller numbers to permit more interaction among students and instructor.

In those public universities where monies are appropriated to the institution based on formulae tied to semester credit hours generated, the administration must resist the argument advanced by the high-enrollment schools and colleges that funds should be allocated by the same formulae within the institution. If the president were to bite on this seemingly rational hook, the departments that cost more to operate than they generate in semester credit hours . . . classics, philosophy, linguistics, many foreign languages, geography, and, indeed, most departments not involved in teaching the general education requirements . . . would be shut down and the institution would cease to be a university. The popular, high-enrollment departments must, in a financial sense, carry the low-enrollment departments to give the institution intellectual breadth and depth.

However, fighting off requests for new faculty positions from the high-enrollment departments is not the only front in the budget battle. Departments with low enrollments will also demand new positions. In this case the argument will be that, although the department is temporarily down in enrollment, all the national surveys show that there is a great need for students in the discipline and the university must anticipate the student surge that is surely coming. Further, the department must sustain a critical mass in the number of faculty so as to be able to offer a full complement of courses. The department must keep faith with its students and provide them with the courses they need to complete their degree program, even though some of the courses have only four or five students enrolled. The department is a center of excellence (the faculty is of high quality and because of low teaching loads can publish at a high rate) and the university should maintain the centers of excellence that it has. The department with chronically low enrollment may also argue that, if the university is to insist upon a truly liberal education, the students should be required to take a course in that important intellectual discipline.

Other departments requesting new positions will argue that they are beginning an innovative new program that in just a few years will reflect great credit on the university. They are on the cutting edge and need seed money to hire faculty to develop the program in advance of the hordes of students who will fight for a place in it. The administration that refuses to innovate has no vision and is in for a great deal of criticism.

As president, you will respond to all these arguments for new faculty positions by recognizing their substance, expressing strong support in principle, explaining that there are insufficient funds to meet all the requests (which will be true), and then allocating the available new positions to the areas of greatest need. It is not difficult to determine where the need really is. In the unhappy event that the university is in such desperate financial straits that not only are there no funds for new positions but also the only solution is to take positions away from some fat departments to staff lean departments at a minimal level, you have two choices. You can resign immediately, announcing that you have accomplished what you set out to do or pleading ill health, or you can wield the budget scalpel as fairly and effectively as possible. In the latter case, you will be the target for a torrent of criticism and vituperation, probably an investigation by the American Association of University Professors, and, inevitably, demands for your resignation. This will test how well your board understands what goes on in a university. The board that approved a budget reduced by financial exigency might be expected to support the president who is trying to implement that budget. But do not count on it. The board members will be under a great deal of pressure and may find it easier to seek new leadership than to stand behind the president.

Faculty salaries and benefits will make up about half of the university's educational operating budget—less in the big research institutions, more in the small liberal arts colleges. Salary increases are, of course, a major budget problem. Academic departments will resist your request to put their recommendations for faculty salary increases in priority order. If the president and dean insist, the list will finally come forward with three or four individuals in a tie for first priority and three or four tied for second priority. Then there will be special recommendations outside the priority list for individuals who "we are going to lose" if their salary is not significantly improved. You should not become too annoyed at the inability of an academic department to develop a priority list for salary increases. The culture makes it impossible. The members of the budget council are voting on themselves, and the chair, for all practical purposes, serves at their pleasure. The dean will have to develop the list and he or she should know the faculty well enough to do it right.

You should be sensitive to how the departments have treated minority and women faculty members in their requests for salary increases. You may have to ask some questions to make sure they are given a fair evaluation.

Social and political activists on the faculty are another problem. Those who are found wanting in their performance as teachers and scholars and not granted a salary increase commensurate with their egos may very well claim that they have been denied a salary increase because of their political or social action activities, and they may honestly believe it. You will be accused of discriminating against the activist faculty member because of his or her political views and it will be charged that your attempt at coercion through salary discrimination is violating their constitutional right of free speech. Some of the activist faculty members who know they are not carrying their share of the departmental load may indeed set you up for such charges. Of course, a disproportionate commitment of time to social and political activism cannot help but be reflected in the faculty member's performance, if not in class, then in his or her scholarly research.

In order for the administration to be on sound ground in making decisions on faculty salaries, the policies and procedures in place must set forth clearly the criteria on which evaluations are made and produce a record of fair and objective consideration based on those criteria. The process must make certain that those who fail to perform, indeed who attack and subvert the purpose of the institution, are not rewarded at the expense of those who are diligent in carrying out their teaching duties and have made a record of first-class scholarship.

Planning is an exercise that works only if the people who have to implement and realize the plan are also the principal architects of the plan.

If in the public sector a state planning department located in some agency of state government develops a master plan for public higher education without the involvement of the public universities in the state, it will surely fail. In the same way, if you are part of a university system and the system bureaucracy has the responsibility to plan for you, it will be a meaningless exercise. The five-year plan for a university must be built from the bottom up with the direct involvement of all the university constituencies affected. The support of the faculty leadership is critical. It may be very difficult to sort out and put together the plans from the various departments, schools, and colleges into a coherent whole for the university, but even if the final product is less than optimal, the process will have been beneficial to the institution.

With the day-to-day pressures on department chairs and deans, and all the other committee responsibilities the faculty have to discharge, it will be difficult to excite the university community about planning unless the president pushes hard to get it done. Thus, although the staff responsibility should be assigned to a vice-president, and the planning committee chaired by a faculty member with a high degree of credibility and experience, your personal leadership will be required to produce a useful product.

In evaluating the plans put forward by the departments, schools, and colleges of the university, and by the various administrative units of the institution, you should pay particular attention to the goals and objectives advanced by the operating entity and the schedule for accomplishing the goals and objectives of the plan presented. An operating unit that lists twenty or thirty significant goals and objectives to be attained for each year of the plan has produced a product that cannot be taken seriously. The planning process is much more meaningful if there are three to five annual goals and objectives that are material to the operating unit and are possible to achieve than if an impossible task of attaining twenty or thirty is announced at the beginning of the year. It is bad for everyone's morale if year after year the unit achieves only 20 percent of the plan's goals and objectives. Since you are the institution's chief planner, make sure that the process is practical and useful and not just an empty, time-consuming exercise . . . as, unfortunately, so many annual planning efforts are.

CHAPTER 11

Intercollegiate Athletics

THERE WAS a time in the universities of the United States when intercollegiate athletics, like recreational sports and intramural sports, was a student activity. Those involved in it were students. They were a part of the student body and recognized by students as fellow students. Indeed, in most universities and for most sports, intercollegiate athletics remains a student activity. However, in the big public universities and in some of the well-known private universities, men's football and basketball have become a business that is not related to students or to the academic mission of the institution. In these institutions, those involved in the men's football and basketball programs are not students in the traditional sense. They are individuals with exceptional athletic talents who are preparing for careers in professional sports. Through their athletic performance at the university level they are seeking to win professional contracts. Academic performance is a consideration only because a minimum level of performance is necessary for the athlete to stay in school to continue to be eligible to participate in the athletic program. These professional athletes live apart from the other students, eat apart from the other students, and study apart from the other students. The only time during the football or basketball season that they encounter the ordinary student is when they attend class.

University intercollegiate athletic programs in football and basketball in this group of institutions have, in effect, been captured by network television and the professional leagues, and what was a university-controlled student activity has been converted to an activity through which games are produced commercially for national entertainment and professional league farm clubs from which athletes are recruited. The corruption of what was a proper and popular dimension of university life was driven by the financial rewards for winning and the attention and acclaim lavished on nationally contending teams.

It costs money to support intercollegiate athletics. Although in terms of the total budget of the institution the amount may not be great, it is money that is difficult to come by. Revenues come from gate receipts, television and radio contracts, and benefactions—usually from alumni who support intercollegiate athletics but few other university programs. As a rule, public universities cannot use appropriated public funds in support of intercollegiate athletics. A consistently winning team has an enthusiastic regional and even national audience. Universities with winning teams have the opportunity to appear on national television and these appearances result in substantial revenue. There is extensive press coverage and coaches become national figures who not uncommonly go into sports broadcasting or politics. Alumni benefactions are greater if the team wins. Thus, athletic programs with winning teams operate in the black as against losing teams that result in red ink. Winning football and basketball teams produce enough revenue to support other athletic programs for both men and women, very few of which break even. Thus, universities in the big leagues of intercollegiate athletics have a powerful incentive to field teams that win and contend for the national championship.

To sustain a winning tradition, turn around a losing record, satisfy fans and alumni, and enhance revenues, universities recruit winning coaches with high salaries, contracts for TV and radio shows, endorsements for athletic equipment and other products, and "perks," such as automobiles and country club memberships. In universities that play in the big leagues of intercollegiate athletics, the head football coach will have total compensation substantially in excess of the president of the institution. That should not perturb you. The head football coach does not have tenure in the position anymore than you do as president, but in all probability you have a tenured academic appointment. The coach has only a contract that, with luck, was negotiated at a time when the coach was winning. The coach must win to hold the job. The only way the coach can win is to recruit the exceptionally talented athletes. There is fierce competition for these athletes. Some of them, regrettably, are for sale. The pressure on the coach to cheat in the sense of violating the rules of the National Collegiate Athletic Association is intense and, again, regrettably, some do. The coach's problem is exacerbated if your university demands a minimum level of academic performance from athletes recruited on what are called "athletic scholarships." If the coach and his or her staff violate the rules it can bring down the president as well as the coach. The "her" in this case should be included because of the growth in popularity of women's intercollegiate athletics. Women's basketball is currently the women's sport that draws the largest audience, but volleyball, swimming, tennis, and golf are growing in popularity.

Understanding the pressures on a coach, it is incumbent upon you as president to support and protect the coach who plays by the rules and the athletic director to whom he or she reports. It will be a great deal easier for them to play the game straight if they know the president understands their problems and is behind them. But by no means should the program report directly to the president. You should have a good, strong, canny vice-president between you and intercollegiate athletics. It diminishes the president for him or her to be directly involved in the management of intercollegiate athletics. But, although you should not be visible in the management of the program, you must insist that the program be clean, even if the price is losing against those institutions that cheat. When an institution that has for years had a very average win-loss record suddenly vaults into the top ten ranked teams, there is a good probability that they are breaking the rules in the recruitment of what are for all practical purposes professional athletes.

The relationship between the big-time coach and the president of the university is commonly an uneasy one. They are in very different businesses and have different goals and objectives. The president must be concerned about the integrity of the institution and the ethical standards it espouses or should espouse. The coach whose only objective is winning can very easily damage both. The winning coach, while he is winning and has not been caught cheating, has the support of powerful alumni and the admiration of regents. The coach is, during these fat years, better known, more respected, and more highly compensated than the president. During these happy times, the wise coach supports the president and says nice things about him or her. The wise coach does not make unreasonable demands for space and money. The wise coach, anticipating the day when his loss record will move him out of the job or at best into the position of athletic director, does not criticize or sneer at the president while holding court with alumni, regents, or legislators. Few university presidents can challenge a winning coach but few coaches have an endless string of winning seasons. If you should become president of a university whose football or basketball coach is riding a high wave of popularity and who is foolish enough to treat you with indifference or arrogance, just be patient.

The easy way to replace a football or basketball coach who has run the course is to make him athletic director. In a university with a substantial athletic program this is probably a mistake. Today, the athletic director must be able to manage a significant business, deal effectively with personnel problems, negotiate radio and television contracts, operate major facilities, raise funds from individuals with big egos, interact with NCAA and conference officials, handle the press and media, and maintain mutually supportive relationships with very tense head coaches. A few old coaches may be up to this level of management, but not many. As long as your university is in the athletic business, you need a professional director of athletics.

If your university is not known for big-time athletics, income from gate receipts will be low, your games will not be featured on television, and alumni benefactions will be modest. You may or may not be able to fund athletic scholarships. Paying the salaries of coaches and building and maintaining facilities will be a perennial problem. Count your blessings. And if a group of alumni persuade one or more of your regents that the institution needs a more competitive athletic program, study and plan as long as possible—with luck until the athletically inclined regent goes off the board.

It is a shame in every sense of the word that intercollegiate athletics in the form of men's football and basketball has been professionalized at the big public universities and some of the private universities. Intercollegiate athletics, before the games were produced for television and before the players were competing for professional contracts in the millions of dollars, brought a great deal to university life. The fall weekends with 50,000 to 80,000 people in the stadium, the bands and the cheerleaders, the traditions, panoply, and excitement, the glory of winning and the gloom of defeat, the crowds flowing in and out, the traffic jams, all were a part of university culture. That culture is, of course, alive and well in most of the colleges and universities of the United States; perhaps it will come back to the schools that have lost student involvement in intercollegiate athletics when the athletics *business* is separated from universities.

Indeed, there are some signs that men's football and basketball will again become an activity for students. Federal legislation requires that women's programs receive a level of funding appropriate to what the men's programs receive and that will broaden the base of intercollegiate athletics. On another federal front, the Internal Revenue Service is taking a hard look at nonrelated business income earned by tax-exempt institutions. There is a probability that television proceeds from athletic events may be taxable. Questions have also been raised about the legality of TV contracts as currently negotiated between universities and the networks. These initiatives from the nation's social architects and revenue seekers may be beneficial to universities in the long run. Together with a tougher stance by the NCAA and a growing distaste for the corruption of both intercollegiate and professional athletics, taking some of the profit out of the game and spreading the proceeds more equitably among the institution's programs may bring us back to an activity that has some relation to what a university is supposed to do for society.

As president of a university that is currently involved in intercollegiate athletics there is no way that you can unilaterally take your institution out of competition and expect to survive as president. If the board of regents makes the decision to discontinue participation in intercollegiate athletics you will still be placed in a very difficult position. You will have to choose sides. You can be sure the issue will be hotly debated.

What you can do for your university is insist on a clean program. You can support national efforts to deprofessionalize university athletic programs. You should determine for your university if there is a correlation between winning athletic programs and donations to the institution. You will in all probability find that winning teams increase gifts to the athletic programs but have little or no effect on support of the academic programs. Review the list of donors to identify those who give to both athletic and academic programs. If you find individuals who support both programs in a substantial way, it is a good idea to talk with them individually to ascertain how they feel about your efforts to maintain a clean intercollegiate athletic program that involves students. With this information you can address the argument that without winning teams donations to the university will diminish. If your academic program is as strong as it should be, that argument should be without substance. You do not need or want the support of alumni who will do anything that it takes to win football or basketball games.

The growth of intercollegiate athletic programs for women, although accelerated by federal legislation, is a result of the desire of women to move beyond their traditional roles in society and of the growing emphasis on sports and physical fitness for both men and women. As president, you should encourage this development and support it financially to the extent that you can. However, except in a very few universities where women's basketball has become popular and draws big crowds, women's intercollegiate athletics does not pay its own way. It is very difficult to squeeze additional dollars out of the university budget to finance expanded intercollegiate athletic programs. It is particularly difficult in public institutions where there is commonly a proscription against using appropriated funds for the purpose. If there are no additional resources available to build the programs incrementally, and federal law requires an equitable distribution of funds between men's and women's programs, then the men's programs (traditional programs established for many years) must be taxed to support the women's programs. This is a situation that will divide the university community as well as the alumni and pose a very severe problem for the president. Even though in absolute dollars intercollegiate athletic budgets are only a small part of the total budget of the institution, you will have to spend a great deal of time working out a solution. One approach is to constitute a committee with representatives from both the men's and women's programs and alumni who have been active in supporting intercollegiate athletics. If you can educate the alumni to the realities of the situation and involve them in a consideration of alternatives, you can head off a great deal of criticism when the hard decisions are made.

As president, you should attend at least the home games of your principal sports and involve yourself in the associated ceremonial and social events. Entertaining major university supporters and other important people in the president's box is beneficial to the success of your development programs and, if you are a public university, your political success. It is not considered good form by the board of regents or the alumni if, on the occasion of "homecoming" or "parents day" when the university is engaged in meeting its traditional rival on the football field, the president is at a committee meeting in Washington or backpacking in the mountains. If you are a sports enthusiast and enjoy intercollegiate athletics, so much the better; if you are not . . . fake it.

CHAPTER 12

Academic Ceremonies and Official Occasions

ACADEMIC CEREMONIES are important elements of university culture and tradition. They serve a purpose. They provide an occasion for students and faculty to ponder the great intellectual traditions of Western civilization and they demonstrate to the larger society that the institution that is the university is fulfilling the responsibilities that society has placed upon it. Those who participate in or merely watch an academic procession with the faculty in academic regalia marching behind the university maces are moved to think about what it all means in historical terms. The caps, gowns, and hoods in different colors and styles provide a link with the past and demonstrate the international character of higher education. The president should give academic ceremonies his or her personal attention, participate in them, and use the authority of the office to encourage participation by faculty, staff, and students. If early in your tenure as president you make it clear that academic ceremonies are important and must be well planned and executed, the academic officers of the schools, colleges, and departments will follow your example.

In the decade of the sixties, the foolish decade, academic ceremonies were declared "irrelevant" by student activists and the faculty that pandered to them, and they were either boycotted or used to draw public attention to protests and demonstrations. Indeed, they may be irrelevant to those with no sense of history and those committed to single-issue causes. They are most relevant to what a university is chartered to do. With the return to the campus of a modicum of reason, interest in traditional academic ceremonies increased and attendance by faculty and students grew.

Ceremonies that draw a crowd are still exploited by activists who want to focus media attention on a cause, but those demonstrations that occur at a ceremony such as commencement are in these times rarely disruptive. There may be some chanting, singing, whistling, or shouting, but for the most part the activists wear arm bands, drape banners from windows or trees, or raise signs upon some prearranged signal. These are literally "signs of the times," and excepting them, university commencement ceremonies today are cheerful, even boisterous affairs, well attended by students, faculty, and family members. Those inclined toward disruptive activity find little or no support among the university community. At the last commencement at which I presided the students cheered the university police when they removed two loud protestors who attempted to disrupt the proceedings. So . . . although at the time of this writing academic ceremonies are much happier affairs than they were just a few years ago, the president should plan for any and all eventualities. On many campuses there are indications that student activism is on the rise.

Commencement is the annual ceremony at which the deans certify to the president that the candidates for an academic degree have satisfactorily completed all the requirements for their degree program. The president, under the authority granted by the board under the institution's charter, confers the degrees. In the process of certifying and conferring, the university is demonstrating in a public ceremony that it is producing educated men and women and thus fulfilling its contract with society. The ceremony usually takes place in middle or late May at the end of the academic year. Some universities also hold a commencement ceremony at the end of the fall semester or summer term for those who complete their degree programs in midyear. It is a smaller, less formal ceremony without the pomp and circumstance of the traditional spring commencement.

Commencement involves a good part of the faculty, the students standing for a degree, and an audience of family members, guests, and visitors. In addition to the conferring of degrees, there is customarily one or more commencement speakers, and whatever else the president wants to include or that may be a tradition at a particular university. Various honors and awards might be presented as part of the ceremony. Some institutions use the occasion to award honorary degrees to distinguished citizens. There is traditionally a baccalaureate service at some time prior to commencement. There may be an ROTC commissioning ceremony held in connection with commencement. However the ceremony is structured, it should be limited to an hour and a half or two hours at the most. In big universities this requires that individual recognition of students be accomplished in separate college and school ceremonies, usually held the day before or in the morning before the university's main ceremony. In the big university commencement ceremony, although graduate students may walk across the stage and receive the scroll, the hood, and a handshake from the dean and the president, the thousands of undergraduate students will be recognized and asked to stand in groups by school or college. In smaller colleges and universities the president still has the pleasure of personally congratulating the baccalaureate students as they walk across the stage to receive their degrees. This is one of the attractive features of the presidency of a small institution.

When you assume the presidency, there will already be a commencement committee in place. You should have an early conference with the chair of the committee, review the charge, and, in particular, ask some questions both of the chair and of independent sources about how commencement has been going in recent years. The committee will have the responsibility for planning the event, but since a poorly planned and executed commencement is a source of embarrassment for the university, you should review very carefully what comes out of the commencement committee and not hesitate to intervene if plans are poorly conceived and deadlines are missed. By all means have the copy for the program reviewed in your office. In many institutions it has been many years since anyone took a critical look at how the commencement ceremony might be improved. You should select the faculty member for the position of grand marshal or senior marshal. This is the individual who carries the mace and leads the procession. It is a position of honor. If your university holds the ceremony out of doors, you personally should study the rain plan and the arrangements for security and crowd control. After all, you will be the one standing at the podium.

When you welcome the students, faculty, and guests, you will have a great opportunity to say a few things about the university that should be said. Take advantage of the "bully pulpit," but do not be too long about it. You should also entertain the commencement official party at dinner the night preceding the event. The faculty on the commencement committee will appreciate a little attention and recognition, and making a two-day package of the occasion will ensure that your commencement speaker arrives the day before the ceremony. Just in case the commencement speaker fails to arrive, because of illness or for whatever reason, have a commencement address in your back pocket. You may have to step in and deliver it yourself.

Commencement should be a time of coming together for the university community. Invite former presidents, deans, and other retired or departed university officials to share in the occasion. It is a way to maintain good relations and to show the flag.

If you are president of a private university, selecting the commencement speaker and recipients of honorary degrees does not present any particular problem. You will be aware of sensitivities on the board of regents and can make your decisions with them in mind. But in a public university, an injudicious selection can raise a political storm. Politicians are always seeking a forum that will reflect them in a favorable light, and, of course, to be invited to give the commencement address at a prestigious university is an honor. Thus, it is not uncommon in the spring of the year for a political figure to seek such an invitation. He or she may very well suggest to a supporter on your board of regents that an invitation to be the commencement speaker would be welcome. Or the suggestion might come to the board member from the governor who appointed him or her. Or . . . it might come to you directly from the governor. Members of the other political party may not be at all enthusiastic about the proposed speaker. This is a real dilemma for the president of a public university. The best way to avoid this kind of squeeze is by making the selection yourself and making the selection early. You can then tell the members of your board who are trying to get into your business that an invitation has already been issued and accepted. You should never—under any circumstances—delegate the selection of the commencement speaker to a faculty-student committee. The committee's choices will range from controversial to bizarre and will provoke a negative reaction from the larger society. If you find yourself in a situation where a faculty-student committee to advise the president on the selection of a commencement speaker is already in place, make sure that the committee understands it is advisory and make sure they recommend at least six names and that the recommendation is in hand by the first of January. Do not feel obliged to take the advice this committee gives you if their list does not contain the kind of speaker that you want.

You want a thoughtful address that deals with great issues delivered by a distinguished individual with impeccable credentials. Commencement is not the occasion for "a fun address" or for putting barbs into the establishment . . . or for a political campaign speech. It is better to have a speaker who is a little stuffy than one who is a vaudevillian. The students may grow restive if a serious speaker is overlong at the podium, but it is more likely that they will remember what is said at commencement than what they have heard at many other presentations where they constitute the audience. The commencement speaker should make them think and give them something to think about. The commencement address should be given *before* the degrees are conferred. If the address is presented afterward, the speaker, however distinguished, will receive scant attention from the students who will have begun celebrating.

Private universities can award honorary degrees to good purpose and commonly do. Alumni who have achieved great distinction in their fields of endeavor, benefactors who have made major contributions to the institution, and distinguished public figures who merit the honor are all potential candidates. The selection process should be a very careful, formal process that produces enough information about the potential recipient to make you comfortable about what you are doing. There is always a risk, however, that a great benefactor or an official at the center of the national public stage will next year be indicted for felonious conduct. The recipient of your honorary degree may dishonor your university, so be very careful. A formal selection process with deliberate procedures may slow down an enthusiastic regent with a great idea long enough for you to do the necessary with due diligence.

Public institutions should not give honorary degrees and you should persuade your board of regents to make a clear statement of policy to that effect. If you permit the awarding of honorary degrees to start, or if you do not put a stop to such a practice already in place, some of the more aggressive elected and appointed state officials who control your destiny in the appropriations process will seek to be so honored or, more likely, will seek the honor for a close friend and supporter . . . indirectly, of course. To confer an honorary degree as a result of a "suggestion" from a powerful political figure will demean the institution and destroy your credibility with the faculty. There may be a former governor or speaker of the house who has truly done a great deal for higher education in the state, and who merits the honor under any test. But if the university grants an honorary degree to such a deserving individual, it opens up a political door that will be difficult to close. You will have trouble living with the precedent. If you cannot persuade your board to adopt a policy prohibiting the awarding of honorary degrees, try to put restrictive language in the policy that will eliminate political figures currently or recently in office. In these times, even conferring an honorary degree on a head of state poses a risk.

One final piece of advice about commencement—more and more students of Hispanic and Asian descent and more foreign nationals are taking degrees from universities in the United States. Make sure that whoever is announcing the names of the degree recipients can pronounce their names correctly. There is no excuse for a university that offers degrees in foreign languages and represents itself as a pluralistic, multicultural institution publicly to demonstrate provinciality by mispronouncing the names of its degree recipients.

Many, if not most, universities conduct a ceremony in the spring to recognize and honor outstanding students and to confer awards to faculty members who have distinguished themselves in the classroom or laboratory. The ceremony may be identified as "honors day" or by some other name of institutional significance. If you as president find that your institution does not have such a ceremony on its academic calendar, it is a good idea to establish an honors day. As with commencement, you should encourage strongly all faculty to attend and pay due respect to the students who have demonstrated through their performance their commitment to the academic values espoused by the faculty. It is an occasion that provides the president with a great opportunity to address the assembled students, faculty, and guests on an academic theme. Take advantage of it. The deans should be given some time on the program to make some remarks about their school or college before proceeding to recognize their outstanding students. Faculty recipients of prestigious teaching awards should be recognized at this ceremony.

If the university has not been able to fund some significant awards for excellence in classroom teaching, you should give your personal attention to raising funds to endow such awards. The top awards should be of a magnitude equal to the annual stipend paid by an endowed professorship. They should be designated for outstanding teachers in the required undergraduate lower-division courses, such as English, government, history, economics, foreign language, and mathematics. These very significant awards will be tangible evidence, much appreciated by nontenured assistant professors, that the university does value classroom teaching. They will do a great deal for the morale of your faculty "work horses."

An honors day ceremony focuses public attention on what a university stands for and is an occasion that reminds both the university community and the larger society that, despite the media's obsession with scandals in intercollegiate athletics, drug abuse, cheating, hazing, discrimination, and the fanaticism of protestors, the university is educating the human resources of our society. As the students with 4.0 grade point averages and 3.5 grade point averages are recognized, you, as president, will feel that what you are doing is eminently worthwhile, and by this time in the spring term, you will need that kind of psychic income.

When you are elected to the presidency, you will have to decide whether the university should recognize the event by a formal inauguration. This is the ultimate in university pomp and circumstance, and it makes an impression on the community. People remember it. Delegates come from colleges and universities all over the world, and the academic procession, if staged properly, is a magnificent sight. You as the new president have a chance through your inaugural address to declare yourself and let the university community and the external society know what your values are and what goals you have for the institution.

But a presidential inauguration, if properly done, costs a great deal of money. In general, it is worth the money, but there are circumstances in which it is wise to forego a formal inauguration. If, for example, your predecessor had a formal inauguration with a great deal of fanfare and lasted only a year or two, it is probably best not to repeat the performance so soon. If the institution is close to a historic milestone, such as a centennial or sesquicentennial, it is probably best to hold off on a formal inaugural ceremony and spend the money on a centennial celebration. If you are coming in as president of a public university that is beset with severe financial problems, and where all expenditures are a matter of public record, it is wise to delay any public inaugural ceremony until you have a good sense of the climate that prevails. Talk informally to members of the board and other key public officials about the propriety of holding a formal inauguration. The decision should be made on what is best for the university.

In addition to presidential inaugurations, commencements, and honors days, other events occur during the academic year that are not ceremonial in the sense that the participants wear academic regalia and engage in formal and traditional ritual but are important to the academic mission of the university. These are known collectively as "official occasions," a designation that indicates it is all right to spend university funds on them. There is the annual meeting of the general faculty at which the president delivers a state of the university message or, less formally, talks about the issues before the university. At some institutions the general faculty meets fall and spring. Unless some burning issue has aroused the faculty, your problem will be to devise some attraction that will produce a quorum. When the academic community is at peace, the faculty will not be moved to attend meetings without an incentive, such as an award ceremony or social event held in conjunction with the meeting.

Other occasions that require thought and planning include the president's reception for new faculty, freshman orientation, a president's reception for minority students, the president's reception or dinner in honor of scholarship and fellowship recipients, the president's dinner for the deans, a reception and dinner in honor of holders of endowed chairs and professorships, dinners and other social events revolving around meetings of the board of regents, alumni functions, and all those luncheons and dinners hosted by the president in connection with distinguished visitors, and with the conferences, symposia, convocations, special seminars, and lecturers that grace the academic year.

There will be meetings of visiting committees, advisory councils, and development boards. There will be many requests from deans and department chairs for the president to host a luncheon or dinner for important visitors to their school, college, or department. These occasions must be well managed and someone in your office must be on top of the detail. Name tags must be readable; flower arrangements must be appropriate, not too lavish but not sparse; where elderly people are expected to stand in receiving lines there should be a carpet and a few chairs nearby; there must be enough bars and bartenders so that it does not take your guests fifteen minutes to be served; the time for cocktails should never be overly long; food service should be efficient and the food should be absolutely first class but not pretentious and not heavy; there should always be a podium for speakers with bifocals who speak from a text; microphones should be tested so your guests will not be irritated by loud whistles and squawks; someone should worry about access and egress, particularly when elevators will be expected to accommodate a large number of guests arriving at about the same time; your office should have a supply of umbrellas that can be produced at a moment's notice; and, above all, the individual in your office who plans and directs these events should be there, on hand, with enough back-up staff to handle crises and emergencies. If, for example, you are having a party on a Sunday night and a group of guests are being delivered by bus, van, or limousine, your director of special events should have one or two Sunday telephone numbers in case the arranged transportation does not show up to collect the guests. Your director of special events should have a good working relationship with the people who are necessary to the success of the function . . . caterers, musicians and entertainers, police who control traffic and parking, security, and the university engineers who can control the temperature and the sound system in the rooms in which the function is being held.

Of course, it costs money to run the president's office in a first-class way and if you are president of a public institution the amount of money you spend on official occasions can be ferreted from open records. You should not play into the hands of an investigative reporter by holding too many black tie affairs with a per head cost that will raise even the eyebrows of your supporters. Official entertainment should be paid for from discretionary funds raised from private sources for that purpose. And you should always be able to make a convincing case that the affair was an official occasion that contributed to the development of the institution and its programs. A dinner party for your personal friends is not an official occasion. Whether you are president of a public or a private institution, you must take the trouble to separate what you spend on behalf of the university and what you spend personally. It is a nuisance but in this day and time you must make sure that the record will answer any charge that you have appropriated institutional funds for a personal purpose.

The way that you plan and conduct academic ceremonies and official occasions, the way in which you entertain, will put your personal stamp on the institution. If you do it well, it will soon be known that you are a "class act," and it will accrue to the benefit of the university. When you invite important people to the campus they will be delighted to accept your invitation because it will be generally known that a university affair is worth attending. Of course, the converse is also true.

Development

THE ACADEMIC ear is very sensitive to terms that are crassly materialistic and connote activities offensive to a community devoted to cultivation of the intellect. Thus, "development" is preferred over "fund raising" although they mean the same thing. Whether you are president of a public institution or a private one, raising money to support the academic enterprise is an important part of your duties. Lobbying the legislature for appropriations, however, is not included in development.

Development refers to raising funds from individuals, foundations, corporations, and alumni to endow faculty positions, endow scholarships and fellowships, provide monies for faculty travel, provide monies to support research and scholarly activity, build buildings, buy equipment, and provide discretionary monies for the president and deans to enhance the programs of the university. It would be very easy for the president of the university to spend all of his or her time on development work. But if you do, the institution will be managed by the vice-presidents and you will lose control. You cannot abandon the internal affairs of the university to someone else and expect to be a successful president. At some universities there appears to be a successful arrangement where the president is "Mr. or Ms. Outside" and the executive vice-president or provost is "Mr. or Ms. Inside." But over a period of years the success of such a partnership is fleeting. A president who spends too much time off the campus becomes invisible to the faculty and loses their support. You should maintain a firm control over both internal and external affairs, including development, and thus you must be effective in the use of your time.

No matter what institutional arrangements you make to support the development effort, the president is always the chief development officer. Depending on the size and complexity of your university you may have an assistant for development working in your office, a director of develop-

ment heading up a development office, or a vice-president for development with an office and staff. Whether few or many, all these people can
do is help you in the development effort. You must lead it. The director of
development and the staff of the office can do research on prospective
donors, maintain a data base on past and prospective donors, conduct
annual giving campaigns, design and operate targeted programs by telephone or mail, staff meetings of the development board and advisory
councils, operate an effective mail service, organize functions on and off
campus, and develop personal contacts with the executive directors of
foundations and the corporate officers responsible for contributions to institutions of higher education. In short, they can free you to concentrate
on the key individuals—wealthy individuals, board members of foundations and corporations, and chief executive officers. Social as well as professional contacts with this relatively small universe of important people
will have to be cultivated by you. It is unlikely that your development
officer will be invited to a house party that includes the rich and famous.
That invitation will come to the president of the university.

It is difficult for the university faculty, staff, and students to understand that, if their president is to be successful in raising money to benefit
them, the president has to travel first class, belong to exclusive clubs, move
within the highest social stratum, and entertain with style. Hamburgers
and barbecue will not do it. In the development business it is linen table-
cloths, fine china and silverware, flowers on the table, and good wine. You
do not meet the people with the financial capability to endow a chair at
the university by visiting the local laundromat. You meet them in the first-
class cabin of airplanes, at country clubs, and on yachts. You meet them in
boardrooms. It will help a great deal if you sit on several corporate boards.
The people you must cultivate want to be associated with a winner—with
an institution that does things in a first-class way and a president who can
make things happen. You will be criticized for what you do to develop
funds for the university and, ironically, the more successful you are the
louder will be the criticism. The same people who carp about the cost of
a first-class ticket will complain that you have not raised enough money
for scholarships, and they will profess to see no relation between raising
money and associating with wealthy people or those who represent them.
You must be very careful about the sources of funds for development-
related travel and entertainment, and you must keep detailed records of
where you go, what you do, and why.

To be successful as a fund raiser, the president needs a strong volunteer development board, a capable, experienced support staff, an extensive,
up-to-date data base, some discretionary money, some time, and, above all
else, something to sell. The institution and its programs must be presented
in a way that persuades the donor that a reasonable investment will really

accomplish an important educational and social purpose. Donors like to see their contributions leveraged so that a modest gift will set in motion a major project. It helps a great deal if the president and his or her spouse have charm, but, in the final analysis, class is more important than charm. The president must be seen as a person of stature, a decision maker, a leader at the state and national levels. To the extent that, in the public sector, university system bureaucracies and state departments of higher education or coordinating boards have moved the decision making off campus and into a state office building, the president's ability to be suc-cessful in development will be reduced. If the president must call some other official before he or she can make a decision or commit the univer-sity, he or she is little more than a high-level clerk and will not be able to do much in the way of raising funds. Individuals who make gifts to universities want to deal with whoever calls "the shots," not with a subordinate.

The development board can be enormously helpful to you. The board should be a mix of people who in themselves have the capability to make substantial contributions and people who are of consequence in their fields of endeavor who can open doors to sources of funds. Some of these people will have political influence and that can be particularly helpful for public institutions in projects where public matching funds for significant private gifts are an issue. In public institutions where open records and open meetings laws have made it impossible for the president to have an effec-tive interaction with the board of regents, the development board can serve the president well as a kind of shadow governing board. The more a development board feels involved in the affairs of the institution, the more committed it will be to support and assist you. If you are able to use your development board in this way, schedule quarterly meetings and lay out in a forthright way the management issues with which you are confronted. If there is a liaison member from the board of regents meeting with you, so much the better.

A frank discussion of issues and alternatives with the development board is not a substitute for such a discussion with your board of regents, but since society, prompted by the media's self-serving cries of alarm about "open government," has seen fit to burden public institutions with absurd strictures, the development board can help you by providing a forum of experienced, knowledgeable individuals willing to serve the university. Take advantage of them. They will be pleased to give you the benefit of their collective wisdom. It is likely that members of the development board will know members of your board of regents; the development board may include former members of the board of regents. Thus, they can help you educate and inform regents outside formal meetings. They can also be effective lobbyists for the university because they will be informed. With all this in mind, you must, of course, be very careful in making appointments to your development board.

At the college and school levels, indeed at the department and program levels, you will find that some of your more able and ambitious deans, directors, and chairs have organized foundations, advisory councils, boards of visitors, visiting committees, and other support groups to raise money for their programs. This is good. If some schools and colleges do not have some kind of structure in place to develop outside support, you should ask why not. The president should know how these groups are organized, what they are doing, and who the principal players are. There should be some loose, flexible university guidelines to make sure that appointments to these boards and councils are approved by the president and that there is a modicum of coordination among them. You should not try to take over these efforts, but neither should you give them free rein. When your schedule permits, you should attend the meetings of these boards and councils to present some informal remarks on the "state of the university" and attempt to relate the efforts of that support group to the university. Your attendance and participation will be very much appreciated. You should be knowledgeable about what they have done and thank them on behalf of the university for the money they have raised and for the time and effort these dedicated individuals are spending to help the institution. You may consider these boards and councils as farm clubs from which members of the university development board can be recruited, but do not express that idea to either the dean or the members of the board or council.

The alumni are a constituency that because of past associations have an interest in and loyalty to the university. Upon taking the president's chair you should review alumni relations and begin to develop a personal relationship with the director of the alumni association. Some of these are in-house organizations and some are independent, outside organizations. The president has direct control over the former, the latter have the advantage of being able to support the university in the political arena more effectively.

Your goal is to develop strong, enthusiastic alumni support for the university that compares favorably in annual giving with national norms. If the alumni of your university do not measure up in terms of the level of their support and the general level of their activities, you will need to formulate and implement a plan to correct the situation. It will require your personal involvement. You will have to travel to speak to alumni clubs around the country and you will have to invite alumni leaders to campus. Ask your director of development to work with the alumni leadership to establish programs to revitalize the alumni. If they perceive that under your presidency the university has clear goals and objectives and is picking up momentum they will be delighted to help. Again, everyone wants to be associated with a winner.

Alumni are apt to be particularly interested in involvement with students and student groups. An organized volunteer student effort to call alumni to solicit support . . . a "call-a-thon" . . . may produce surprising results if it is well done. With student help you can do a great many things that you could not afford to do if you had to hire permanent staff. And looking down the road, students who are involved with alumni are more likely to become involved alumni following graduation.

Alumni clubs should raise money locally to offer scholarships, endow professorships or lectureships, and establish awards for teaching excellence. They should also be in the high schools identifying and recruiting for your university the most outstanding students. They can be effective in recruiting minority students. With the right leadership, your alumni clubs can be enormously helpful outreach organizations for the institution. It may take several years to build alumni support to a desirable level. Stay with it.

There was a time when alumni interest and enthusiasm appeared to be focused mainly on intercollegiate athletics. This was the most visible alumni interest and alumni who were involved in your athletic programs were the ones who visited the campus most frequently and they were the ones from whom the president heard. There are few university presidents who have not received weekend or late-night telephone calls from alumni who were moved very strongly to comment on a coach. But alumni interest in the academic programs of the university, although less organized and less visible, has always been there for the president to develop. Currently, it is in fact a broader, deeper, and more dependable interest than the interest in intercollegiate athletics. It is gratifying to note that at the halftime of televised college and university athletic events, universities use their allotted time to extol the quality of their academic programs. I am not persuaded to the common wisdom that winning athletic programs are necessary for successful development programs. It is true that several consecutive losing seasons may diminish the enthusiasm of supporters of the athletic programs and that their contributions to the university in support of the athletic programs may decline. But it is rare if more than a few of those donors also support academic programs. A losing football season will not move supporters of the academic programs of the university to decrease their contributions . . . as long as the institution is an academic winner! That is where the president's emphasis should be.

In your efforts to raise money for the university you will encounter potential individual, foundation, and corporate donors that have established principles, rules, or priorities to guide and control their benefactions. Some will make contributions only to private institutions that do not have access to public funds through legislative appropriations. Some will make grants but will not establish endowments. Some require certain commitments from the institution receiving the donation, and these commitments will range anywhere from a requirement that the institution match the gift in some proportion to "strings" that may be unacceptable. Challenge grants are more and more common. The donor as a condition of the gift challenges the university to raise additional funds from other sources.

In working within and around a donor's wishes and conditions, it is necessary that the president have as much flexibility as possible within the rules and regulations of the university. For very large gifts, you may make a case to the board that established policy be waived. If, for example, a donor wants to give the university $20 million to build a new fine arts building on the condition that it be named for his dying mother, you may decide to waive the university's rule against naming buildings for living individuals. It is not likely that the good lady will be indicted for fraud in the waning months of her otherwise exemplary life.

Some donors will attach so many conditions to their gift and require such specific performance by the university that both parties' interests are best served by refusing the gift. Obviously, you should not through accepting a gift bind yourself or your successor to do something that is not in the university's interest. Not uncommonly the university will be offered a piece of property under the condition that the university maintain it in its current state and warrants never to sell or otherwise dispose of it. The property may be a magnificent old house in which the donor's family has lived for five generations. The donor proposes that it be used by the university as a conference center or as a museum. Or the property may be an old family farm of historic value. The donor proposes that it be used for faculty retreats or as a writing center. Unless it is indeed an unusual piece of property, you should graciously refuse such a gift. The cost of maintenance will be a burden that cannot be justified by the usefulness of the property. The university should never agree to retain and maintain a piece of property in perpetuity. Perpetuity is a very long time and the university's circumstances will surely change. Do not accept a gift of property with the restriction that it can never be sold!

Gifts to the university will be tax exempt. The university should not accept a gift specifically designed to benefit an individual selected by the donor if the donor then takes a tax deduction for the gift. If such an arrangement were lawful, every family with the means would endow a scholarship designated for their own son or daughter and thereby take a tax deduction for the cost of educating their progeny. The university should never put itself in the position of establishing a value for a non-monetary gift. The value put on property, art works, book collections, furniture, or equipment should be between the donor and the Internal Revenue Service. If the university supports a value for a nonmonetary gift that is in excess of its real or market value, the university is a party to a tax fraud.

In soliciting funds, the president of a private university will argue that donors should favor private institutions because they depend on tuition revenues, endowment income, and benefactions for their very existence and it is in the national interest to maintain a strong system of private higher education as an alternative to public higher education. It is a persuasive argument. The president of a public university will argue that, since the basic costs of operating public institutions are funded through legislative appropriations, private gifts to a public university enjoy a very high leverage whereby a relatively modest gift can provide the margin of excellence. That is also a persuasive argument. Most donors want the academic impact of their gift to be visible. They do not want to make gifts to the university to pay the utility bills. The endowment for a chair in a private university usually has to carry the full costs of the position; in a public university, income from the chair endowment may be over and above the regular faculty salary paid from state appropriations.

Although some donors as a matter of principle will exclude public institutions from their benefactions, and some donors will seek institutions, private or public, where their gift can be most effectively leveraged, most donors will give to the institution in which they have a personal interest or which is best able to accomplish the purpose for which the gift is intended. A donor contemplating a major gift to support a program in Japanese studies, for example, will consider universities that already have programs in Asian studies and a record of experience in instruction and research in the language and culture of that region. Experienced donors are more inclined to inject funds into an existing program to enhance its quality than to fund a start-up program.

You may be lunching with the president of a corporation to discuss a major gift to the university shortly after one of the faculty members in your department of economics has written an article attacking corporate America. Why, asks the corporate president, should my corporation give the shareholders' money to an institution that is antibusiness? Why indeed? This is a question being asked more frequently in the boardrooms of American corporations and it is a question that will have to be addressed by presidents of universities seeking private support. It is not difficult for you to deal with an occasional antibusiness article or speech by a liberal or radical member of your faculty. Corporate executives are sophisticated enough to know that university faculties, particularly in some departments, tend to be politically liberal. They also understand that they depend on the university for the new recruits they need to conduct their business. You should be prepared to address the larger question—is there a growing antibusiness bias in American colleges and universities and what do you, the president of a university, think should be done about it? You will be well advised to develop a position on this issue and be able to speak convincingly to the need for a partnership between business and higher education. If you are not so persuaded, do not ask for money.

You may be approached by an individual or a corporation that wants to do something about what is perceived to be an antibusiness, anti–free enterprise, anticapitalism bias in American higher education. They may propose to endow a chair or professorship in capitalism or fund some other mechanism to counter what they perceive as an undesirable trend in higher education. Very probably the prospective donor will not know much about universities and how they function. Your problem is to handle this generous gift and the press releases about it in such a way that the faculty do not charge you with "selling out" the university, and the faculty of the department receiving the new endowed chair are delighted to have it. It is to be hoped that the donor can be persuaded to style the endowment as a chair in American economic systems or a chair in business enterprise. If it is called a chair in capitalism, there will inevitably be demands that there be created a parallel chair in Marxism. The donor's purpose can be achieved with less faculty debate in a school or college of business than in a department of economics, but in economics you can reach a broader group of undergraduate students and a different population of graduate students than in a professional school. Remember also that, no matter how the chair is styled, the faculty of the host department will have the responsibility for recruiting the chair holder.

It is best to discuss frankly and honestly with the prospective donor the problems of how to style the chair and where to put it, even at the risk of losing the gift, than to attempt to conceal or minimize the faculty problems that the gift may provoke. At the appropriate point in these kinds of negotiations the board should be informed so there are no surprises on either side.

Other prospective gifts may come your way that you cannot in good conscience accept because your institution cannot realize the donor's intent. If someone offers to endow a professorship in Japanese language and literature and you have no oriental language programs in the university, and no resources with which to initiate an oriental language program, you would be deceiving the donor if you accepted the gift. There should be a good match between the donor's intent, the mission of your university, and what you can deliver.

Occasions may arise when the university has such an urgent need to raise large sums of money that you or the board may decide to employ a professional fund raiser, either as a consultant or to undertake most of the work necessary for a major capital funds drive. If the goals are ambitious and the time is short, it may be impossible to direct, plan, and staff the project in house. But professional fund raisers are expensive and sophisticated donors will want to know how much of the money raised in a successful capital funds drive will the university get and how much will go to the fund raiser. Make sure that your contract with the outside firm will stand up under scrutiny. It is better to pay a stiff fee up front than to burden the capital funds drive with too much overhead. Moreover, it is unlikely that the demands on your time will be significantly less if the work is contracted to an outside firm. Whether the work is done inside or outside, the director will have to be able to produce the president to bring in the big gifts. If the professional fund raiser explains to the board that the effort was unsuccessful because the president would not schedule important meetings with potential donors, the blame for failure has been successfully transferred to you. You will have to be involved in the effort in a major way, so you should be comfortable with the contract and the principals at the outset.

In summary, in nearly all universities the president is expected to raise money for the institution. In some small, private universities fund raising may consume a very large part of the president's time. In a large, public university the president will have to devote more time to management of the institution, but fund raising is nevertheless an important part of his or her responsibility. When you are offered the presidency you should have a clear understanding with the board of regents as to their expectations for your performance as a fund raiser. If it is apparent that a successful development effort will be required for your tenure as president to be a success, and if you do not enjoy that part of the job, you are well advised to decline the offer. There is no way that you can hire someone to take the responsibility for development off your shoulders. You can depend on staff to do preliminary and organizational work but the chief fund raiser is the president.

CHAPTER 14

State University Systems, State Government Bureaucracies, and Other External Constituencies

THE POINT was made early in this Primer that the distinction between public and private universities is no longer as clear as it once was. Private institutions depend on public funds for research contracts and grants, for tuition grants, and for student loans. With public money comes the obligation to report, account, certify, and comply with federal and state law and with a vast array of rules and regulations. However, in the area of institutional governance and management the private university is blessed in comparison with public universities. Although presidents of both public and private universities answer to a board of regents, trustees, or directors, the president of a public university must contend also with additional governance and oversight organizations, such as university systems, state coordinating boards, state departments of higher education, state human rights commissions, committees of the state legislature, state auditors, state purchasing commissions, state comptrollers, and the office of the governor of the state.

Some of these external agencies impose little more than a reporting requirement on the university, but of course they all insist that the report, commonly containing the same information as in reports submitted to other agencies, be filed in their unique format. Like federal agencies, these state agencies, under the authority of state law, are mission oriented and in carrying out their mission they have little or no sympathy or regard for the mission of the university. Some of the external agencies have the authority to intrude into the internal affairs of the university and will question or demand justification for program, budget, and personnel decisions; they will attempt to influence the direction of your planning process. The directors and staff of these external agencies will have little knowledge of what universities are and how they function.

Thus, one of the great challenges to the president of a public university is to shield the institution from these intrusions and to minimize the threat that they present to the independence and integrity of the educational enterprise. In this role the president's political and diplomatic skills are put to a severe test. The battle is conducted above the awareness of faculty, staff, and students. The president's victories will not be appreciated; the president's defeats will be manifest over time in an increasing bureaucratization of the institution for which he or she will receive the blame.

Unfortunately, victories will be few. The best that the president can hope to accomplish is to slow down the inexorable invasion of government into the affairs of the university. In our democratic society's passion to protect everyone's rights and to confer new ones on citizens, noncitizens, and animals alike; in the determination to protect all living creatures to the ultimate extent of taking all risk out of life; and in the determination to make everyone equal regardless of talent, ability, and productivity; the public university's tradition of intellectual freedom will be eroded and its meritocracy perverted. Signs abound from constraints on research using animals or radioactive or hazardous materials, to hiring and firing based on criteria other than merit and performance, to admission and advancement of students on criteria other than their academic record, to enormously expensive construction and transportation standards to accommodate a small minority of the population.

No society has the resources to do all things for all people. That way lies bankruptcy. A bankrupt society cannot do anything for anybody. So . . . our own humanity puts us at risk. As president you will be attacked as inhumane for making decisions based solely on merit, for insisting on a rigorous, demanding curriculum, and for defending the freedom of the university to pursue inquiry. It comes with the job.

University systems are organizations created to administer more than one institution. Although some systems in a *de facto* sense have been around a long time, they are as formal organizations a relatively recent phenomenon that is restricted to the public sector. If the operating academic institutions within the system are headed by presidents, the chief executive officer of the system is called a chancellor; if the system head is the president, the institutional heads are chancellors. Henceforward, in this Primer, it will be assumed that the institutional heads are presidents and the system heads are chancellors, although it may very well be the other way around.

At one end of the spectrum of systems is the multicampus university; at the other end is the federation of more or less autonomous universities. There is one board—regents, trustees, or directors—for the system. In some states there is one system for all the public senior colleges and universities, while in other states there may be as many as six or eight systems.

Systems grew and developed for a number of reasons, some political and some bureaucratic. A board of regents faced with the responsibility to govern more than one institution found it necessary to expand the staff of the secretary to the board in order to organize and coordinate the business of the board. The staff serving the board grew and it became necessary to employ an executive officer. Members of the board with business experience decided it was good practice for the presidents of the component institutions within the system to send their business through the board's executive officer—the chancellor—and the "University System" was formally constituted. In those states where a number of public universities were competing for public funds, boards of regents saw political advantage in creating a university system with a broad base. Institutions in large cities or in legislative and senatorial districts with powerful elected officials were more able to influence the appropriations process than institutions in small university towns.

The process of "systemization" was also promoted by state officials and elected representatives plagued by requests from a multitude of university presidents. They preferred to deal with a system chancellor who could analyze, screen, and put priorities on requests from a group of universities. The perception in some large states that higher education was "in chaos" drove the establishment of university systems. It became the common wisdom in state government circles that state universities were poorly managed and that public funds were being spent unwisely or wasted. Costs, it was alleged, were out of control. Under fire, public universities attempted to demonstrate that the cost of higher education had not risen out of proportion to costs for other public services and that management costs, compared with other public and private organizations, were actually low. But a popular delusion is difficult to dispel. Higher education was reorganized and institutes for higher education management appeared. The additional layer of bureaucracy represented by the university system will be with us for awhile.

All this is bad news for the president of an operating academic institution. Traditionally, an academic community on a campus is composed of faculty and students who interact in educational and research programs. The faculty and students are resident in a university. In the worst manifestation of a university system, the faculty becomes a system faculty and the students become system students; the system becomes an operating entity and engages in teaching and research. The ramifications of this organizational structure are obvious. Policies and procedures become standardized over the system. The university that has more rigorous requirements for promotion and tenure and higher performance requirements for faculty and students is brought down to the average. The presidents of the component universities become assistant or associate chancellors for their campuses, even though they retain the title of president; they function more as chief clerks than as chief executive officers. The important academic decisions are made off the campuses at the system level. The academic community is diminished and the institution ceases to be a university in the traditional intellectual sense. You should eschew the opportunity to be a university president in this kind of university system.

In the best kind of university system, the system office functions as a kind of corporate office and does not become an operating entity. The system does not offer academic programs or engage in research. The system does not confer tenure or award academic degrees. The system does not have a football team. Academic programs and decisions concerning them are campus based. The academic leadership is on the campuses and the chancellor does not function as or represent himself or herself to be the chief academic officer of the campuses. In fact, if the chancellor understands the job, he or she will make sure that the visible academic leadership is vested in the presidents of the component institutions. In this ideal, the system provides services, including planning, architectural, engineering, budgeting, financial and investment, and legal services. The system undertakes lobbying efforts. It is the continuing responsibility of the chancellor to evaluate the performance of the presidents and maintain a high quality of leadership across the system.

But when a university system is created, whether it is benign or malignant, the authority and responsibility given the chief executive officer are authority and responsibility taken away from the presidents of the universities that make up the system. To the extent that the authority and responsibility of the president is diminished, the university as an institution is diminished. This may not be immediately apparent to faculty, students, and alumni, or even to the board of regents that created the system, but it is nonetheless true. It is up to the board of regents to constrain overly ambitious system executives if the board wants to protect the quality and integrity of its operating universities.

If you have an opportunity to become a candidate for the presidency of a university within a system, it is wise to exercise a little due diligence before committing yourself. Is the board of regents involved in the recruiting process or is the process handled exclusively by the chancellor? In the latter case the job is certainly less attractive. Talk to the other presidents of institutions within the system. What is the relationship of the president to the board? Does he or she have access to the board? Is the president regarded by board members as a colleague or an employee? If the system offices and the university are in the same community, who does the community look to as the leader of the university? If it is the chancellor instead of the president, you will have your work cut out for you. Does the chancellor encourage or permit entrepreneurial faculty members, department chairs, and deans to go around the president and come directly to him or her? If you take the job, you have to have an ironclad agreement that this will stop.

You should also conduct a discreet investigation to determine how the chancellor stands with the board. These relationships may in fact be quite different than indicated on the official table of organization. If your candidacy proceeds to a discussion with the board or a committee of the board, you should ascertain what the board considers to be the president's role as against the chancellor's role. Do not be content with a general answer. Pose some specific examples. You may have to remind the board of their answer in the future. Inevitably, the chancellor and the system staff will be involved in your planning process and in the approval of your budget. They should under no circumstances be involved in hiring or promotion, in basic decisions on academic programs, in admissions or any other student-oriented function, or in intercollegiate athletics. From the point of view of the president of a university, these are the ultimate tests of the quality of life within a university system. If decisions in these areas are made at the system level, do not take the job.

Development is a sensitive area. If the chancellor and the system are active in attempting to raise private funds they will be soliciting your prospects and trying to bring your donors into support of the entire system. If the system attempts to co-opt your development board you have to fight or resign. You cannot, in view of your responsibility to the institution, acquiesce.

In your interview with the board of regents ask if the president is permitted to deal directly with the legislature. Although on paper the political representation function probably rests with the chancellor, in a crisis, when the chips are down, you must have the authority to make your case directly. If the chancellor shuts the president off from legislators and other public officials, the presidency is a weaker position. If the chancellor is good at his or her job, the presidents of the component institutions will be brought into the political arena in a planned and coordinated way. The chancellor must be an advocate of the "we're all in this together" strategy if he or she is going to build a team of strong institutional presidents. If that is not the management philosophy that prevails, if the chancellor is secretive or evasive, you do not want to be a member of the team.

Although chancellors and system bureaucracies can be a serious threat to the independence and integrity of the flagship university within a state university system—usually a nationally ranked comprehensive undergraduate and graduate research university—presidents of smaller, regional component institutions may regard them very positively. Flagship institutions are big enough to supply in house the services provided by the system. Smaller system components cannot with their resources provide the quality of architectural, engineering, planning, budgeting, financial, legal, and investment services that can be centralized in a university system. Interinstitutional arrangements and programs can be promoted by the system so as to share existing program and staff strengths among the institutions of the system. The political strength of a big, well-administered university system can be vital in tough economic times.

Looking at the system from the vantage point of the institution, the character, ability, and personality of the chancellor is all important. The president has to get along with the chancellor, not vice versa. The president has to deal effectively with the chancellor on a day-to-day basis. There must be mutual confidence and trust. If it is not there, you should leave. After a number of successful years in the presidency you may be able to challenge the chancellor on an issue and win it in the boardroom. But it is far better to resolve issues with the chancellor at the working level. If it comes to a fight with the chancellor at the board level you will have to put your resignation on the line and the board will then choose between you. If you are right on the issue and the chancellor carries some scars, you may win. Soon thereafter, you may have to decide if you want to be chancellor. When the president of a component institution within a university system accepts the chancellorship, it is usually because he or she is afraid of who might be appointed if the offer is refused. The presidency is a better job . . . unless, of course, the chancellor has assumed a good part of the authority and responsibility that should go with the presidency.

In summary, although university systems properly limited and directed in their mission can contribute to public higher education, they represent an expensive layer of administration that is probably not needed. Abolishing them would cause some short-term dislocations until their essential functions could be assigned either to the operating universities or to a well-organized, expanded office of the board of regents. If, for political reasons, system bureaucracies cannot be abolished, they should at the very least be regularly pruned to keep them out of the teaching and research business of the university. University systems are not universities and should not be permitted to take on the trappings of universities. The university system bureaucracy that through either ambition or ignorance is intrusive into the affairs of a component institution presents a difficult problem for the president. Resisting these intrusions, and they must be resisted to protect the university and the presidency, diverts the president from productive activities.

Coordinating boards, departments of higher education, and commissions of higher education came into being, like university systems, in states that spend a great deal of money in support of public higher education and where there was a public perception that state universities were growing rapidly without adequate control and coordination. The statutes that created these new state agencies stressed the need to eliminate unnecessary duplication of academic programs but, once established, these oversight and regulatory agencies sought and received authorization to review and approve not only degree programs but also course inventories, plans to construct buildings, long-range campus master plans, and research programs. They have varying degrees of authority for budget review and approval. In some states they have the responsibility for developing and administering the formulae under which public university elements of cost are funded by the legislature. In addition, state legislatures gave these new agencies responsibilities for student loan programs, core curricula, and affirmative action programs and authorized them to make a wide range of studies. In their zeal, and following the bureaucratic imperative, these boards and commissions moved to standardize university personnel policies, including policies on promotion and tenure, faculty work-load policies, admissions policies, and grading policies. Course numbering systems in the states' universities had to be altered to fit a standard system compatible with the agency's computer.

Coordinating board staffs are very uncomfortable with excellence. It is much easier for them to deal with the norm and thus they attempt to standardize on the average. The expanding authority of these higher education regulatory bodies put them into conflict with boards of regents charged by law with the governance of the institutions. Where the state agencies have prevailed, boards of regents have diminished authority and, if the trends continue, regental appointments may well become little more than honorific. The state university that has a constitutional shield against this kind of interference is fortunate indeed.

So . . . in addition to chancellors, public university presidents now have to deal with commissioners of higher education. The staffs of these state agencies demand voluminous reports on the university's operations. The burden of reporting, accounting, complying, and certifying is heavy. Of course, when faced with additional rules and regulations the faculty will blame the president for the bureaucratization of the university. All you can do is try to explain to the faculty the authority that the legislature has given to the coordinating board. The staff of a state agency under whatever name is not nearly so concerned about academic freedom as is the university community. Conflict is inevitable and you are caught in the middle. A departmental faculty that traditionally has had sole control over a degree program does not take kindly to dictates from a state bureaucracy about how the program should be structured, and the very minimal academic qualifications of the regulatory staff constitute a gratuitous insult to the faculty.

Another problem for the university is that the additional layer of review and approval required by the existence of a state higher education agency causes delays in implementing new programs and even in some states new courses, as well as a great deal of additional work. After all of the university's internal review procedures are completed, and after the university system and board of regents have reviewed and approved the new program, the coordinating board staff will begin a lengthy review, and the review will be conducted from the viewpoint of a regulator that has a mission to control the growth of higher education and stop the proliferation of degree programs. It may well be decided that, since a program similar to yours is offered at another state institution, your request should be denied. Then you must begin the appeal procedure to demonstrate that the two programs are not similar and that, if the particular academic department involved is to remain nationally ranked, it must move with the discipline into new areas. By this time, the departmental faculty is totally discouraged and the new faculty member hired to develop the new program is looking for a position elsewhere. You are moved to wonder why so many people seem determined to keep you from doing your job and begin to contemplate seeking the presidency of a private university. Do not give up. This is but a sign of the times. Take a long walk and devise a strategy to get the program approved.

The president of a public university cannot do much about the authority given by law to a coordinating board or other state agency. When the authority is abused by an overly zealous staff, you can try to reason with the commissioner and, if this fails, in concert with other universities and with the support of your chancellor and board, you can make representations to the board of the agency and as a last resort pursue a remedy with the legislature. But pick the issue carefully. It should be one for which you can make a persuasive case that an intractable state bureaucracy without knowledge or vision is preventing the university from moving into a new, fast-moving field with great economic potential for the state. If a Nobel Laureate testifies before a legislative committee you will get the attention of the coordinating board members and the commissioner. They will take care of an obdurate staff. It is nearly always the staff that is the problem.

It is easier to reason with a commissioner of higher education, or with any other state government official, if you have established a personal relationship with him or her. People who make decisions about higher education in the state should be on your invitation list and you should know them well enough to talk to them informally over lunch or dinner. If they are informed about your university and your ambitions for it, they will be more likely to give a receptive ear to your argument than if they do not know you and are uninformed. Personal diplomacy is always to be preferred over confrontation. Conversely, you may receive valuable guidance from them as to what positions they are going to take and why. If you have recently come into the state, you will have to work to develop the necessary relationships. This is why the chairman of your board and your chancellor, if you are part of a system, should have a series of receptions to introduce you to the decision makers. If they are just too busy to do so, you will have to depend on your own resources to get the important social introductions, and you will have learned something important . . . that either they do not know the important people or they do not want you to know them. Remember, you have the position working for you . . . you are the president of the university . . . and with a little aggressiveness on your part, the university will provide the entry.

In addition to the commissioner of higher education, you should develop cordial relationships with the head of the state purchasing commission, the state comptroller, the state auditor, and key members of the state legislature and their staffs. Your relationship with the legislature should be carefully planned and orchestrated. It is not becoming for a university president to be too visible in the halls of the state capitol. You are not a lobbyist and it will not do the university any good for you to be perceived as a lobbyist. You should avoid hanging around the capitol and concentrate on building relationships with the governor, lieutenant governor, speaker, and the chairs of a few key committees. It will help to be on a first-name basis with the top staff in their offices. Do not forget about these people when the legislature adjourns. You can perhaps do more to build the relationships when the legislature is not in session than during the session when the press of daily business is heavy.

Although it is not seemly for you as a university president to conduct yourself as a lobbyist, it is proper for you to stand publicly as a strong advocate for higher education. The public university president who leads the institution during a state fiscal crisis when legislators must make tough choices on funding priorities among higher education, public schools, highways, law enforcement agencies, and other established state services should rise to the occasion, set aside regular duties and activities, and campaign actively for higher education in general and his or her institution in particular.

The best way to get the attention of legislators is through influential people in their home districts, contributors, and supporters. The public university president who embarks on a crusade to sustain appropriation levels for higher education will make a large number of trips throughout the state to carry a message to newspaper editorial boards, television program directors, civic groups, and influential alumni. Good press relations are important. Many of the people who must be convinced that higher education should have a high priority in the allocation of scarce funds will not know a great deal about the university, its mission, and its critical importance to the economic, cultural, and intellectual development of the state. If you as president find yourself with such an assignment, you should prepare a tight, cogent, and practical message that will result in favorable editorials, television commentary, and phone calls and letters to targeted legislators. Make the case through a commonsense presentation on the importance of the contribution the university makes to the state through its graduates, research, and cultural programs. High-quality programs can not be stopped and started annually. A drastic cut in funds in one session of the legislature, even if coupled with a promise of restoration during the next appropriation cycle, will make it difficult if not impossible to recruit the faculty you need and indeed may set off a flight of your most outstanding faculty to aggressively competitive institutions. But remember who you are talking to and leave the academic rhetoric on campus. The argument must be made on the state's interest in maintaining the quality of its institutions of higher education.

As president of a public institution you will receive many requests for political contributions from candidates and officeholders of both parties. In addition to the solicitations for outright contributions, you will be asked to buy tickets for "appreciation" breakfasts, lunches, dinners, and receptions. A considerate board of regents will establish a fund for the purchase of these tickets so that you or a designated member of your staff can appear and shake hands to establish the university's presence at the function. Requests for contributions are the most difficult problem.

As a first law, the president of a public university should not be politically active and certainly should not be closely identified with a political party or movement. You should be identified as independent and bipartisan, and you should maintain friendly and cordial relations with politicians of all parties. If you have strong conservative or liberal beliefs, conceal them while you are representing a public institution. This will not be easy because some politicians, both candidates for office and officeholders, will attempt to pressure you into declaring yourself as "for" or "against." It will take some creative evasion and fast footwork to avoid being forced into one camp or the other. You must seek the image of a strong advocate for higher education who is above partisan politics and working only for the best interests of the state and the university. Obviously, if you have the support of the leaders of both political parties your relations with the legislature and the governor's office will be successful.

However, the role of a bipartisan statesperson for higher education will not relieve you of the problem of political contributions. You should make a distinction between those running for office and those holding office. For candidates running for office you can establish a rule that you will not make any contributions in a contested race. Under this approach you should write a nice letter to the candidate and explain that as president of a public institution you do not believe it is good policy to take a partisan political position, and extend your best wishes. Some candidates will understand this position; some will not appreciate it at all. Another approach is to make an equal, token contribution to all serious candidates in the race. These contributions must come from after tax personal funds so this policy is expensive and puts you on a great many lists. The lists are public so it is clear to all who read them what you are doing. However, memories are short and, no matter who is elected, you are on the record as a supporter. If you pick and choose, contributing to candidates who are strong supporters of higher education or who are personal friends, there is always the risk that your candidate will lose. That, of course, is not fatal. You can always get aboard with the winner by contributing to a fund to retire his or her political debts.

You should respond, judiciously, to requests for contributions from officeholders who have a great deal to do with higher education and with whom you interact on the public's business. The obligation comes with the job. Your contributions will not be of such magnitude as to suggest that you are buying influence, but it will benefit the university if you have easy access to the governor, lieutenant governor, speaker, and the chairs of important house and senate committees. If you are more comfortable by removing yourself one step from the process, ask your spouse to write the check and make the contribution in his or her name. If you do not like any part of the political process through which universities are funded and governed, you should take yourself out of the public arena and seek the presidency of a private university. An institution supported by public funds appropriated through a public process by a public body in an open debate cannot expect to be above politics just because it is a university. The best that can be expected is that the state constitution will offer some protection to the institution and that the board of regents will protect the president against the most cynical political attacks.

The alumni of your university are a constituency whose members are tied to the institution by the memories of happy days, and a varying degree of interest in what the university is doing. Some students graduated from the university, or left the institution, and in effect said "good-bye" to it; others joined the alumni association the day they graduated and are constant and loyal supporters, making annual gifts and coming back to campus frequently. You must work this constituency in a planned and organized effort to increase alumni interest, participation, and support. Some ex-students who in the early years after graduation were consumed by their own careers and interests can, at some point in their business and professional life, be brought back into the university orbit. In addition to the alumni association, there are visiting committees and advisory councils that might arouse their interest.

Cultivation of alumni requires your personal time and attention. Your data base should include as much information as you can develop on your ex-students so that you can call up a profile on their association with the university over the years, their business and professional interests and achievements, organizations to which they belong, and the growth and development of their children. A personal letter from you offering congratulations on awards and achievements, congratulations on births, and condolences on deaths will strengthen ties to the university. When travel plans take you to a city for business reasons, you should schedule a lunch or dinner with prominent alumni.

The director of your alumni association will be enthusiastic about organizing for you a tour of alumni groups. You should host events on campus designed to bring alumni back for a few days once or twice a year. They can be planned around football games, artistic performances by students, or lectures on campus by distinguished national or international figures. A university newsletter designed for alumni will keep them informed about campus activities. Through your continuing education program alumni can participate in travel and study abroad. These efforts may not pay immediate dividends but in the long run they will surely benefit the institution.

Alumni can be invited to join an exclusive president's council. Dues of $500 or $1,000 per year will entitle them to special invitations and certain perquisites and provide you with some badly needed discretionary funds. If you are president of a public university, an active and interested alumni can be organized into an informed and therefore effective lobby to work on their local representatives and senators during legislative sessions when the university has important bills under consideration.

The local community, whether small town or big city, is a constituency that can hurt you or help you. The president plays a key role in building the necessary bridges to the community and developing community support for the university. Although the university is likely one of the most important economic and cultural assets that the community has, and is indeed its "cleanest" industry, relations between community and university will deteriorate if you do not take an active role in maintaining good relations. Notwithstanding what the university contributes to the community, there will always be frictions over zoning, tax exemptions, rights-of-way, law enforcement, and the inevitable radical and provocative attacks by campus activists on community traditions and social institutions. When you become president, a few informal conversations with community leaders will tell you where the problems are. You should not be too busy with state and national affairs to serve on a few selected city boards and commissions.

If a town-and-gown club is not already established, start one. If there are other colleges and universities in the city, take the leadership in bringing the presidents of them together at regular intervals for lunch and a discussion of mutual concerns. It may be useful to organize a higher education council that would include all the degree-granting senior colleges and universities, the community colleges, and, perhaps in associate status, such cultural institutions as museums and galleries. Such an organization can be very effective in the community and may be a mechanism to effect a sharing of library and computer resources.

Make sure that the mayor and other city officials are invited to important campus events. If there are barriers to community residents who want to take or audit courses at the university but who are not seeking a degree, make it as easy as you can for them to study at the university on a space-available basis. Find a way to make other university facilities, such as athletic facilities, available to members of the community when they are not in use by students.

In summary, whether private or public, universities in our time cannot function successfully as an ivory tower or refuge. It is up to you as president to reach out to the larger society. To the extent you are successful in dealing with the external constituencies, you may go down in university history as a great president. Put another way, you may be well regarded by faculty and students for your management of the internal affairs of the university, but history will not record you as a great president of the university if you are not well regarded by the world outside the institution.

CHAPTER 15

Establishing the University Agenda

THE MOST important responsibility that the president of a university has is to establish the institution's agenda. Operating the institution in an effective and efficient way is not enough. If the university is to have direction and purpose, the president must direct his or her attention away from operating problems long enough to develop a vision of where the institution can be in five years, or even ten years. If the president's vision is to become reality, a carefully crafted grand strategy must be devised to move the institution in the right direction with all deliberate speed.

The president's agenda and the president's grand strategy are separate and distinct from the annual ongoing institutional planning exercise that involves all the university departments, schools, and colleges and establishes goals and objectives against which performance is measured. Indeed, the president's agenda may be for some time, in whole or in part, held as a private agenda. Considering the independent, contentious, and commonly fractious nature of the university community, you should not be in any hurry to disclose in any detail where you hope to take the institution during your presidency. Initially, at least, make your comments about direction and purpose in very general terms. If after only a few months in the presidency you present the faculty with a grand design for the university, it will be challenged, disputed, and resisted.

During the first year of your presidency you will be learning about the strengths and weaknesses of the university, the extent of its resources, and the magnitude and urgency of its needs. You will be wrestling with what appear to be an overwhelming number of operational problems and crises. You will be organizing your administration and assessing the capabilities of your staff. You will establish operational priorities, smooth out and speed up the flow of paper, and develop the confidence of your management team in their ability to make good decisions on time. But all the while that you are building the university ship you should be thinking about where you are going to sail it.

When your management is working well and with confidence, it is all too easy to relax and spend more time off campus going to national meetings. But if you are content with a presidency known for its operational efficiency, you will have a reactive presidency, perhaps a calm presidency, but one that will be almost invisible when the history of the institution is written from a future vantage point. An institution that makes no waves is an institution adrift. It may not sink and it may not go aground, but it will be pushed this way and that by external forces beyond your control; it will have no headway under its own power with you at the wheel.

If you as president aspire to more for the institution than good management, all the while that you are working on next year's budget, trying to recruit two new deans, pushing to get the faculty to move on curriculum revision, contending with student protests and demonstrations, raising endowments to support faculty positions and scholarships, presiding over university meetings, keeping a full appointment schedule, entertaining at official functions, and calming an unhappy member of the board, you must be thinking about the great issues of our time and how the university can address them, lead society to a higher level of development, and improve the human condition. When you awake in the wee hours of the morning and your mind turns to these considerations, have a pad and pencil by the bed so that the ideas conceived with great clarity in the peace and stillness of the night do not evaporate with the dawn. Likewise, when you are alone on long flights or sitting in airports, record your ideas for subsequent refinement. You will not have the time for such contemplation while at your desk.

The university as an institution, with its responsibility to develop the human resources of society, the intellectual power of its faculty, and its traditions of free inquiry, has a great capacity to improve the human condition. The great challenge to you as president is to position the university so that it can maximize its potential to serve society. The university can lead, but if it gets too far out in front of the larger society it will not be followed. It will lose public confidence and support. Universities are the keepers of society's history and traditions and guardians of knowledge and wisdom. They must be at one and the same time conservative as stewards of the past and innovative as leaders of the future. Universities should not be too eager to embrace the social science fads of the moment or the new political dogma. The decision on what is relevant to higher education cannot be left to sophomores. You must decide. Those universities that are institutions of a democratic society must recognize that truth and right are not determined by a show of hands and that law must be built on precedent rather than the whimsy of individual judicial conscience. This view of institutional responsibility will be anathema to those radicals within the university community who want to proselytize students and convert the university from an educational institution to a social action agency. Although you should investigate and consider new programs and new organizational structures, you cannot let an activist minority dictate the university agenda. You have the power of the office. Use it astutely.

After you develop your vision of the university's future and after it has been refined through reflection and tempered by experience, you can profitably test your ideas informally in conversation with associates and friends, presenting ideas not in the form of a grand design but more indirectly, relating them to issues of current interest. You can incorporate them in addresses to various groups and see how they are received. But keep your own counsel about how you plan to change the institution. Implement your grand strategy a step at a time. For all their liberal and even radical ideas, university communities are very conservative when it comes to change. Although they complain about "weak leadership," the faculty does not want to be led and will resist the strong leadership that they believe they seek. To establish his or her agenda, the president must work through suggestion, reason, persuasion, blandishment, coercion, intimidation, and indirection. To implement your grand strategy it will be helpful to read or reread Machiavelli's *The Prince*.

In devising the grand strategy, you will appraise the university that you inherited from your predecessor and consider the institution that you will build and leave to your successor. It will help to be systematic in approaching the problem.

What is the image and reputation of the university? Is it really as good as it is reputed to be? Is it better? The image does not always reflect the reality. Clearly, as part of your efforts, you want your university to be the finest in its class and to be perceived as the finest in its class. What will it take to build both the substance and the reputation? The faculty is the key. The general public will not have a higher regard for the university than does its faculty. If the faculty is grousing, complaining, and feeling sorry for itself, you will have to find ways to reanimate them and instill in them the feeling that they are part of a great enterprise. It takes a while and the judicious use of resources, but it can be done.

And what about the faculty? You must conduct a very careful and thorough evaluation. A faculty profile of each department is a good place to begin. What is the ratio of tenured to untenured faculty? How are the departmental faculties regarded by their peers in other institutions? What are the departmental promotion standards? Do they reward merit when it comes time to allocate monies for salary increases or do they just spread it around equally without regard for performance? Are the departments really making an effort to recruit women and minorities or are they just

paying lip service to university policies and initiatives in this very important effort? What can be done to support the strong departments and
build the weak departments? What is the caliber of departmental leadership? Is there really a sense of department, a departmental obligation to
the program, or is it each faculty member for him- or herself? Do the
senior faculty teach undergraduate courses and do they do a good job of
it? Is the department defensive in recruiting and program or are they on
the offensive? Are there department chairs who have been too long in the
job? Should some departments be phased out or merged? Should new
departments be created? The answers to these latter questions depend, of
course, on an analysis and evaluation of the university's academic program.

You should have moved early in your administration to make certain
that the deans of the schools and colleges are members of your team. As
chief academic officers of the faculties of those operating divisions of the
university, they must be people you are able to count on to support your
program, and that includes the grand strategy as it may be revealed to
them. You will never be able to make changes in the academic program of
a school or college without the enthusiastic support of the dean. Your
relations with the dean should be such that in frank conversations about
his or her college the dean will lay the problems on the table and not
attempt to conceal weaknesses or potential trouble spots. Frank discussions with the dean on his or her vision for the school or college are a
good starting point from which the dean's ideas and your ideas can be
melded and blended so that, when the plan is made, the dean is convinced
that what you want to accomplish is consistent with his or her vision and
in fact what you want is really his or her idea.

Give the dean all the credit for what success is finally achieved. You
want the grand strategy to succeed; the dean can have the credit. The dean
will have earned it. Phasing out programs, instituting new programs,
changing the direction of a department, changing departmental, school,
or college practices and procedures, relieving a popular but ineffective
chair, and making tough decisions on salary and promotion recommendations are not easy, but they are essential if your grand strategy for the
university is to be successful. The quality of the institution must be built
department by department, school by school, and college by college. If the
dean is not up to what you want to accomplish or cannot be brought
around to share your vision, you will have to engineer a replacement. If
the recalcitrant dean is the head of one of the core colleges of the university
you will have to move sooner; if the problem dean leads one of the peripheral professional schools you can wait until later.

It is through the academic and research programs of the university
that the institution can be brought to address the great contemporary issues. But it is unlikely that a focus on great issues will occur through the

traditional discipline-oriented departments. It is here that the president will have to use the authority of the office to create and fund new multi-disciplinary university structures. You will have to identify the faculty from several departments who are working in or around the issue and provide the assurances and incentives necessary to persuade them to focus their teaching and scholarly efforts on the problem. These innovations will be resisted. Faculty committees will have to be appointed and manipulated to legitimize the new multidisciplinary or interdisciplinary structures being established as part of your grand strategy for the university. You will have to be very persuasive. Some of the innovations may have to be labeled as "experimental" programs to win faculty approval and support. Students are generally more receptive to new ideas than faculty who are being asked to change their patterns of activity. Students who are persuaded that the proposed new program is their idea can exert pressure on reluctant faculty that the president cannot. This is a situation where student demands for "relevance" can be put to good use.

Your review of the university's programs will, of course, focus on both content and quality. The quality of any program is a function of the quality of the faculty involved in the program. As you are successful in enforcing high standards in recruitment and promotion of faculty, and as the quality of the faculty improves, so also will improve the quality of the university's programs. Student performance standards must also be enforced, but students in general are proud to be graduates of a tough, demanding program. They may complain while under the pressure of a faculty member who insists on high standards, but when the course is over, that faculty member will get high marks from the students. In your grand strategy to advance the university, the students will be your allies.

If you push too hard and too fast to change the content of the university's academic programs, the affected faculty may raise the flag of academic freedom. It is a formidable defense against any university president who wants to redirect a program and cannot persuade the faculty themselves to make the desired changes. When that flag is hoisted, even though the cause is spurious, the president should back up and come at the problem from a new direction.

As president you must be a strong defender of academic freedom. It is the university's defense against external pressures directed against the institution and its faculty for mean or base political reasons. The faculty in the final analysis must be the judge of what is taught and the qualifications of those who teach. The principle of academic freedom should be enshrined in the charter of the university and in the rules and regulations promulgated by its board. Academic freedom is so important to the intellectual freedom of the university that it is deplorable to raise that defense for trivial or spurious reasons. A young instructor or assistant professor who believes that he or she has the absolute right to teach "his" or "her" course any way that he or she sees fit may balk at the departmental requirement that the course syllabus be approved by a committee of the senior faculty or that certain approved textbooks be the only ones used, and may indeed claim a violation of academic freedom. The courts have found, however, that academic freedom does not give the instructor the absolute right to flout departmental authority over course content and textbooks.

At the classroom level, academic freedom is a qualified right to free expression of views and opinions within the overarching right of the institution through its established faculty-approved procedures to determine course content. As president with an agenda for making some changes in the institution's academic programs, you should craft your strategy so as to avoid giving cause for the faculty to oppose you on the grounds that your efforts to improve the academic program in any way constitute a violation of the principles of academic freedom.

Early in your presidency you will review the student body and ask questions about the students' academic qualifications, the ethnic mix, the male-female ratio, the age profile, where they come from, and the number on scholarship or receiving some form of financial aid. Is the size of the student body appropriate for the number of faculty and the capacity of the university's facilities? Should enrollment be managed so as to increase or decrease it? In developing your ambitions for the university you may conclude that some change in the character of the student body is desirable. Perhaps too many of the students come from one region of the country and you believe a greater geographic diversity would be beneficial. The mix of foreign students may not be appropriate for the kind of university you envision. The minority student recruitment program might be lagging. Endowed scholarship funds in all probability will need to be increased. Do the university's admission policies produce the kind of students that fit the institution you want to build? You will most likely begin work on this problem by appointing a carefully selected committee. Based on its recommendations you can start to put this part of the grand strategy into place. The problems inherent in managing the enrollment are discussed in the chapter on operating the institution.

What is the condition of the university's libraries, research equipment, buildings, and grounds? Efforts to make improvements in the institution's support facilities and infrastructure will be well received unless it is perceived that the improvements are taking money away from faculty and staff salaries. How does the campus look? Unless necessary maintenance has been deferred for some years, a little money spent sprucing up the campus will pay a big dividend. A shabby campus has a depressing effect on morale and performance. A project to improve the general libraries will always be well received by the faculty. Has the university moved appropriately to integrate the new computer technology into its operations or are you still doing business on 3 x 5 cards? Unless your predecessor developed a capital budget sufficient to stay on top of these institutional needs, your grand strategy will have to address the imperative to develop the capital resources essential to modernize the campus.

So . . . unless you see yourself as a caretaker president preserving the status quo for the next president to come along and do something, you must do more than manage. You must lead an institution composed of very independent constituencies that jealously guard their traditional prerogatives, and to do this, you as president must establish your agenda and push it through to a successful completion. If you can make it all happen, history will record you as one of the great presidents of the university.

CHAPTER 16

Exiting the Presidency

The day that you assume the presidency of a university you had better begin thinking about how you are going to get out of it with your health, sense of humor, and reputation intact. It is not good for any chief executive officer of any organization to remain in the position too long. It is not good for the organization or for the executive. There are exceptions, of course, that flow from extraordinary circumstances and extraordinary individuals, but saving those exceptions a president should attempt to realize his or her vision, achieve his or her goals, and make his or her contribution to the organization within a tenure of five to ten years.

The point has been made in this Primer that the presidency of a university is a consuming job. No matter how many hours a day you work, there is always something else that you can do to advance the cause of the university and higher education. After some years it is not surprising that the president's energy and enthusiasm are somewhat diminished. If you have been able to accomplish those goals you set for yourself and the institution when you acceded to the presidency, and if your agenda for the university is well established and moving along, you will have a good solid record of progress to your credit. It is far better to quit a winner than to be fired or forced to resign after a couple of difficult years when circumstances and events not of your making and largely beyond your control have troubled your presidency.

If you came to the presidency relatively young, exiting the job after five or ten years presents a different problem than for the older individual who retires from the presidency. For the younger man or woman who has had a successful tenure as a university president there will be opportunities to take a presidency at another, larger or more prestigious university, to seek a position within a university system, or to accept appointment to a high position in government service. Foundations commonly look to university presidents to fill their executive positions. Ex-presidents are commonly in demand as consultants. For a successful university president who is still some years from retirement, opportunities to move to another position will come frequently and the offers will be attractive. The board of regents of your institution will be anxious to retain your services and will make counteroffers. Do not leave before you have made a solid record of accomplishment; do not stay too long after you have made the record. If you move too soon without having made a significant contribution, those who read your résumé will wonder if perhaps you are one of the academic "charmers" who "con" their way into a university presidency, survive for two or three years on charm, and leave before their incompetence catches up with them.

If you elect to move to a new position as chief executive make sure that you take at least a month's leave between jobs to rest and prepare yourself for the new challenge. Or, if you are tired of the rigors of administration, you can elect to return to teaching and research as a faculty member. The board will probably give you a year's leave to prepare for a return to the classroom. The faculty will understand this decision and admire you for it. The transition will be difficult and after the excitement and challenges of the president's office you will probably regret the decision to rejoin the faculty as a teacher and scholar, at least for a while. For the first few months after you leave the center of the storm you will find it difficult to take the time to read a scholarly paper with deliberation. After five or ten minutes you will be seized with the conviction that there is something urgent you should be doing. But if you make a successful transition back to life as a faculty member you will find that your years as president have prepared you well to chair important university committees and, if you want it, to occupy a place as a senior faculty statesperson.

The president who has put eight or ten years into the job and is close to retirement may be tempted to hang on past the time when he or she should exit the presidency. This is a mistake. It is better to take early retirement as a successful president and graciously accept the title of president emeritus from the board than to stay for a "few more years" and see the institution get away from you. It is far better to leave when the board is urging you to postpone your retirement and stay for another year than when the board, with regret, is moved to engineer the departure of their reluctant president. You can make a much better deal for the support of an office of president emeritus in the former case. If your retirement from the presidency is timely, a great many nice things will happen to you. In addition to the emeritus title, there will be a round of dinners in which your colleagues and associates express their appreciation for your service and regret at your departure, an endowment may be created in your honor, your portrait may be hung in a place of honor, or perhaps even a bronze bust may be commissioned to enshrine your likeness in the halls of university history. The university may provide an office for the president emeritus. Even the press may write laudatory articles about what you have accomplished.

Circumstances may arise, of course, when as a matter of principle you have to make a sudden and unanticipated exit from the presidency. In any conflict with the board your resignation is the only weapon you have. If you use it, the board may very well accept your resignation. In that case, you will have your integrity and your tenured professorship, and little else. If, however, you have conducted yourself well in the battle and the academic community concludes that you have the right of it, there will be offers of a presidency from other universities. You will be remembered as a man or woman who would not sacrifice principle to hold on to the job, and however traumatic a resignation under those circumstances may be, if your conscience tells you not to "go along" with a board decision you are well advised to stand firm.

If you move to another presidency, there will be new issues, new problems, and new challenges. You will have the experience of one presidency behind you. There is no substitute for that experience. In fact, if you aspire to be president of a big, complex, public institution it is better to start with a smaller, simpler university to build the experience you will need. On the other hand, if you retire from a university presidency, your life will change dramatically. After all the pleasant ceremonies that accompany the retirement of a successful university president, you will have to decide what you are going to do. Of course, you will have already thought about that a good deal before you made the decision, but until the reality is upon you all that planning and analysis about retirement will be "academic."

The president who retires after a successful tenure in the office, whether to return to a faculty position or simply to enjoy the status of president emeritus, should, out of consideration for his or her successor, disappear from campus for a year. The new president will have enough problems without a highly visible, well-liked, and well-respected former president in evidence at university functions and events. Obviously, it does not help a new president if his or her predecessor is commenting formally or informally on university affairs.

If you are on campus, it is inevitable that colleagues and associates will express their regret that you are not still in the president's chair, complain about decisions made and actions taken by the new president, and then quote whatever you might say to friends and associates about the campus, slanting your comments now and again to make a point. Reporters will call you and ask for a comment about university issues that have caught the media's attention. So . . . the way that you can be most helpful to your successor is to take a long trip, accept a visiting assignment at another institution in another city, or just stay home. If the board of regents has named you president emeritus and provided an office on campus, make plans not to spend much time there for the first year after you have left office. The office of the president emeritus should certainly not be prominently located in the administration building. You will do your successor and yourself a favor if you find an office in a more remote and secluded area of the campus.

If you are returning to the faculty as an active teacher, take a leave of absence for at least a semester and preferably for a year. After a year or so, the world will have turned, the new administration will have established itself, the new president will be confident and secure, and you can return to campus without arousing much interest. The campus will have adapted to the new administration and few will remember that you did things a little differently. Memories are short. Your successor will be grateful to you for making the transition easier and will be more likely to call on you for advice and counsel when it is clear that you are not a critic. It is very good for an institution when at important university functions the current president is seen talking in a friendly way with one or two former presidents.

As soon as word of your impending retirement has circulated you will receive calls from a number of organizations who see you as an able individual who suddenly has a great deal of time to devote to *pro bono* activities. You will be asked to serve on boards and committees of charitable and nonprofit organizations and to raise money for them. While these are worthy activities and some of them may hold a particular interest for you, be careful you do not promise them too much of your time. Unless you have retired from the presidency as a wealthy man or woman, you will want to supplement your income from investments, annuities, and a pension by consulting work for a fee or from fees as a corporate director. You may very well want to write, either because you have something to say that you believe is important or because you expect to earn income from book royalties, or both. Very probably you will have the option to teach part time. Since in all likelihood you will not know how long you will live, and since inflation is a serious threat to the standard of living and independence of retired people, you will seek, at least in the early years of retirement, to continue to build your estate and enhance your income. Take some time . . . you will have earned it . . . before you fully commit yourself to any course of action.

As president of a university you will have had an active social life in association with civic, business, professional, and political leaders of the community, state, and nation. You will have grown accustomed to a flow of invitations to luncheons, receptions, and dinners; you will have been invited to spend weekends at the coast, the lake, the ranch, or the mountains; you will have been invited to events in the state capital and in Washington, D.C. You will have flown as a guest in private aircraft and cruised aboard pleasure boats and yachts. You will have a very wide circle of friends. When you are no longer the president of the university this will all change. A great many of the invitations came not to you, but to the president. And many of your friends were really friends of the position of president. This is to be expected and should not leave you in any way bitter or even disappointed. After all, this is the way of the world and you are no longer in a position to reciprocate through entertaining as president of the university.

Accept the fact that you will upon leaving the presidency live a quieter life and a life without many of the perquisites that went with the presidency. It will all be put in perspective when you encounter an acquaintance in a local club and are greeted by an irreverent, "Well, hello, . . . didn't you used to be somebody?" You had your day, did well, and should sympathize with the poor devil who is wrestling with the problems that used to plague your days and nights. When someone asks, "What are you doing now?" they probably are really not all that interested. They are more interested in what they are doing and will appreciate a chance to tell you about it. So . . . give them the short answer and inquire about their activities. While they are discussing their own involvements they will not be looking over your shoulder to see if there are any important people in the room. If you want to cut the conversation short, begin an account of your last vacation trip. That will accelerate the "Great to see you, just great!" that will terminate the encounter.

When you have successfully exited a university presidency you will also have exited this Primer.

Index